£1·50

MY LIFE *as a* SCRIBE

MY LIFE
as a
SCRIBE

~

GEORGE L. THOMSON

CANONGATE

First published in 1988
by Canongate Publishing Limited,
17 Jeffrey Street, Edinburgh

The publisher acknowledges subsidy of
the Scottish Arts Council towards the
publication of this volume.

British Library Cataloguing in Publication Data
Thomson, George L. (George Lawrie), 1916 –
1. Great Britain. Calligraphy, Thomson,
George L. (George Lawrie) 1916 – Biographies
745.6'1'0924

ISBN 0–86241–171–8

Typeset by Buccleuch Printers, Hawick
Printed and bound in Great Britain by
Billing & Sons Limited, Worcester

for
BECKY BLUE
live long and prosper!

MY FATHER
ANDREW THOMSON
was born in Causewayside in

Edinburgh in 1888, the eldest of a family of six boys and one girl. About the age of three or four it became apparent that he was not growing normally, and as he grew older it was obvious that he was a dwarf. Full grown he reached the height of four feet six inches.

In the last decades of the nineteenth century, the reasons for dwarfism were unknown outside a small section of the medical profession. In my father's case, no dwarfs had ever been heard of in either parent's ancestry, and they believed he was stunted because of a bad fall at the age of three or four. He was a very lively infant, and when playing a chasing game with some older children, followed them up some scaffolding. He fell off and was knocked unconscious. The rest of the gang, who at first feared he was dead, were too scared to tell anyone what had happened. With good reason, as quite apart from the accident they would undoubtedly have been punished for climbing the scaffolding in the first place. The truth was not known for years.

Achondroplasia is a form of dwarfism which manifests itself in a stunting of the growth of the limbs, while the head and torso grow to normal size. Though thought to be undesirable in humans, this condition is diligently bred into some breeds of dog, such as dachshunds and beagles, and into some types of cattle, notably the Hereford and Aberdeen Angus. The intention is to breed animals which develop as much body meat as possible in relation to the amount of leg meat and bone. Bone is of course waste weight to the breeder. These poor animals are therefore subject to the same diseases which plague the human achondroplasic, such as arthritis and pulmonary conditions.

The genes which cause the condition are recessive. That is, the achondroplasic manifestations will gradually disappear with each

1

succeeding generation. They may reappear suddenly out of the blue, maybe five hundred or a thousand years later, indistinguishable from a first generation mutation. In the case of the animals, the dwarfism is made permanent by breeding like to like. But if an Aberdeen Angus were crossed with a normal breed, and its descendants likewise, in one or two generations all the offspring would be normal.

Back in the Thirties, in a book called *Art without Epoch*, I was fascinated to find a carved and painted representation of an achondroplasic dwarf, discovered in an ancient Egyptian tomb. With him were sculptured figures of his wife and three girl children, all apparently normal. He had been a respected member of his community, in a position of some responsibility. He was overseer of a weaving shop. His disability had not precluded him from rising in his society's esteem. It may even have bestowed some advantage — the ancient Egyptians worshipped a God of Laughter, *Bes*, represented as an achondroplasic dwarf.

A master plumber in the 1890s though, would never have heard of genes and chromosomes, and would have shown very little interest if he had. My grandfather, George Thomson, had much more interest in soaking up beer. He always reeked of beer and 'baccy in my recollection. My grandmother died before I was born, worn out by the struggle to keep a home going. Eight children to feed and clothe with whatever money was not spent in the nearest pub. She was a quiet and gentle soul, kind and hardworking. When my parents were very young, many children went barefoot throughout the year. The Thomsons and Lukes aspired to something better, and their children wore boots during the winter months and, of course, when they went to church.

We should not, I think, judge the old man too harshly. No doubt he was caught in the poor man's trap of too little money, too little leisure, boozing to forget, forgetting too well and finding another child on the way with consequently still less money to go round. But he was, they say, a good plumber.

When he stayed with us for some months in the late seventies, I remember him at mealtimes chewing up a mouthful of food and feeding it to Flossie, our Yorkshire Terrier — who loved the sloppy beer-scented morsel.

In appearance he was rather like a weedy, beaten down 'Old Bill', with the same tobacco and beer-stained drooping moustache, the same ripe nose and alcoholic complexion, the same quiff, but with rather beadier eyes. He always wore an ancient greenish bowler hat and superannuated overcoat, a greasy wrinkled waistcoat with watchchain draped across it, and his trousers always seemed too long for him and concertinaed over his boots. When he was short of cash,

2

which seemed to be most of the time, he tapped my father for the price of a pint, and no doubt any other of his sons he could find. To be fair, as an old age pensioner he received only 10/6d per week, which was little enough even then.

My mother, with the chronic shortage of cash during the Depression years, had strictly forbidden any handouts, but my father and the other uncles had a soft spot for the old reprobate, and he usually got his drink. He must have served as an awful warning, for none of his children would touch drink, apart from the traditional New Year tot. He *did* make an effort to stay sober during his few months with us, but inevitably slipped up occasionally, and finally he came in blind drunk one afternoon after a reunion with some old army mates. My mother was out. When she returned she found him asleep and half undressed on his bed in our bedroom. (We four kids slept in the other bed.) His state of undress was the last straw to her, and he was ordered out of the house next day when he had sobered up.

WHEN my father left school at the age of fourteen, most ordinary jobs were closed to him because of his stature. He once told me he had been approached by a man who saw him in the street, not long before he left school. He worked for a travelling circus and offered my father a job as a clown. This of course is one time-honoured profession open to dwarfs, and must have been old before the pyramids were built. He thought he might have taken the job, but his mother was outraged and vetoed any suggestion that her son might earn his living by allowing people to laugh at him. Later he was offered an apprenticeship as a jockey — something that happened to me also, much later.

He eventually became apprenticed to George Meikle, a watchmaker and jeweller who owned a shop in East Adam Street. This was only a few minutes from Surgeon's Hall, a busy junction in Edinburgh about five minutes' walk from Princes Street. It showed considerable faith and understanding on the part of Meikle, as I know from personal experience that the majority of people take one look at the stumpy fingers and immediately dismiss the possibility that they might be capable of the most delicate and precise workmanship. I have seen my father working on a lady's wrist-watch less than half-an-inch in diameter, manipulating almost invisible, dust-grain-like screws, and fragile tiny wheels which could be crushed by the tap of a fingernail.

3

He had incredible patience too. On the rare occasions when one of these minuscule components fell to the floor, to become invisible in fact, he never lost his temper. He just got down and swept around under the bench, and when he had collected into a pan whatever debris there was on an already clean floor, he worked painstakingly with a magnet until he recovered it.

On finishing his seven-year apprenticeship with Meikle, he served another year or so with him, then decided to start his own business. Meikle hoped he would stay, and even hinted that the business would be handed over to him in the course of time, but accepting that his mind was made up, Meikle gave him an excellent reference, and in addition told him he could take his choice of any watch in the window display. There were metal, silver and gold watches, some to the value of £60 which was an astronomical sum then. My father did not want to appear greedy. He was well aware of which watch was the most valuable in the shop, but he chose instead a moderately priced silver watch with, as he put it, 'a good movement'.

Meikle had it engraved inside with the date, 1909, and the inscription, 'presented to Andrew Thompson for Honesty and Diligence in Business'. He or the engraver added the redundant 'p' to the surname. That watch was still keeping excellent time until quite recently, but the mainspring broke and it seems impossible to find a replacement.

During these apprenticeship years my father attended night school. At the end of the course, he won a first prize for excellence in English. This was a dictionary, the most useful book among the few in our house. We also had the complete works of Shakespeare and Robert Burns, one or two tatty copies of lives of missionaries (Livingstone and Mungo Park), *Spud Tamson*, *The Iron Horse*, *Ungava* and of course the family Bible. The dictionary was bound in black, and was illustrated. His evening class work was so good that he was offered the chance of further study, aided by a scholarship, which would have led on to university. This he was obliged to turn down. As the eldest, his weekly wage was now indispensable to the family. Nowadays generous living grants are available, but then and even in my own time, the parents had to be relatively well off to be able to afford a non-earning son on a scholarship, which normally paid only the college fees. I am sure that given the chance he could have gone far.

He had the temperament to work hard and *do* things. He was almost painfully honest and generous. He was the most courageous man I've ever known. Not just in facing society with his pretty daunting physical handicap, but in his personal life, particularly during the last two years of his life, when he suffered from gradually worsening *angina pectoris*. For two or three years previously, his little shop had begun at last to offer a living above subsistence level, and he had actually managed to save about £170. He felt he now had a chance to provide properly for his wife and family. Then came this shattering blow. After the first attack, the doctor advised him to ease off — to retire, in fact. As my brother and two sisters now had jobs of a sort, we could have supported our parents. But he knew we were all of marriageable age, and there was no predicting how things would turn out. He carried on, working if anything even longer hours. He would work in his shop on his Wednesday half-day, saying it saved him walking home till evening. Latterly Charlie or I would meet him at the shop and walk home with him. He would walk fifty yards, then stop, grey-faced, until the pain abated enough to let him carry on. He had to stop maybe twenty times between shop and home, pretending we'd just stopped for a chat to fool passersby who might be concerned if they thought he was unwell. Since we lived at the top of a tenement building, four flights of stairs up, my brother or I would give him a hand upstairs, a final ordeal after the long walk home.

The business he started with such pride — 'Andrew Thomson, Watchmaker and Jeweller' — was at 1 West Adam Street, not far uphill from Meikle's establishment. One would have thought this proximity rather unfortunate. I have to assume that it was difficult to find premises further away, which I am sure he would have done had it been at all possible. Perhaps one reason was that the shop was leased by the same factor who rented him the flat at 13 West Nicolson Street. But they still lived on amicable terms, passing on customers to each other when they themselves could not fulfil their requirements.

At the age of twenty-nine, just before he opened his shop, he married Eliza Fogo Luke. They were the same age and had known each other and their respective families for all of their lives, living so close — Causewayside and Ratcliffe Terrace are continuations of the same street. She was also the eldest in her family, of six girls and three boys.

MY MOTHER was the survivor of twin girls. The other died at birth. Her father, Charles Luke, was a house painter and decorator, with a business at Causewayside. I still have the step-ladder he used. He died before I was born, but from photographs he appeared to be a pleasant person, white-haired and moustached. My mother remembered him as cheerful and kindly. He died of lead poisoning from the paint used in his daily work. It was known that paint containing lead was dangerous, but most paints then contained a percentage of the metal. Knowing this, he was meticulous in scrubbing his hands clean every night, cleaning his nails of every trace of paint, but the poison still built up gradually in his body, and he died at the age of sixty-five. Unusually for adults of his age, he still had a perfect set of teeth, but to his disgust and discomfort, in his last few years a new set had started to grow in. Teething at sixty-plus is painful as well as inconvenient.

What my grandmother did before she was married I am not sure, but I think probably she had been a domestic servant. My mother remembers she used to talk about working as a very little girl, when she would be taken with *her* mother into the country. There a gang of women with children were employed as 'barkers'. The women used iron tools to strip the bark off cut logs, and the children collected and stacked the pieces. Probably the bark was used either as firewood or in tanning leather.

At school my mother said she was not of the brightest, and she always claimed to be slow at reading, writing and arithmetic. 'Dic-dictation, is a botheration!' she would say. She and the rest of her family were plagued by schoolmates calling after them 'Plooky Lukey!' (Plooky means pimply.) It was all the more annoying because they never *were* troubled with plooks!

But she certainly was not so dumb as she claimed. Slow at reading she remained all her life, but she wrote many letters, and when it came to managing the housekeeping money, she performed miracles. On leaving school at fourteen, she entered domestic service, living in, and going home when she had a day off. Her mother took her salary, which was very little, I believe about five shillings per month, and gave her pocket money. At the age of twenty, her allowance from her month's earnings was only threepence. Finally she rebelled, for, even allowing for the difference in value of money then and now, threepence for a whole month was incredibly stingy. Though she now had to buy all her own clothes and other necessities from her earnings, she felt comparatively affluent. She even bought a second-hand bicycle for ten shillings and sixpence.

She mentioned a love affair she had during this threepence-a-month period. Her boyfriend lived in Cockenzie, a fishing village which must have been nine or ten miles from her place of work. She used to visit him on her days off, and walked both ways because she had no money for the tram fare. He rarely if ever made the journey into town to see her, and after about a year the affair broke up. She confessed she had been quite broken-hearted at the time.

One of my aunts, also a domestic servant, once might have married a sheikh, long before the discovery of Arab oil. When she was in her early twenties she dated an Arab student who was studying at the university. His name, I was told, was Eek-Ballaly-Sha. It was some years later that I translated this into Iqbal Ali Shah. For some reason the affair was called off. I suspect she discovered that the status of women in Arabia was not all she would have wished. So perished my one chance of having a rich uncle.

When she became a 'skivvy' in domestic service, my mother found it entailed no great change in her lifestyle. Ever since she had been old enough, she had been skivvying at home. Any spare time she had from housework was taken up in caring for the shoal of little brothers and sisters. My grandmother had favourites among her brood, but my mother was not one of them. This may have influenced her attitude to her own children. She would lean over backwards to avoid the least suspicion of favouritism.

While her mother seems to have been unjustifiably hard on her, my grandfather had a soft spot for her, and occasionally spoke up on her behalf, though he seems to have left the running of the family mainly to his wife. In her early years, my mother was very slim, and she did not put on weight until long after she was married. This was a sore point with her, and when she talked about it at home, her father's stock phrase was, 'Ay lassie! Ye're strecht up an doon, like a shit-hoose door!' Though he may have made the occasional earthy comment, I was assured that no swear words were ever tolerated in that household. My mother never used to swear until her brush with her father-in-law, and even then only in moments of great stress.

She always had great respect for the 'gentry' in whose houses she worked, and never seemed to have any great resentment when they threw their weight around, though I do remember her impersonation of one particularly pompous and imperious employer. Her great ambition was to have us children dressed up and acting like 'little ladies and gentlemen'. Maybe she had learned to curb her feelings while at school. She suffered under some callous teachers who would be sarcastic at her expense, and hold her efforts up to ridicule. She was sometimes terribly hurt by their cruelty, but seems to have built up some sort of defensive shell, out of sheer necessity. But she ended her school days with vast relief. You should understand that children who did not pass the equivalent of the 11-plus examination, like my mother, were simply made to stay in the same class until they could leave legally at the age of fourteen.

Anyway, when she was twenty-nine, she and my father decided to get married. My father had also just come out of an abortive love affair. The girl's parents had vetoed the relationship. As I mentioned previously, they had known each other since babyhood, and both families were well known to each other, so this was no sudden and passionate love affair. But there was deep respect and affection between them.

There was an engagement period of about a year, and during this time their resolution was thoroughly tested. Mrs Luke, though she knew my father was a hard worker, and knew his character from personal contact with the family all his life, now ordered my mother to break off the engagement. 'No daughter of mine is going to marry a freak!' she declared. My mother was much taller, of average height, about five feet six inches, so there was a very obvious contrast in stature which gave the unfeeling scope for jokes about orange boxes and piles of books. When my mother refused to accept this ruling, she was disowned forthwith, and told never to cross the Lukes' doorstep again.

So my parents were denied entrance to Granny Luke's house, and she even refused to attend the wedding. I was four years old before she reluctantly gave in to the pleading of the remaining daughters and finally consented to receive us. I cannot recall that first encounter, but I know we visited quite regularly thereafter.

We children were rather in awe of Granny Luke. She was a large, forbidding, sour-faced old lady, fat and sagging, and always dressed in dull black, with a jet necklace. She never seemed to get out of her old upright rocking chair. She never smiled. She breathed mainly through her mouth, and since it was always open, we children could watch a single long yellow fang, which wobbled perilously. I used to wonder how long it would hang on. My sister Betty says she remembers being given a present of a necklace as a token of special favour, but I do not think we ever managed to work up any affection for her, and she plainly regarded us as an embarrassment.

The unmarried aunts did make us feel welcome, and we liked all of them, though occasionally we were trapped and made to submit to wet kisses. There always seemed to be a crowd of them in the little kitchen, with a cheerful fire in the grate and a black iron kettle singing on the hob. Everything was kept spick and span. No doubt Granny insisted it be kept that way.

We did enjoy our visits to Ratcliffe Terrace though. There was a fascinating back garden, reached through a sort of washhouse-cum-conservatory. No-one else we knew then had a house with a garden — only toffs could afford them. Actually, in retrospect, it was a very dull, small mediocre town garden. It was only two long narrow strips of sooty earth with a brick path up the middle, surrounded by brick walls. But the end wall was covered in ivy, with huge dark green glossy leaves. There were lively woodlice and earwigs under the stones. A marvel to us was the path edging of upturned and half-buried bottles; some of them had green ferns inside which had grown there by themselves! This garden was the first place we wanted to see. No doubt Granny was glad to see us go outside, and the longer we stayed the better. But born and brought up in a slum tenement as we were, *any* kind of garden was Eden to us.

Even the house itself was fascinating to us. It was not part of a tenement, like the houses of everyone else we knew. It was a separate building on a corner, and had an upstairs and a downstairs and rooms beyond counting. I don't remember ever seeing upstairs. It must have been out of bounds. The building could have been quite old. In the Old Edinburgh Room in the Central Library, I found an old print of the crossroads from the time when there used to be a toll there. Quite conceivably the building could have been the old Toll House. In my earliest youth, the road beyond the house towards Liberton was cobbled for maybe half a mile, but beyond that it became an unsurfaced red dirt country road.

Most Edinburgh streets were cobbled. The main thoroughfares like Princes Street had finely dressed granite setts, but the side streets and alleys had whinstone cobbles, much bumpier, as became obvious when one cycled from one to the other. Suburban roads were beginning to be surfaced with tar macadam in the twenties and thirties, and in the city itself, slowly replacing the cobbles.

Sometimes we were taken for a long walk out to Liberton Dams, in the heart of the country where lived old Mrs Alexander (Granny Alexander to us). Her house was similar to Granny Luke's. It had been built by a great-uncle (I believe) of my mother's, named Ross, for himself and his family. He had been a stonemason. There was no garden, but there *was* a farmyard, with chickens and a huge, terrifying bubblyjock. I was intrigued by the knobbly blue and red wattles on its head and neck. Did they hurt? There was a tiny enclosed yard at the back of the house, reached through the kitchen. The whitewashed stone walls reached up to the sky. Often we were turned loose to play there, safe from the bubblyjock. It was paved with stone flags, and you would think contained nothing of any interest whatsoever. But there were patches of moss on the stone walls, of different textures and colours, green, brown and yellow. Some had little forests of spikes with little knobs on the end. There were spiders, midges and daddy-long-legs. There were glossy, lively black and orange earwigs. There was the occasional pink and glistening worm, stretching impossibly long, then contracting, writhing by a crack in the paving. The walls were plain stone, but looked at close up every stone was different. The grey was made up of lots of different colours, and they each *felt* different. You could see

9

tiny sparkles of quartz grains, little pebbles, veins of different coloured stone. Oh, there was plenty to see!

This Uncle Ross was a bird-fancier, meaning of course canaries — and so was his friend Granda Luke. His house still was decorated with glass-fronted boxes full of stuffed canaries. But the Ratcliffe Terrace house had more, of all kinds. We gazed with horrified attention at the Fancies — Border Fancies and so on. Some of them had long necks at right angles to their bodies, like little green and yellow vultures. Some had little mops of feathers on their heads, covering their eyes. How could they *see*? And they were all colours — bright orange, clear yellow, browns, greens and parti-coloured varieties. We thought it was cruel to kill all these poor little birds, but we were told that it was only if they died that they were stuffed and mounted. It was a hobby, and it also served as a record of prize-winning strains. My mother as a little girl used to help her father feed and clean the canaries, and prepare them for showing. She used to enjoy this, feeding tiny chicks with chopped boiled egg on the end of a matchstick.

MY PARENTS were married, in church of course, on Hogmanay, December 31st, 1915, and it was soon after this that my father started his own business. It was a real act of faith. He had very little money saved up, but he put it all into furniture and stock for the shop. He told us that on the day he opened for business, all he had in the till was one solitary halfpenny. At the end of the first week, his takings totalled threepence. Things were difficult at first, but improved as he became known. He did mainly watch and clock repairs, with some fitting of spectacles, and ear piercing on rarer occasions. He also could remove wedding rings stuck on someone's finger, and enlarge them or make them smaller. He repaired all kinds of jewellery. During the war, new clocks and watches were unobtainable, so the old ones had to be repaired. Meikle generously directed some customers his way too.

In August of 1916 my parents visited friends living in the High Binn village near Burntisland. It has been in ruins for many years now, but at that time was only nearing the end of what had once been a flourishing shale oil industry. Many years later I saw an old photograph of the place in its heyday, with a row of huge retorts and clouds of smoke. My mother used to suggest that maybe the reason I gravitated to the area in later life was that I had been there before I was born.

10

I was born at home at 13 West Nicolson Street in December 1916, weighing ten pounds and obviously very normal and healthy. The second child, Euphemia, was born the following August, very prematurely, and weighing less than four pounds. She was 'bright red, with transparent ears, and looked like a skinned rabbit'. But she was a determined wee soul even then, and she survived. The third, Elizabeth (Betty), was born four years later. As it was suspected there might be complications, my mother went into Astley Ainslie Hospital for the birth, but the baby was normal and full-time. Charles, the final addition, arrived about a year later, and like the first two, was born in the kitchen of the two-roomed house.

The flat had been taken on a temporary basis by my parents. It was impossible to find a council house; as a newly wed couple they had no priority. But some slum properties were being demolished, and the occupants were automatically first on the lists for a new house. West Nicolson Street, it was rumoured, would be among the first to go, so when the factors offered a room and kitchen on the second storey, my parents were delighted to get it. The lavatory, an unlit box in the lobby, had to be shared with another young couple next door, but that would be no great hardship for only one more year, or two at the most. Actually, the two flats were one house which had been split up by installing a cold water tap and sink in the 'parlour', creating a 'single end' and a 'but and ben'. The original door to the flat was rarely closed. Open, some dim light could enter from the window halfway down the stairs, but when closed the lobby was pitch dark. The door to the single end was at the far end, and the one to our kitchen on the right past the lavatory.

Coal for the open range fire had to be kept in a large wooden bunker in a corner of the kitchen. The single end had the same arrangement. All cooking and baking was done on the open range, with a coal-fired oven beside it, or on a gas ring at the side of the fire. The range was kept gleaming black, the steel trim polished like silver with a burnisher, a square of steel ring mail mounted on leather. On the top, beside the glowing coals, was a big old cast iron kettle holding about a gallon of water. It was always kept blackleaded and polished. In the winter with a good fire in the grate, it would sing away quietly to itself. One or two of our married aunts had little boilers built in at one side of the range, with a brightly polished brass tap which produced hot water to order. We envied people who had such ultra-modern conveniences.

The hearth was pipe-clayed fresh and white. The ash bucket was trimmed with polished brass, and there was a polished steel fender. Decorations on the hearth were a pair of flat irons and a pair of gauffering irons. The poker and shovel were polished steel and brass.

11

The oven had to be fired separately by shovelling live coals from the grate to a little fire box down on the hearth. The heat went up and round the oven and then up a little movable cast iron chimney with a damper in it placed at the back of the chimney place proper. This was a great entertainment for us children, as it was only rarely used, and then for special treats like steak pies or Christmas baking.

In the early thirties we acquired a gas stove, which rendered the old oven obsolete. But hot water still had to be boiled by the kettleful. On Friday nights, bath night, as the eldest I always had the deepest water. It was topped up after each of the others got out. The tin bath in front of the fire had to be emptied basinful by basinful in the kitchen sink.

The only water supply came from a polished brass tap over a very ancient-looking pocked yellow stoneware sink at the window. All the pipes were lead and as old as the sink. Now we are told lead in drinking water causes brain damage. I imagine we were protected by our mother's passion for cleanliness, which never allowed the water to settle in the pipes long enough to create a problem. Occasionally, bird seed from our canary's cage lodged under the wooden rim, and would sprout a bright green grass leaf. When pulled out, there was a translucent white root hair with an intriguing pink tip.

All this was accepted. There was nothing better to be had. The young couple next door had two windows facing south, but only the single room. We had two rooms, the bedroom with the south-facing window, and the kitchen with its window facing north. The south windows overlooked the street. The kitchen window looked out on the back court, reached by the pend through the tenement. This court was completely covered in concrete, and whitewashed all round to a height of ten feet, except for the side to the right, which was a solid plank fence about twelve feet high. There was a gate in this, very rarely opened, which led to a junk yard. It had originally housed a stable, for when I was very young, you occasionally met a vast carthorse filling the pend on its way to the stable. In the far lefthand corner of the court was a flat-roofed garage, usually seen open only on weekends, and rarely at that. Up to around 1930, it had been used as a store by the local scaffie, who kept his tools there, along with many bundles of birch twigs piled up against the walls. Occasionally we could watch fascinated as he made a new broom head with the twigs. The scaffies (scavengers) swept the streets clean, shovelling the rubbish into heavy wooden handcarts. Latterly, they were upgraded to 'street orderlies' and given lighter double-ended aluminium carts with lids. In the far wall of the court beside the garage was a back door to the type foundry. Its wood was so hacked and battered it might have been dug up in some Pharaoh's tomb. We

12

never heard of this door ever being open, but very often you could pick up old lead type which had worked its way underneath to our side.

Stephenson Blake's type foundry with its tall smoking brick chimney, worked all night as well as during the day, clattering and crashing. The left of the court was the wall of a sawmill, from which came the intermittent scream of circular saws. This too went on all day, but mercifully stopped at night. Over the junkyard wall and the buildings beyond, the gilded youth on top of the University dome could be seen poised against the sky.

The drain in the middle of the court tended to get blocked in rainy weather, and sometimes there would be a two-foot deep pond which could persist for days on end. The local children of course loved this, but we were forbidden to paddle in it for fear of germs. Quite reasonably, because certainly at times it did pong a bit.

BUT complications set in. The young couple next door, the Tierneys, were Catholic and Irish. Race and religion did not necessarily cause friction — people of different persuasions in our neighbourhood all lived together quite amicably. There was a large local Jewish community too. The synagogue was just across the street from my father's shop. The Tierney's first child, Charles, arrived not long after me. Mrs Tierney eventually had thirteen children including a set of twins. I think three or maybe four died. Child mortality was higher then. In time their single room became rather crowded, and with our own six-member family next door, the use of that single w.c. became an obsession. One had to wait until the cistern flushed, then make a dash for it. It was bad enough when our families were on speaking terms, but decidedly unpleasant when we were not. Since the cistern supplying the one in the w.c. was in a corner of our kitchen, the sound of running water was rarely absent from our ears. In the mornings when we had to get ready for school, we often had to resort to a bucket at the end of the bed, which my mother would empty later.

It really became impossible at times. On several occasions the Tierneys blocked the waste pipe. With toddlers around this was always liable to happen. But they went on using it until the bowl overflowed. Mrs Tierney refused to do anything about it; it was the landlord's job to send for a plumber. My mother would set to, take out her false teeth, and unblock the foul thing, retching all the while.

13

Then she scrubbed out and disinfected the place with Lysol. After this, they would attempt for a while at least to be more careful. But often it was a filthy and disgusting place to enter. As there was no light (gas mantles put into the light bracket were stolen in a day or two) one always had to take a candle or torch; and ventilation was only a small round aperture high in the ceiling.

Before the 'bagwash', run by the Co-op who collected, washed and delivered weekly, my mother spent most of Monday washing, mangling, ironing and starching. Some things had to be boiled. For the wash, she used Hudson's Soap and A.1. Soap Powder. These were pure soap; detergents had not been invented. For fragile items, she would use Lux flakes. 'For a whiter white', Reckitt's Blue was swished through the hot water. Robin Starch was used for things which had to be starched. Everything was rubbed or scrubbed on the ribbed zinc washboard in the tub.

After mangling to remove surplus water, everything was hung on a pulley from the ceiling to dry out enough to iron, with newspapers spread on the floor to catch the drips. In fine weather, the washing was hung on a T-shaped wooden frame with two ropes strung along each side, which was held in a socket at the kitchen window. Every other window in the tenements had one of these contraptions, and on windy Mondays the whole façade would be a-flutter. Heavy blankets were usually pegged up on ropes in the back court, with long wooden clothes-poles to hold them up off the ground.

Ironing was done with solid, heavy flat irons, heated at the fire or on the gas ring before the gas stove came. Finally it was possible to buy a gas iron, an ultra-modern convenience. My mother insisted on starching and ironing our shirt collars — we wouldn't have been 'decent' otherwise. My father wore celluloid collars until they went out of fashion. We wondered how anyone could endure anything so very uncomfortable.

Our floors were covered with linoleum. Each week my mother scrubbed them clean, on her hands and knees. When dry, they were polished with Mansion Polish. Sometimes, to save her knees, we were given old socks to put on, and we would skate up and down until there was an acceptable shine. The rug at the door was a veritable death trap after this treatment. In front of the fender was a clootie rug, made of hand-looped rags. Most households had at least one of those. They were made by cutting up old clothes, blankets and so on into narrow strips, which were then hooked through a hessian backing — an old sack opened up flat. Some people made quite attractive designs in this way, but it was quite acceptable to make a random pattern, using whatever colours came to hand. We would

14

help to cut strips on winter evenings, but after a while the scissors hurt your hands. Hooking was more fun.

One might think that families living in conditions like these would have priority on the re-housing lists. In the early thirties, there were a dozen persons living in that single room next door to us. All their applications were refused. With only six in two rooms, we of course had no hope at all. We were two boys and two girls, aged from eleven to sixteen, sleeping in one room, with the parents in the kitchen. Obviously far from overcrowded. God knows what kind of condi-tions the authorities would have considered *really* urgent.

When we were all small, we slept in one bed packed like sardines, the boys with their heads at one end, the girls at the other. On occasions when we had visitors, we might have four at each end. Pyjamas we had never heard of. Boys wore a night shirt (which was also the day shirt), girls had 'goonies' — nightgowns. The beds were of iron with brass knobs and trimmings, and they were raised on wooden blocks six to eight inches high to provide more storage space underneath. There were no cupboards or wardrobes, apart from a built-in cupboard under the bench beside the coal bunker, used for pots and pans and other hardware. There were two kists (chests) for clothes and blankets. One, the big one, had belonged to my housepainter grandfather, and was gloriously painted to disguise it as walnut. Some clothing was kept in a modern canvas steamer trunk under the bed, but coats and jackets were hung on coathangers by the front door. Toys and personal treasures we kept in cardboard boxes under the bed. There was an old black painted kitchen dresser for food and crockery, and my mother's best china was kept on two high shelves.

All round our area, slums were demolished over the years. Ours would surely be next. But when I was sixteen, nothing had been done, and the building still looked as if it might collapse at any time without assistance. It is still standing today. Now it has been renovated and preserved as housing for university students. I had always wondered whether one day they would mount a plaque over the pend saying 'George L. Thomson was born here.'!

The year I started at Art College, before I was sixteen, we had at last found a better house to move to. It was at 2 Salisbury Square, a more salubrious sounding address, but it also was just an old tenement near the top of Dumbiedykes Road, at the foot of Brown Street. It had three rooms, a kitchenette — still with only a cold water tap, but with two incredible luxuries, a w.c. of our own, and *electric light*. For some days we all went around switching on and off, and enjoying the sheer novelty of having instant illumination. The lighting too was a vast improvement on what we now perceived as dim gaslight.

15

Between our bedroom in the old house and the Tierneys' room was the old communicating door. It had simply been nailed up and their side had shelves across it, making a shallow open cupboard. So it was impossible not to hear a lot of what went on next door, especially on Saturday nights, when Tierney came home roaring drunk and created hell generally.

He beat up his wife, smashed things, and thumped any of the kids unfortunate enough to get in his way. This happened quite often — not every week, but often. When it did, the noise woke us up in fright and our mother used to come through and would tell us not to listen. In spite of not listening, we learned all the swear words at an early age, though we were dared to use them under any circumstances. The Tierney offspring were not so inhibited.

Though for much of the time it seemed we were not on speaking terms with our neighbours next door, we felt sorry for Mrs Tierney. When younger, she must have been quite a striking girl with long red hair and a slim figure, but I remember her as gaunt, grey-faced and slatternly, with her red hair dishevelled and wearing a tatty old coat and hat. And yet, sometimes we heard her singing as she worked, and to me it sounded terribly pathetic. She sang on key, but her voice was harsh and edgy. Once, when she was ill and again 'expecting', my mother scrubbed and cleaned out the room for her so it would be presentable for the visiting nurse.

OUR back court was a perfect playground for the children of the tenement, safely separated from the street by the pend. Intruders from elsewhere in the street were not welcomed. Whipping tops were popular — wooden tops with a leather-thonged whip. I never mastered the throwing top. You wrapped string round it and threw it to spin on the ground. Girls played with diabolos, which I have not seen for many years, apart from a TV show with Chinese jugglers.

The Bif-Bat, a rubber ball attached to a wooden bat by a piece of elastic, was introduced in the twenties. So was the Yoyo, which still survives. But these cost money. A home-made toy which could be made from scrap was the 'sooker', a circle of leather with a knotted string threaded through a hole in the middle. This was soaked overnight to make it pliable. When it was pressed down on a smooth flat surface, by standing on it, it stuck fast. A hefty pull drew it off with a gratifying pop. Quite heavy stones could be lifted with this contraption and it wasn't too popular with adults as some lads went around pulling up manhole and toby covers and didn't always replace them. This pastime was popular in showery weather since wet, smooth surfaces were required. In fine weather we could always find the necessary moisture somehow.

When I was an infant, I had a wooden horse on wheels. Not a realistic one, like a rocking horse I saw and coveted years later with real hair, glass eyes and real harness, but a painted wood cylinder with a horse's head at one end, cut out of plank. But I loved it for years. One year I was given a tricycle, in the hope the exercise would strengthen my legs. It had a solid frame, a large front wheel with fixed pedals, and small wheels at the back. The brake was a push pad type which pressed down on the front tyre. It had a bell, to warn pedestrians, as I was only allowed to use it on the pavement. My father fashioned a pillion seat so I could take Phemia along when my mother took the others in the go-cart or pram. This gave me endless pleasure, and one of my joys was to pedal it up to the pend entrance, then freewheel, feet off the pedals, down to the far end of the court where there was still enough momentum left for a tight circle on two wheels. This machine survived for seven or eight years, when the pedal grips were worn to smooth metal and the solid rubber tyres level with the rims.

A gentler pastime was playing shops. For this we had to find 'champin' stanes', used to pound smaller stones and pieces of brick into powder — flour, sugar, cocoa and so on. The girls always had tin scales and scoops and dishes saved from Christmas stockings, and these were useful furnishings for the shops. Shops were set out on doorsteps and things bought from one shop were sold in another. Pieces of glass were used for money.

Both boys and girls enjoyed playing with hoops. Bought ones were best, but if money was tight you could get the wooden hoops off the empty barrels of butter at the grocers. Bought hoops came in various sizes. With the bigger ones it was possible to do tricks like jumping through it while it was moving. Or you could throw it away with reverse spin and make it come back to your hand. Boys liked to get steel hoops. These were made by the blacksmith across the road. Some of them had the propelling stick attached to the hoop by a ring at the end, or the stick was bent into a hook. It was purely a toy for running with, but it made a most satisfactory ringing, singing noise.

A toy which could be bought, made, or on occasion acquired as a free gift with a comic was the 'Whizzer'. This was a circle of card with string threaded through two holes in the centre. You pulled on the strings, the card revolved at high speed and made a whirring sound. We sometimes made a more lethal version out of a tin lid, with the edges cut to make a circular saw. This could cut notches in wood. Or your finger.

Inside the house we had humming tops. One I had was quite big, and gloriously coloured. It was spun up to humming speed by pumping a central plunger vigorously up and down a few times, and it sang away for quite a long time, gradually growing fainter. Related to this was the gyroscope I got one Christmas. It was started by string round the centre spindle and pulling sharply, when the toy would do the most extraordinary things, seemingly against the law of gravity.

As far back as I can remember, I always had a box of paints, and a series of drawing books. Long before I started school, my mother would keep me quiet by drawing things on scraps of paper, which I would sit painting for hours. Though tigers and dreadnoughts were beyond her, she often drew bunches of forget-me-nots, which were her *forté* when *she* was a schoolgirl. At Christmas I got a replacement when my paint box was finished, and on occasion I might find myself with *two* boxes, a new one for special paintings, and an old one for everyday. Paint boxes were quite cheap, though most of the paints were of poor quality, little more than dyed clay, especially the big flashy boxes which opened up to show dozens of beautiful colours, exotically named. Like 'Payne's Grey', 'Hooker's Green', 'Rose Madder', 'Ivory Black', 'Crimson Alizarin', 'Green Bice', 'Chrome Yellow' and 'Vermilion'. Only after starting secondary school did I come to understand that a box with only six good colours was worth any number of those tawdry gift boxes.

One Christmas the girls got a sewing machine each. These were all metal and actually worked, producing a chain stitch. The girls used them to make dolls' clothes. On TV recently, I saw one, now a 'vintage toy' and quite valuable. Nearly all the bought toys of that period are now vintage. Many clockwork toys made of tin came from Germany, and very often on the inside you could read 'Lyle's Golden Syrup'. There were clowns, motor bikes, clockwork animals of all sorts, all very cheap. Once I got a toy railway. It was only a circular tin track with a tin loco and truck, but we spent hours winding up the engine and watching it chase its tail. Bassett-Lowkes and Hornby trains were way out of our class, and we envied the wealthy who could afford to fill a whole room with a miniature railway system with all the trimmings. But we had to concede it would have been difficult to fit one of those super sets into our kitchen.

Some splendid moving toys were made of wood. There was the 'Jumping Jack', where you squeezed the ends of two spars together and made him do gymnastics, and the circle of chickens, which pecked away in turn as you swung the weight underneath. There were balancing dolls, and a jointed dancing doll which danced a

18

lively jig when held just touching a springy board, beaten by your other hand.

We had a cast iron 'Black Sambo' bank, which would be valuable if we had it today. It was painted black and red, and when you put a penny in his hand and pressed a lever, he lifted it to his mouth and swallowed it. Later we got pilfer-proof TSB metal banks, not nearly so much fun.

Over our camping years I had a few toy boats which gave me a lot of pleasure. Not model yachts, which would have cost far too much. The best sailer, and the one which provided most satisfaction, was a six-inch-long model which I carved from a piece of cork. I added a thick piece of tin for a keel, which bent at the end for a rudder, and a stick mast with a scrap of rag for a sail. Usually the receding tide would leave a large shallow pool, and here I learned about sailing — tacking, running before the wind, and sailing into the wind. This contraption sailed as close to the wind as any super model yacht I've ever seen.

We probably had the same table games as everyone else; Snap, Tiddlywinks, Ludo, Happy Families, Snakes and Ladders, Draughts, Dominoes, Solitaire. But we had one rather unusual one. This was Bagatelle, played on a green baize board like a miniature billiards table, but with a rounded end with a series of little wooden cups with numbers painted inside. There was a cue for potting the balls into the cups.

Periodically magazines and comics would give away free gifts in the hope of increasing circulation. Usually they were card constructions — I remember a glider in the form of a dove — or a snap-gun, which you flapped to make it bang. Occasionally there were more exciting things, like the luminous paint which came as a powder to be mixed with water; or invisible ink; or transfers. The *Children's Newspaper* brought out a series for the coronation of George VI. There was a striped black and white celluloid holder, into which you pushed card strips with illustrations of the procession. By moving the strips, you made the horses trot, flags wave and wheels turn.

MY FACILITY at drawing was noted even during my first year at school. Miss Eales remarked to my mother that I was so good I would probably become an architect. I had no idea what that might be, but it sounded important. Letters fascinated me from the very beginning. The event of the school year was when we were given a new reading book, which I would take home and read from cover to cover that same evening. I enjoyed spelling, and got quite a reputation in our street. Once a lad of ten cornered me on the stairs and said, 'All right, if you're so good at spelling, how do you spell "owdatious"?' I spelled it as he pronounced it, and there went my reputation. The reading book I was on had a long word which I read as AN-SWER-ED. Until it was read out by the teacher, I didn't realise it was the same as 'answered'. But once I learned a word, it seemed to be there for keeps.

The actual shape of letters interested me. In one of my first reading books I can remember being lost in admiration of a lower case 'h', the beginning of a word 'he' or 'him'. There was a coloured picture on the top half of the page which I can't recall, but I can still savour the shiny black of the ink, the rightness of the straights and curves of the letter, and the smooth glossy white of the paper it was printed on.

In writing, we progressed during the first year or two to *Vere Foster Copy Books.* In these were letters, then phrases which had to be copied in the lines beneath, as accurately as possible. The first few letters were dotted in, to be drawn over. One of my first lessons in the art of compromise was during the course of one of those writing lessons. We were using pencils, and Miss Eales impressed upon us that we must write very, very lightly, hardly pressing on the pencil at all. Always willing to please, I wrote the first line exceedingly carefully. My line was as thin and steady as a spider web, evenly accented all the way. Any lighter and it would have been invisible. I sat back with justifiable pride and waited for Miss Eales to compliment me. 'Oh dear, George! Are you afraid to start? I'll show you how to do it!' And she drew heavy, coarse-looking lines all over my delicate masterpiece. From then on, I matched her line. I couldn't tell her then the job had already been done superlatively. One did not correct a teacher. That was when I had the first suspicion that teachers were not really omniscient. But she was a pleasant, lovable old soul, even if her eyes were not as good as they had been.

In view of my later status as a professional scribe and calligrapher, it was a great handicap to be taught Vere Foster Script. There was no way it could be developed into beautiful writing. With care, it could look tidy, but written fast it developed into a nondescript scribble, difficult even for the writer to decipher. In later years, some of us introduced quirky tails and extra flourishes to try and infuse some character into our writing, but of course there was nothing that could redeem it.

Miss Anderson was headmistress of the Infant school. I do not remember her with affection. She was a large-boned, big-bosomed, craggy-faced lady who ruled the school with a rod of iron. She usually wore dark brown, red-brown or purplish dresses, ornately patterned, with necklaces of tiny jet beads. Her hair was piled on top of her head in the style of Queen Alexandra. She never smiled. During the first week, we children were just becoming acquainted with each other. Bertie Leslie, who lived in a tenement across the street from my father's shop, knew me already. One morning as we stood lined up preparatory to being marched into school, he told some of the boys around that my father was a jeweller, and turned to me for corroboration. 'Yer faither's a jooler, inty? Inty?' I knew talking in the lines, or anywhere else for that matter, was forbidden, and I opened not my mouth. But Bertie was persistent, and at last to shut him up I nodded my head. Miss Anderson's eagle eye spotted this fractional movement, and we were both ordered out, to wait in the hall after morning assembly. Miscreants had to wait beside the central dais in full view of the rest of the school.

Bertie was a tough little lad, and accepted two of the belt as the price you paid if you were caught, which he regularly was thereafter. I was not so tough, and besides, I was innocent. Miss Anderson made us stand and hold out our hands. He was first and she did not hold back because he was only five and it was a first offence. I watched with horror and somehow found the courage to say, 'But I didn't say anything!' But I was forced to accept the 'palmies'. The leather tawse hurt worse than anything I'd experienced up till then. My eyes filled with tears, I could hardly see to walk back to Room One. My hands were red and swollen for at least an hour, and I had no sense of touch.

When I went to the shop for my dinner, I told my parents what had happened. My mother took me back to school in the afternoon and demanded to see the Headmistress. What she said I don't know, but she pointed out that I never told a lie, and using the tawse on an infant for a first offence was excessively severe. I *do* remember Miss Anderson apologising to me, but detected a strong note of insincerity.

Actually I did once tell a lie, before I reached school age. We were expecting visitors for tea, and my mother had set out the table beautifully, with a white tablecloth and her best china, with plates of scones and cakes. She was doing something in the front room when I yielded to temptation. I climbed up on a chair, wet my finger, and stuck it in the sugar bowl. Delicious! Then I noticed the perfect cone of poured sugar now had a glaringly obvious finger mark in it. In panic, I tried to restore it, and thought I had succeeded. Coming back, my mother said, 'Who's been at the sugar?' Full of guilt, I suggested, 'Maybe it was a moose?' She remarked it must have been a pretty big moose, and I was off the hook. But though I was quite sure she didn't know who did it, I felt horribly guilty for days.

My mother always had a pot plant or two in the house. The first one I can remember was an aspidistra. It was an unexciting plant. It never seemed to change or put forth a new leaf. But it was green and a survivor. It seemed to thrive on the occasional protracted drought when nobody remembered to water it. In a hanging pot in the window was a Wandering Sailor (*Tradescantia*) or a Mother-of-Thousands. In a window box in the front room she grew pansies, double daisies or wallflowers.

Though we never had room for a proper aquarium, I had a round glass container about six inches deep, in which I kept a freshwater mussel, a minnow, two water boatmen and some water snails, with some gravel in the bottom to anchor some Canadian pondweed. I spent hours watching this miniature pond. The translucent emerald green of the pondweed, with a shaft of sunlight falling through its fronds, made ordinary pot plants look dull and dowdy by comparison. In bright light strings of diamond bubbles would rise from the leaves, oxygenating the water, while on dull days the stream would slow down or stop, leaving one bright bead on the leaf.

The minnow lived about three years, and I found it endlessly fascinating to observe so close up. In the wild, a minnow is an unexciting little fish, dull brown on top, with the white below only flashing silver when the darting shoal changes direction. Close to, the brown is shot with blue, purple and gold, and the rainbow bloom on the silver of the lower half makes the fish a living jewel. I had wire netting over the dish to keep the minnow from jumping out. It would rise like a salmon or trout when I fed it a fly or bluebottle. But one day, sadly, I came home to find it lying shrivelled and dry on the table, having somehow wriggled through the netting.

The water boatmen were lively little insects, gold and black, with a silver coating of air when they dived below the surface. They were added after the minnow died, or possibly it would have eaten them. They provided some life and movement which the mussel didn't display. The snails moved, but slowly. I found they could travel upside down on the surface of the water, gulping down whatever they found there in the way of food. Their main function was clearing the green algae from the sides of the glass, which they did very well, leaving zigzag coiling trails to show where they had been.

Those insects vanished after one season, and were replaced by a dozen tadpoles. Just little black wigglers? No, looked at closely the skin had a blue and purple sheen, and as they grew older, the skin turned brownish with gold speckles. The heads grew more froglike, and the legs began to grow. Probably because of their omnivorous diet, the numbers decreased to three. I added a cork so they could climb out of the water when they started breathing air. Two did become tiny frogs, but met the same fate as the minnow when they managed to climb out.

At last all that remained were the snails and mussel. Its only sign of life was a stream of water spouted out at one side, only observable by the tiny particles swirling in the current. After one summer holiday I came home to a terrible stink and a dead aquarium. While we were away, the mussel had spawned and died, whether naturally or because of the cloud of spat, I do not know.

The window in our front room was used for 'windae-hingin'. You'd 'hing oot the windae' to call your coalman, throw a jeely piece to your offspring, or just to chat to a neighbour. At public occasions — a wedding, a funeral, a bonfire, the Friday night Salvation Army band, the BB's Pipe Band — all the tenement windows would be packed with sightseers. The Salvation Army band created in me an aversion to brass bands for the rest of my life. It always stopped immediately below our window, and when we were little woke us all up. The BB's band was always enjoyable. It marched along our street on its way to church parade on the occasional Sunday morning. It was of special significance to us, as our Uncle John was the big drummer. We admired and envied him in his splendid uniform thumping away at the huge drum, twirling the drumsticks professionally, and wearing, marvel of marvels, a real leopard skin over his shoulders.

The Bone Fire was on Bonfire Night. It was on the thirty-first of October originally, then with increasing English influence it moved to the fifth of November. Gangs of kids in each street would start stockpiling inflammable material weeks in advance. Occasionally raids were staged on a neighbouring street's hoard. The universal war chant was 'Ello, Ello, Bone Fire Wid!' We were not allowed to join the local gang. On these forays someone was sure to get a bloody nose or knee. The actual fire was a sight to behold. Usually there was enough material for a really big fire, and it was always built in front of our window at the widest part of the street. At its most splendid, the flames would be level with our window. Now and again, we heard of shop and house windows being cracked with the heat. If we woke during the night, we could still see the reflected red glow of the embers on the ceiling. Next morning there was only a huge circle of white ash, smoking gently. The dustmen came later and carted it all away, hosing the cobbles clean again.

The spectacle of spectacles, though, was probably the funerals. On the other side of the street was Hugh Harkess' funeral parlour. He must have run for election to the town council at one time, for I

23

remember crowds of children being recruited to march through the streets bearing placards showing his picture (in tile hat), chanting 'Vote, vote, vote for Shuey Harkiss! He is sure tae win the day. If ye dinnae let 'im in, we will bash yer door in, and ye'll never see the guizers any mair!'

Some funerals were restrained affairs. A small hearse, and one or two horse-drawn carriages for mourners. But for a really first-class funeral, there was a huge, ebony black, ornately decorated hearse, with glass sides so you could see the expensive coffin, with silver trimmings, and six horses to draw it. These midnight black steeds were a magnificent sight, pawing the ground, snorting, and tossing their heads in impatience to be off. Their trappings were polished black leather with silver buckles and decorations. Their manes were black silk. Their hooves were polished black. On their heads were huge feather plumes of black or purple. There might be six or more glossy black carriages for favoured mourners, and sometimes there was a long procession of people on foot. Six undertakers in funeral black and wearing top hats reverently and slowly bore the coffin from the funeral parlour to the hearse, and carefully slid it into position between the silver rails, before piling in the many floral wreaths. From the arrival of the hearse to the departure of the cortege never took much less than an hour, and we enjoyed every minute. That was the way to go — in style!

Father's business did reasonably well for a few years, but the pinch began around 1920, and became desperate at the time of the General Strike of 1926, which started on May 3rd and went on until May 13th. The miners continued on strike until November 30th. From 1924 to 1928 was the worst period. Often there was not enough money to buy food, but my mother never allowed the rent to fall into arrears. That was always paid first — we had to stay 'respectable'. But very often she had to go to the shop to see if any money had come in since opening, so she could buy something for us to eat. She said that at one period she had to feed us all on about a shilling a day. It says a lot for her that none of us remembers being really starving at the time. Often enough we felt we could eat a lot more, but we were luckier than some. She would do without herself, so that we could have enough. Many years later she confessed to me that she had decided it was just impossible to go on, and somehow managed to save twelve pennies. The day she achieved this, she was going to put her head in the oven and turn on the gas; since this came through a penny-in-the-slot meter, she had to be sure it would not cut off too soon. Twelve pennies worth would have been ample. After sending us off to school, she would have the whole afternoon, undisturbed for three hours. But that day, I complained of a headache, and she allowed me

24

to stay off school. She had to postpone her suicide attempt, but by the next day she had thought it all over again, and realised she would leave her four children without a mother, and her husband with an impossible burden. We should all have been put in a 'home', the ultimate shame and degradation. So she decided to carry on for a while at least. After all, there was a shilling in hand. This gas oven solution was one familiar to everyone who read the newspapers during the Depression.

One shilling (five new pence) was little enough even in the twenties to feed two adults and four growing children for a whole day. Food prices were low, but still too high for the people in our neighbourhood. One of my mother's ploys was to send one of us to the butcher's shop and ask if he had 'any bones for the dog'. Bones were generally given away free with your half pound of sausages or mince. I am sure the butcher knew the bones were not intended for the dog, and he would give a generous bagful, some with meaty scraps still adhering. These were boiled up for soup stock, *then* they went to the dog. A sheep's 'pluck' (stomach, lungs, intestines) cost about sixpence, but you had to clean it yourself. My mother would spend hours washing and scraping the tripe, but the result was nourishing food for several days. On occasion she would use some of this for making haggis, and I have never tasted commercially produced haggis which even approached the flavour of her master-pieces.

She was a good cook and baker, but for some reason she never baked her own bread. Odd, because her pastries, scones, buns, biscuits and shortbread were first-class. During affluent periods, her mincepies were delicious, but most times the sweet filling had to be searched for. She used to economise on jam by making it so runny that only a minimum amount could stay on the bread.

For minor ailments, my mother always had some sort of medication at hand. Occasionally we were lined up for a dose of brimstone and treacle, and this we rather enjoyed unless she had overdone the amount of sulphur. 'Scott's Cod Liver Oil Emulsion' fortified us during the winter. Hot sugary toddy was a cure-all for colds and flu, or upset stomachs. A blob of cottonwool soaked in neat whisky eased our toothaches. Even today whisky to me tastes like medicine. Coughs were treated with camphorated oil rubbed on the chest, or if really bad with a hot poultice. Warm almond oil was used for earaches. We liked the taste of 'California Syrup of Figs', far preferable to castor oil, but the after effects of both were not so enjoyable. Strains and sore muscles were cured with liberal applications of 'Sloane's Liniment'. A cough and sore leg together meant you could be smelt from afar, with 'Sloane's' and 'Wintergreen Cream' together. Doctors' medicines in bottles were helped down with the proverbial spoonful of sugar.

Shopping was done in small family businesses — greengrocers, little bakeries and dairies. 'Low's', now a supermarket chain, was a little grocer round the corner on the main street. There was a dairy directly below us. When I was sent down for a pint of milk, I had to take our own jug, and the wifie in the shop would dip the milk out of the pan or churn with a tin measure of the quantity required. They sold cream, double cream and butter too, but we had cream only on red letter days. When the Co-op arrived, delivering milk at twopence-halfpenny the pint, in bottles, the dairy stopped selling milk. Theirs was fresh milk, not pasteurised. Maybe they were forced to stop. The public was just now being made aware of 'germs' in everything.

The dairy also sold sweets. These were kept in the old-fashioned tall glass jars and shaken, or chipped out into the pan of a highly polished pair of brass scales. Then they were tipped into a 'poke', a square of newspaper twisted into a cone. There was ice-cream too. Ice-cream cones at a halfpenny or penny each we called 'ice-cream pokes'. There were also 'sliders', a flat slab of ice-cream difficult to eat without drips.

And what a cornucopia of goodies glistened there to tempt our Saturday pennies! Dolly Mixtures, Doddles, Sherbet Dabs, Coconut Taiblet, Lucky Bags (only a halfpenny, with toys and sweets inside), Soor Plooms, Acid Drops, Ogopogo Eyes, Kali Sookers, Jelly Babies, Rosebuds, Stickjaw Toffee, Locust Beans, Wrigley's 'Spirrimint' Chewing Gum, Tiger Nuts, Nelson Balls, Aniseed Balls, Toffee Aipples, Liquorice Allsorts, Liquorice Straps and Laces, Barley Sugar, Sherbet Pralines (very expensive), Snowballs, Sugar Mice, Chocolate Drops, Easter Eggs and many more. The wee greengrocer's, 'Duffy', which later opened across the street, also sold sweets, but had the added attraction of a 'Vantas' soda fountain. The carbonated and colourless beverage was kept in a globular glass container. The flavour and virulent colouring was chosen by the customer and added to the glass first. A great part of the enjoyment came from the preliminary ritual preparations, and the impressive sound effects when the lever was pulled.

Also in our street was a fishmonger's, just a small shop with a limited choice of fish. This is where we went for twopence worth of fish for the cat. Usually this was cods' heads or haddocks that were just 'going off'. This was boiled up in the cat's own iron pot, and lasted him for a week. Near the end of the week, if you lifted the lid in the dark, the remaining fish would glow with pale phosphorescence. This wee shoppie served our needs, but there was a palatial establishment out Newington way where we always had to pause when our walks took us that way. It was a huge tiled hall of a place, with coloured tiles illustrating sea creatures, and water running constantly down the inside of the window if the weather was warm. In cooler weather the water was turned off, and the splendidly arranged collection of seafoods on the huge marble slab became more clearly visible. The centrepiece was usually some huge fish — a turbot, skate or salmon, with lesser fish artistically laid out around it. Colour was added with large crabs, lobsters and shellfish. Everything was nested in jewel-like crushed ice, and garnished with parsley.

Another shop worth visiting was the poulterer's further along near Nicolson Square. Here the window was full of poultry and game. Strings of rabbits hung up outside. At Christmas time they really spread themselves, and most of the shop front was covered with festoons of carcasses — chickens, turkeys, geese, guineafowl, pheasants, hares and rabbits by the score. A few would be on sale prepared, plucked or skinned ready for the pot, but mostly the skins and feathers were left on. There were no oven-ready, plastic-wrapped, pre-cooked, deep-frozen, standard-sized, chicken-flavoured chickens.

In the mid-twenties, a new shop took over what had been a plumber's premises, across the street from us. It was a ladies' hairdressing 'salon'. (We thought it was a mis-spelling of 'saloon'.) It seemed unlikely that the local ladies could provide sufficient patronage to keep it going, but it flourished with its 'water waves', 'marcel waves' and 'perms'. Around this time all the female population went 'thoroughly modern', and most had their hair cut short, in 'shingles', 'bingles' and 'bobs', though no one in our area dared to go so far as an 'Eton Crop'. My sisters and cousins all had their hair bobbed. I thought the new styles were unbecoming. Girls with long hair looked far more attractive. Besides being the 'fashion', it could be that short hair was much easier to deal with. Certainly my mother had to spend hours washing, drying, combing and brushing. In the case of our straight-haired Betty, she had to do her hair up in rags to make it curly; and she curled her own hair with hot curling tongs. Why they should *want* curly hair, I couldn't understand.

Male hair styles were conservative, short back and sides. A moustache was permissible, but any man with a beard would attract a gang of urchins shouting 'Beaver!' Long hair was only acceptable on known eccentrics and the occasional public figure like Lloyd George. Our 'respectable' unadventurous short hair is now considered outrageous enough for skinheads and pop groups, who would no doubt be horrified to have their grandparents' approval. But any of our friends who suddenly appeared with very short hair, clipped close all over with maybe a little patch of short fur left as a quiff in

27

front, was immediately classed as an untouchable. This was the 'convict crop', compulsory for all those who didn't pass the 'Heid' Nurse's periodical examinations. This nurse came to our classrooms and examined every head for livestock or disease. Those heads shaven for impetigo or ringworm and anointed with vivid patches of gentian violet would pass as punks today without comment.

At the far end of the street was 'Leggat's Fish and Chip Shop'. On a Saturday night, when cash was available, I would be sent along for two fish suppers and sixpennyworth of chips. Leggat had been in music hall, but had given it up. He had been a Scots comic, and his signature tune, which he'd written himself, was *A'm the saftest o' the faimly*, stolen, he claimed, by Harry Lauder. His idea of fun was to lift a large chip out of the frying basket with fingers immunised to hot fat, and drop the sizzling morsel into your eager waiting palms. As often as not you had to drop it in the sawdust, a cruel waste. But he would give you a cooler one later. On frosty winter nights it was great to carry home the fish suppers, wrapped first in plain paper, then newspaper, clasped to the chest like a hot water bottle, with delicious savoury smells wafting around one nostrils. This was enough for the six of us. During the leaner spells, we had to make do with the sixpennyworth of chips only. If you split your chips down the middle and put them between two slices of bread, it made a tasty chip piece. (Chip butty is the English equivalent. To us a butty is a friend — a buddy. Bread with butter was a butter piece, or piece-'n'-butter.)

'Pie Davey's' was another wee shoppie beside the fish shop, and they sold chips too. Instead of fish they sold penny and twopenny pies, scalding hot. But their chips never seemed as good as Leggat's. They always seemed soggy and limp, or overbrowned. Like the rest of the shops in this half of the street, it was two steps down from street level. At Leggat's end, they were two steps *up*, which suggests the street may have been levelled off at some time in the past.

The far end of the street, round the corner from Leggat's, was strictly out of bounds to us. This was Bristo Street and a den of vice (so we thought) called Potterrow, where a lot of unsavoury characters lived. At the time when the potters *did* live and work there, it was a famous and respectable thoroughfare. 'Wha saw the Fortysecond, comin' doon the Poatterraw?' as the song has it.

Now and again our street was visited by Newhaven fishwives in their colourful costumes, with creels of fresh fish on their backs. Other more static fishwives sat on stools at busy junctions, selling a saucerful of ready-cooked buckies, whelks or mussels at a few pence a time to passers-by. Newsboys called the latest editions as they went along. Vendors sold firewood made up into bundles from their loaded pony-carts, sometimes coal briquettes too. Occasionally a fruit vendor's cart would clop by, loaded with oranges, apples or strawberries. All had their own, distinctive calls. Now and then we were treated to music from a barrel organ, an evocative sound reminding us of fairs and carnivals. The one we liked best had a monkey on top. It wore a jacket and a little red fez, and carried a cup to receive your penny. By the end of the thirties they had all gone.

We used to get a Saturday halfpenny when family finances allowed, which was raised to a penny when I was nine or ten. Later this was augmented by twopence so I could buy a weekly boys' paper. My choice was *The Adventure*. It was an investment really because you could swap it later for someone else's *Rover, Wizard* or *Hotspur*. Just as well, because I read them cover to cover in thirty minutes, and I would never have spent two whole pence on something so soon finished. Fortunately, one of my aunts was a member of the Public Library, and as soon as I was ten, she got me enrolled. Children *under* ten were not allowed into libraries. This was a real milestone in my life. With two tickets the following year, and eventually four, when my brother and sisters also joined, I could read as much as I liked — free!

From the time any of us could read, there were of course the comics. With the Sunday papers which I went to collect at the newsagent's beside 'Pie Davey's', there was also our regular family comic, *The Funny Wonder*. It was printed on pale green paper. Each comic had a different colour. All the comics cost a penny, except for the more upper-class ones like *Bubbles, Rainbow, Puck* and *Tiger Tim's Weekly*, which were in colour and cost a prohibitive twopence. *Film Fun* also cost twopence, but was in black and white. We never bought these, and though as swaps we read them faithfully to the last page, we always felt they were a bit sissy and aimed at the posh classes. Like the boys' magazines later, we saved our comics to swap for others. Other penny comics were *Chips, Comic Cuts, Jester* and the *Monster*. Dad always claimed first look at the outside page of *The Funny Wonder*. Like us, he followed the adventures of Charlie Chaplin and Pitch and Toss every week. I can still recall every character of the inside strips.

Occasionally we got batches of American comics posted from aunts or uncles who had contacts abroad, usually months or years old, but very welcome nonetheless. The sheer size and brighter colours appealed to us, and we got to know their characters too — Maggie and Jiggs and the Katzenjammer Kids spring to mind.

But to me, comics were froth, entertainment certainly, but without any real substance to them. They were finished in no time. *The Adventure* and its equivalents gave maybe half an hours' reading, but I wanted more than that. In some swaps, *The Gem, The Magnet* and the *Boy's Own Paper*, I found stories with slightly more meat to them, but they all seemed a bit lah-de-dah, with their variations on Bob Merry and Billy Bunter and all that completely alien public school stuff. My schoolmates simply could not equate their own experiences with day boys, boarders, impots, monthly postal orders, tuck shops, cricket and rugby. Imagine going to school wearing Eton collars and top hats! *We* were in school uniform if we wore the school tie, and the more affluent even wore school caps. One unfortunate lad's parents even bought him a blazer, which took a lot of living down. We read it all as we would read of life on another planet.

Without exception, all these publications reflected the same ethos. Some facets of this were naive, if not actually reprehensible, like the attitude to foreigners. In a fight, one 'Britisher' was worth any ten 'Dagoes', 'Wops', 'Frogs', 'Huns', 'Chinks', or 'Lascars'. Members of any other race were known to be inferior in every way, apart of course for the sons of immensely wealthy rajahs and those of similar status. But most of the attitudes displayed had much to recommend them. Courage, patience, fortitude and patriotism were prime virtues. Fair play was a major theme. Our heroes fought with bare fists — only 'Wogs' were so cowardly as to use weapons, and then only when the odds were overpoweringly in their favour. Our heroes never hit below the belt, and kicking an opponent when he was down was utterly unthinkable.

Yes, with 'Morgyn the Mighty', 'Strang the Terrible' and 'Tarzan', there was plenty of violence, but it was clean and honest, and the baddies were always defeated in the end. Old people were respected, given seats in trams or buses and helped across the road. A granny beaten up for her pension would have been headline news.

After I was twelve or thereabouts, occasional swaps brought in sixpenny novelettes like *Dixon Hawke* and *Sexton Blake*, both single issue complete detective stories, and eventually boringly repetitious. There were also 'Westerns' in the same format, each story remarkably similar to the others. But I read everything, boring or not. Sandwiched between all this rubbish was *The Modern Boy* and *The Children's Newspaper*, an excellent publication, but perhaps marginally too edifying. This I first saw at school, but eventually it was bought for us at home.

I was nine or ten when my father bought *The Children's Book of Knowledge*, an encyclopedia in eight volumes. The idea was to help us all when we came to take our qualifying exam, and I've no doubt it did. I started at the beginning of 'Volume One' and read solidly through to the last page of the 'Index'. It kept me busy for a long time, and gave me a solid if elementary basis of general knowledge. I was able to look through one or two of the volumes a year or two ago, and noted the great changes in scientific theory, and the tremendous advances in knowledge in every field since then. But at that time it was a well informed publication, well produced and written in sound English.

All this reading, rubbish and educational, was really only an obbligato to my library books. It was a great joy to have access to books that would last more than one evening. I read the classics — *Robinson Crusoe, Alice in Wonderland, Swiss Family Robinson, Tom Sawyer, Gulliver's Travels, Pilgrims' Progress* (boring), *Hans Andersen, Treasure Island, Grimm's Fairy Tales* and the rest. With great affection I recall *Doctor Doolittle,* with Hugh Lofting's original drawings; E. Nesbit's books; *Maya the Bee; At the Back of the North Wind; Old Brindle* (a dog story); Kipling's *Jungle Books* and so on. The Junior Library was really well supplied, but I had mined out everything of interest by the time I was fourteen and entitled to join the adult section. There were of course plenty of girls' books, and I often took some home for my sisters. The others would read books I took home, but they were not so keen to walk as far as the Central Library to change them.

LIGHTING at Number 13 was a single gas mantle in each room. Because we had a penny-in-the-slot gas meter, a penny had to be kept in reserve at night, or you were stuck in the dark until you could find one. When I was in the house alone reading, the gas always seemed to fail at the best part of the story. I discovered that if I produced a long and resonant hoot, like a foghorn, the light would brighten long enough to read one more sentence. The light dimmed after the sound. When it finally failed, sometimes the fire in the grate could be stirred up to provide enough light to read by.

But we were trained to poke the fire as little as possible, with the cost of coal so high — one shilling to one and twopence for a hundredweight bag. Coal was bought straight off the street. One of us would be detailed to watch at the front window and catch the eye of the first coalman to pass on his horse-drawn dray. As we lived two storeys up, some were not too keen. Some 'poachers' who didn't have a regular beat ignored anyone above the first storey. But one made a point of not buying from them when they came around next time, short on sales and prepared to supply top flats and attics. There were maybe half a dozen or more regular coalmen who came about the same time on each round. Since it was impossible to distinguish the sound of one iron-tyred horse-drawn dray from another, they announced their presence with individual cries. The simplest was a bellow of 'Coal!', but most managed to infuse some originality into their variations — 'Bay-ay-coal!', 'Ole-be-dope-bope!', 'Ole! Ole!', 'Beg-a-coal!' and 'OUL!!' This last is almost impossible to describe — a cross between a foghorn and the Hound of the Baskervilles. When your coal was finally humped up the stairs, it was deposited in the coal bunker. My mother would hurriedly spread newspapers all over the floor first. Some coalmen were remarkably careful and tidy; others barged in, dumping the coal with a crash and raising a cloud of dust which settled over everything in the room.

Like the coalmen, the occasional rag-and-bone man also had his own distinctive call. The most affluent merchant, who had a large pony drawing a flat-topped lorry, shouted 'Regbottleandbones!' on a falling cadence, alternating with raucous toots on a battered copper bugle. This could be heard streets away, warning the local children to start looking for castoffs and jam jars. He gave the best gifts in exchange — 'birlers' (windmills), multi-coloured balloons, brightly dyed papier maché birds attached by a length of string to a stick which flew when waved about, tails revolving in the wind. But what we all coveted were the goldfish, each in its own little bowl. I suspect they were only window dressing. Only once did I see one handed over, to two little girls who had brought a tin bath heaped with old clothes.

The merchant second in the hierarchy, with a smaller pony and cart, called 'Rags-'n-bones!' and had no bugle. Lesser dealers only had handcarts. Though they all accepted bottles and jam jars, I only once saw one with a heap of bones. I expect these were only available in reasonable quantity from some butcher.

Christmas was a time of enchantment for us. All the shops put up special Christmas decorations. One that specially drew us was 'Mackenzie's', the toy and sports shop near the Empire Theatre. Every year their window displays became more colourful and glittering, and always there was some moving centrepiece, clockwork trains, clowns, animals and so on. I could only look with hopeless envy at the vast Meccano working models, and the huge and temptingly displayed Meccano Sets, dismayingly expensive. I had got my first set from Santa Claus at the age of seven. It was a 'Number 00', the smallest available.

The next Christmas I wanted to add to it — a 'Number 6', if possible, — I had so enjoyed playing with it. But my parents explained to me that there wasn't *really* a Santa Claus, and they simply could not afford anything so expensive. They asked me not to disillusion my brother and sisters, and for a few years more they still believed. But the inevitable had to come. Santa Claus and economics did not mix.

By the time I was fifteen and past playing with it, I had built up my set to a '2a', plus one or two extras like an expensive seven-and-sixpenny clockwork motor. I then presented it to my younger cousins in Glasgow, after pieces of it were requisitioned by my father to build a clockwork gadget which flashed the lights on his shop window Christmas Tree in a complicated sequence. Flasher mechanisms were not yet on the market, but he worked out himself how to do it.

He really had an inventive turn of mind, and was interested in scientific progress. Just after the war, he had collected all the equipment necessary for taking, developing and printing photographs. I remember his dark room, which was the short lobby at the front door. It was screened off with a heavy curtain, and there was a red lamp inside, with magic equipment like hypo trays and photo developing frames. This was abandoned when wireless came along. He built crystal sets with esoteric plans and unlikely looking collections of wire and vulcanite. And they worked! You could actually *hear* sounds, voices and music, through the headphones. He had three sets of these, so each of us could listen with one earpiece each.

The first thing to come over the air which connected the whole process with reality was the news that Middlemass's biscuit factory, about a mile to the south of us, was on fire. Sure enough, when we looked out of the window, there was this great red glow in the sky. We went out specially next day to see the blackened and smouldering ruins.

From the cats' whisker crystal set he progressed to the more advanced wireless sets, with one or more valves, though for these one now had to buy batteries and accumulators. We always thought, watching him bend and solder intricate mazes of coloured wires, why wire-*less*? Here again he showed initiative, fitting up a loudspeaker from an earphone and a gramophone horn, long before they became generally available to the public. But he envied the outfit built by our Uncle Davey Anderson, who had a vast and dauntingly complicated set, all dials, knobs and black ebonite, which used the entire side of a room to a height of six feet. This formidable apparatus could receive shortwave messages and signals from all over the world.

Though I appreciated the radio as much as anyone, it had progressed to the loudspeaker stage by the time when I had to do an hour or so of homework after school. There was no problem during the summer. I could work in the bedroom in comparative peace. But in the winter the kitchen fire was the only one lit, so it was the only room warm enough to sit in. It took real concentration then, with

33

three younger children playing around and my mother working about the house. The total of clear floor space in that kitchen was maybe sixty square feet. My capacity for concentration paid off when I wanted to read, though I was accused of deliberately ignoring requests to do this or that.

We children would listen to *Children's Hour* on '2LO', so we tried to keep that period clear. 'Auntie Kathy' once read out my name on a birthday list — instant fame! With 'Uncle Leslie' their birthday catch phrase was 'HELLO-O-O, TWINS!'

At this time my father was also dabbling in photography, and his interest in electricity led him to make his own wet cell batteries, which he used to power an electric door bell. This outfit remained in use until the advent of dry batteries in the shops.

One achievement in his own field of watchmaking which gave him the greatest pride and satisfaction was the repairing of one particular watch. This was in the mid-twenties. Quite a number of seamen used to bring watches and clocks for repairs. They apparently recommended 'the wee jeweller' to each other as being quick and reliable, which, as they might be in port for only a few days, was of prime importance to them. One day a ship's captain brought in a silver watch for repair. He had tried to get it repaired in nearly every big port in the world, without success. 'It can't be done', they all said. He had even tried the world-famous Bond Street jewellers in London. Then from some colleague he encountered in Shanghai or Hong Kong, he heard about my father, and on his next docking at Leith, took the first opportunity to bring in his watch. The watch did keep perfect time, but on the hour it was supposed to chime out a little tune, like a music box, and the mechanism had been out of order for several years.

My father took the watch and promised to 'do his best' — one of his favourite business phrases. He studied it for several days, and finally spotted the fault in what was a very complicated piece of machinery. One tiny lever, about one eighth of an inch long, was missing. Deducing its size, function and shape, he fashioned a new piece in fine steel, fitted it, and lo and behold, it worked perfectly. For the next few days he enjoyed the hourly chimes, then the captain returned. He was overjoyed to find his watch again in perfect working order and asked how much he owed. Typically, my father said there was no charge; he had enjoyed doing the work, it was such a challenge and out of the usual run of jobs he had to do. The captain said he had been prepared to pay at least £20 to have it mended, but my father refused to accept so much. Finally he was persuaded to accept £5, a lot of money then, more than two weeks' wages.

When Phemia was ten or eleven, she was having difficulty in walking, and the surgeons at the Sick Children's Hospital decided she should have the thigh bones broken and re-set. For six months she was encased in plaster, and of necessity, spreadeagled on her back. Her transport was a 'spinal coach', rather like a long fish box on high perambulator wheels. Urination was a real problem, and the hospital practice at that time was to use nappies, for adults as well as children.

But again my father rose to the occasion. He designed a shaped bottle-like container which he cut out of tin and soldered together. This very efficiently fulfilled its function. When a surgeon at the hospital saw this ingeniously designed receptacle, he advised my father to patent it, as it was a thing that had long been needed and would certainly be bought by the thousand. But he refused. He would not want to make money from something that would make the lives of sick people more bearable. His royalties, he thought, would make them more expensive than they need be. This surgeon then undertook to show the thing to the surgical glass manufacturers (glass being obviously more hygienic than tin), and this was the ancestor of all those odd-shaped but handy bottles everyone has seen in hospitals. I imagine even the smallest royalty on this invention could have brought him in enough revenue to allow him to stop work when his doctor advised him to, instead of working on until he dropped.

He was quick to pick up a new idea. Just before the war we decided we'd like to be able to play chess. It seemed an excellent pastime for the long boring nights the press had been preparing us for. Other people obviously had the same idea, for it took me a long time to track down a shop with a set to sell, and even then two of the original pawns had been lost and replaced with smaller ones; but I got it at a slightly reduced price because of this — one pound. This was quite a lot at a time when a reasonably expensive board game cost seven and sixpence. But they were genuine boxwood pieces. I undertook to learn the game from library books and teach it to him and the others. We played with each piece separately until we knew how they moved, then added another piece, and another, until we were using all of them. I kept ahead until we had learned all the moves, then things evened out, and I had to work for any victory. We must have worked up to a pretty fair standard of play, though we were unable to measure ourselves against seasoned players, as no one we knew played chess. It was regarded as a highly intellectual, but boring game, played by dome-browed professors who took forever to make a move. We found it interesting and exciting, and played fast, at least until someone got into a tight spot.

My first chance to assess our skill came when I was working in Rolls-Royce, Hillington, during the war. I found that a Mr Marcus, in charge of the photographic department working with our drawing office, was a chess addict. I spent many a lunch hour playing him. The first game I won. He explained later that my opening was so unorthodox that he kept expecting some terribly subtle and devastating move, which of course never came. I never won another, and was quite delighted on those rare occasions when I managed to scrape a drawn game. No one else would play with him because he always won.

Before we started playing together, he made a point of telling me he was Jewish. Because of this there were some who did not care to have any social contact with him, and certainly would not have had lunch with him. Racial intolerance was not a Nazi monopoly. He told me this because he was aware that this prejudice could apply to anyone who associated with him, though most of the drawing office people were more tolerant. But I enjoyed his company. He influenced me to join the Works Chess Club. One night there was a knock-out competition and I was drawn against Fox, the head of the drawing office. He was a bit of a snob and had obviously classified me as something very far below him socially and intellectually. It gave me great pleasure to defeat him without difficulty, though it did not improve our subsequent relations.

Our main family entertainment prior to this was card games, along with Ludo, dominoes and draughts. When Monopoly arrived, it took its place with chess as our main recreations, along with listening to the radio. This was about the time when people stopped calling it 'the wireless'. We were interested in the possibilities of television, which was in its infancy at the beginning of the war. As a science fiction addict, I predicted that one day there would be *colour* television, but everyone was sceptical. I went further and said there would be three-dimensional television. Pure fantasy, they said; but now it seems only a matter of time.

Occasionally we would try the Ouija Board or some variation, though we never had any significant results. We skirted the borders of spiritualism, as many people did at that time when so many had friends or relatives killed or missing. Though quite a few of our friends were believers or even practitioners, we ourselves seemed to be lacking in 'faith'. The 'other side' would have nothing to do with us. Not long before father died, we agreed that whoever died first, (knowing that the odds were on him), would make every effort to make contact in one way or another. We knew several 'Spiritualist Meeting Houses' where people who knew us could take a message. Nothing ever happened.

My father had always enjoyed playing games with us, even when we were little. When he bamboozled us with his disappearing penny trick, he'd use the magic words 'Abracadabra!' or 'Sacramento!' This latter he may have picked up at music hall acts like the magician Chung Ling Foo who died in a fire while working at the Empire Theatre. Another baffling word he used was 'Sakkaboney!', which I only recently deciphered as 'Sakubona!', the Zulu greeting. This must have had its origins in the Zulu wars or the Boer War. Apropos, there were all the French phrases brought back by returning soldiers after the first world war; 'San Fairy Anne', 'Toodle-oo!', 'Napoo!' and 'Billy Doo'. A familiar German word was 'Kamerad!'. 'Achtung' only arrived with the second world war.

When Howard Carter discovered the tomb of Tutankhamen in 1922, it was immediately headline news in all the papers. My father used to frighten us in the dark with ghostly knockings, saying, 'Here's auld Tutankymum comin' tae get ye!' It must have been around this period that we had a nocturnal visit from a peacetime German zeppelin. The gas was turned off, and I was held up at the window to see a tiny silver sausage held in the searchlights, slowly drifting with a distant hum past Stephenson Blake's chimney. The adults of course remembered the wartime zeppelin bombing raids during the war. I believe one bomb landed in the Surgeon's Hall area, very close to us.

ONE of the first family holidays I remember was about 1925. We stayed with friends, the Bruces, in a house in Pottery Street, Kirkcaldy, when there was still a working pottery there. We kids would play with the rejects in the back garden, which was contiguous with the pottery yard. The brightly coloured designs on the plates and shards were similar to those on Wemyss Ware. But our most persistent memory of this holiday were the nights. Our friends also had five or six children, and the sleeping arrangements were that we all slept in one room, on improvised mattresses filled with straw which covered most of the floor. The pillows were filled with hen feathers, including the quills. We townies did not sleep soundly. The sharp straws stuck into us at all angles, and the quills in the pillows poked into your eye or ear. Worst of all was the flea infestation. We visitors did get *some* sleep, but in the morning looked like bad cases of measles. At home my mother would suffer no crawling insect to survive, but it took days to kill them all off on our return home. Oddly enough, the resident children seemed to be immune.

The following summer, our uncle Robert (Bunt) discovered it was possible to rent a tent for a camping holiday. He invited us to join him for the week of the 'trades holiday'. Accordingly, we all took the train to Kinghorn, and made our way to Pettycur Beach, which was the spot my uncle had heard of. The tent was delivered by horse cart from the station, and my uncle drew on his army experience and organised us in erecting it. It was an ex-army bell tent with one central pole, simple for even beginners to handle. This tent was inscribed above the entrance flap, 'The Old Nest'. It certainly *was* old. There seemed to be more patches than original canvas. One wet day in a later year, we counted them; over 140, and every one leaked.

None of us had ever camped out before, and we learned the hard way. We had ho idea what camping gear was needed. Cooking was done on a bath brick soaked in methylated spirit, in an old biscuit tin, and took forever. Bedding was two large sacks filled with straw and was only big enough to accommodate the eight children; us, our cousins, and their cousins. The six adults sat up each night round a driftwood fire, with coats or blankets round their shoulders.

Fortunately that first holiday was seven days of the most glorious summer weather, so there was no real hardship. We children lived in an ecstatic daze for the whole week. Miles of sand, sunshine all day, sea that came up to within yards of the tent door, rocks to climb, pools to explore, and fishing. Paradise! At night we could see the stars through the open tent flap, heard the hush and roar of the waves and the cry of the gulls, the crackle of the fire, the friendly moo of a distant foghorn; smelt the wood smoke, felt the sand between our toes, and fell happily asleep knowing it would all still be there waiting in the morning.

Eddie Mackay, the other uncle, had brought along a gramophone. It was a toy really, made of tin printed with garishly coloured cartoon characters. It came from Woolworths, in the days when it still was a 'threepenny and sixpenny' store. It could have cost as much as a shilling, because some of the more expensive items were sold in two parts at sixpence each. Maybe the spring was classed as a separate item. But he had brought along only two records. They must have been one-sided, because I remember only the two tunes, played *ad nauseam* all week, — *Bye, bye Blackbird* and *Tiptoe through the Tulips*. What made them almost unbearable was that the machine had no speed regulator, so when it was fully wound up and released, the singer's voice started off at top speed, sounding like a mad chipmunk, and got slower and slower until he sounded like a *basso profundo* spinning out his royalties.

38

Eddie offered to teach me to swim. I loved playing around in the water and I was very keen to learn. The sun was hot, the beach golden, and the sky and sea blue. The waves were small and friendly as he led me out chest deep. Then without the slightest warning he pushed my head under water and held it there, for so long I believed he was trying to drown me. I had breathed in sharply with the shock, and while struggling to get free I swallowed a lot of salt water. When he finally let me go, I fought my way to the shore, choking, coughing and retching. I was sick, and had a headache for an hour. After this experience, I was completely terrified of the water. Had he had the sense to warn me to hold my breath all would have been well. As it was, I refused to go to swimming lessons at school, and was the only one in the family who never learned to swim.

Probably what finally decided me to learn was a frightening experience at Pettycur during the summer before the war. It was one of those rare hot sunny days with a strong wind from the west. We were all down at the water, swimming and paddling, and someone had brought down a Lilo airbed on which we all had a go. When my turn came, I had great fun paddling around in only a foot or so of water. After five minutes or so I suddenly realised I had been carried out of my depth. The wind had driven the Lilo along and into a strong undercurrent setting straight out to sea.

Normally there were no currents on this beach, but the combination of the west wind, a projecting curve of rocks at the end of the beach, and an exceptional digging away of sand in a line beside the rails had caused a scoured channel to form. I shouted to Charlie, but the roar of the surf prevented anyone hearing me. Fortunately my mother, up on the cliff beside our hut, had spotted my predicament and managed to catch his attention. Betty meantime had struggled out to me, but was almost swept off her feet by the current and could not get a grip on the airbed. Now Charlie had got out to me, and being taller still had a toe-grip on the sand. It was touch and go. Another few seconds and they would have had to swim back, and against that current could have made little headway.

I had been using all my concentration to keep my balance, but in the heavy swell it was not easy. On my own, and further out from the shore, I could easily have capsized. Of course, had I been even a poor swimmer, I would have been perfectly safe for hours, holding on to the Lilo. But I would almost certainly have panicked with the whole of my body in the water. After this scare, none of us took chances with anything inflatable, and we tried to discourage anyone who did.

It was not until I was twenty-four that I decided it was illogical to remain afraid of the water because of a stupid incident when I was a child. I borrowed some books from the public library and proceeded to teach myself to swim, to such good purpose that I became a confident swimmer and actually taught several others to overcome *their* fear of water. I never ever ducked anyone, with or without warning. Normally the water temperature in Infirmary Street Public Baths was around 67°, more bracing than comfortable. Only once was the water at 80°, in preparation for an evening gala. I swam fifty lengths that day. Once the heating boiler was out of action, and I was warned the temperature was only 44°. I mistakenly assumed this would be no more unbearable than a similar air temperature. I dived in for my daily swim, swam the fastest length ever, and shot out of the water at the far end frozen to the marrow, and pale blue.

Joe and Andra were two old fishermen who lived in a shanty at the far end of Pettycur Beach all through the salmon fishing season. They were employed by some commercial syndicate. Out on the sand flats, they had two sets of nets, long lines of poles stretching seawards, with one fish trap midway along and another at the far end. In the early years we sometimes watched them struggle home with shoulder bags stuffed full. The salmon were gaffed from the traps at half tide, when the fisherman edged his way along a rope stretched just above the water line. We children would gather at their shanty to see the day's catch before it was boxed and sent off to the markets. These silver fish were a beautiful sight, and so were the occasional grilse or sea trout. The biggest salmon we ever saw was a 75 pounder, but there were many of over 20 pounds. But over the years the catches grew less, with smaller fish, and finally with the war the fishery closed down.

And shall we ever again see the herring shoals? On bright summer days we would see a dark shadow drifting over the water, and not a cloud in sight. These were the herring shoals, perhaps acres in extent, with white gulls and gannets wheeling and plunging above them. These shadow shoals were not at all uncommon in the early years, but became rarer and rarer up till the outbreak of war. Just recently we were told of a splendid and unusual catch of herring being dumped back in the sea. Housewives now do not want the trouble of preparing fresh herring themselves; what they want is pre-packed, hygenically processed fish fingers.

In time, we all picked up a great deal of camping know-how from the veterans who in some cases had been coming for twenty years or more. They were mostly Glasgow folks, a friendly lot, always ready to show the tyro how things should be done. Camp furniture, for instance, was improvised from crates loaned by the bottleworks at the far end of the beach, and covered with curtain material. Ultimately this kindly and free service was stopped. New and less responsible campers proliferated every year, and many crates were stolen, broken

40

up and burned. Similarly, women campers were allowed to use the washroom facilities at the factory, but this generous dispensation was abused by the newcomers, and these privileges also were withdrawn.

The real campers were always meticulous in tidying up when they left, and the only sign of their occupation might be a rectangle of bleached grass where their tent had been. New campers left all their rubbish, and we children would tidy up after they had gone. Even worse, latterly, was the litter left by day-trippers. We cleared up each night with a bonfire, and buried bottles and tins. In the early days children could play barefoot through the entire holiday, but broken bottles made it dangerous without shoes. Charlie had his knee slashed open to the bone when he knelt on a piece of glass. One of the old timers efficiently took over, and cleaned out the wound, scraping the sand out with a pair of scissors. He made a very professional job of it, and when the doctor saw it later, he commented on how well it had been done. It should have been stitched, but the sticky tape used was so artfully applied that there was only a minimal scar.

Occasionally we were treated to a spectacular thunderstorm. I remember one that went on most of the night, with vast flashes of lightning and shattering rolls of thunder like all the guns in the world firing at the same time, shaking the ground. The dark inside of our tent would light up bright as day, and with it the crack of doom immediately overhead. Slowly the storm passed, and we counted the seconds after the flash, until finally even the most distant muttering of thunder could not reach us. But for a long time after that, there were flashes of sheet lightning, lighting up half the sky, silhouetting the hills on the far side of the estuary.

The city of Edinburgh seen from our beach lived up to its title of 'Auld Reekie'. Even during the summer months there was often a pall of smoke maybe five or six hundred feet in depth hanging over the houses, drifting in whatever direction the wind took it. No wonder every building ended up a sooty black. But then, every large city was smoke-blackened.

We and our cousins often found baby rabbits lying dead at the foot of the cliff, and we devised a game which kept us happy for hours at a time. We conducted funeral services for each furry little corpse. I had the job of finding suitable flat slabs of stone for gravestones, and we would compose a suitable inscription to scratch on them, like R.I.P.. Little black baby Rabbit. Died 3rd July, 1929. Sadly missed. Jim Thomson had once kept pet rabbits which escaped and bred with the wild population, so that black or white rabbits kept appearing each year along with the wild ones. I am told they still do, nearly sixty years later, in spite of the myxomatosis epidemic. We dug little graves in the short turf at the foot of the cliff, put up the gravestones and held short but moving services. Finally there was a row of little headstones, lovingly tended each day, when we would place fresh wreaths of flowers. People passing along the path would stop and photograph our cemetery. (Jim Thomson was the son of Oliver Thomson, the operator of the Sandhills Company which dug the sand from the beach. He kept all the machinery in working order, cared for the horses, and ran the holiday camp during the summer.)

Eventually we decided we could save money by buying our own tent, which would be new and waterproof, unlike many of the hired ones like 'The Old Nest' which had probably started its career during the Boer War. My uncle was unlucky enough to re-hire this relic one year when we had a wet spell at the beginning of the holiday. He complained vigorously and damply to the hiring firm, who sent a newer replacement. But in subsequent years we saw it regularly, housing greenhorns who didn't know any better. My uncle bought a new pristine white bell tent the following year.

Our new tent was from Black's of Greenock, a ridge-pole cottage design, green and rot-proofed. We chose it because we had spotted a site just off the sand which was too narrow for a bell tent, but perfectly fitted this rectangular shaped one. We looked on this as our own personal site for some years after this. It had the great advantage of being some feet higher than high water mark. In the later years, any tent on the sand risked inundation at neap tides. The beach was depleted by the removal of thousands of tons of sand every year by the Sandhills Company. The Kinghorn Bottle Works also removed a great deal of sand from *above* high water mark, until its quality deteriorated to the point where they had to *import* sand more suitable for glass making.

The Sandhills Company took all their sand from below high water mark during the years we holidayed at Pettycur, and each year we saw the high tide mark creep closer inshore. Pettycur Beach at last had no dry sand at high tide; but when I visited it many years later, it was beginning to rebuild itself, with even a sign of regeneration of the original marram grass dunes. The erosion became so bad that the railway embankment was endangered, and thousands of tons of stone and rubble were tipped as reinforcement. When we started camping, there were extensive grassy dunes; when we stopped years later, they had all gone. Square miles of wet sand showed when the tide was low, reaching out to the Black Rock off Burntisland, near which one could sometimes see the remains of the wooden ribs of a sailing collier wrecked there a hundred years previously.

Oliver Thomson told me that around 1900, all that vast acreage had been farm land, and cows grazed as far out as the Black Rock. His job, with one or sometimes two labourers, was to lay out narrow gauge rails on wooden sleepers far out on the beach, dig sand and load it into tipping wagons carrying about three tons apiece, then hook up a horse to tow a train of six to twelve along to the foot of the hill. There they were coupled to a steel cable powered by a steam engine at the top, hauled to the highest point, then down by gravity to a wooden gantry over the railway siding above Pettycur Bay. Here the sand was tipped into waiting trucks. He was tremendously strong, but several times I saw him strapped up in bandages after straining muscles. The trolleys occasionally jumped the rails while traversing the hill, and to save time emptying one and then re-filling it, he would tip out enough sand so that he could hump the whole thing back on the rails — by himself. This was no mean feat; the trolleys were solid iron and very heavy.

The Thomsons would store our tent and equipment from year to year, and he would deliver our coal, toting a hundredweight bag as though it weighed no more than a briefcase. Our two families became friends.

RETURNING to West Nicolson Street: below us lived Mr and Mrs Guthrie, with son Willie and daughter Eleanor. They were Catholics. The children were some five years younger than I. There was a third, Patsy, who died very suddenly of meningitis when only about a year old, leaving the family heartbroken. They often came up to spend the evening with us, and we still kept in touch even after moving to the new house.

Willie the elder was a bit of a ladies' man (young Willie followed in his father's footsteps) and on festive occasions tried once or twice for a kiss and cuddle with my mother, but she would have none of it. She put up with him for the sake of social amity, but found him repellent in his amorous moods, when he was left in no doubt as to the coolness of his reception. But he was a cheerful soul and meant no harm.

Mrs Guthrie was a well-meaning lady, with a very high-pitched voice which I personally found irritating. Sometimes she was quite justifiably cool to us children, when we had been thumping around overhead for too long. Then she would knock on her ceiling with a broomstick. If we made excessive noise when my mother was out, she always reported it, and we were reprimanded.

In the earlier years, I was not too keen on Willie's company. He had a formidable lisp. Sometimes, as the oldest, I was saddled with the care of the Guthrie's children as well as our own. Normally I found it easy enough to keep some kind of order, and only once something went drastically wrong. It was a winter afternoon near Christmas, dark by four o'clock. My mother had gone to her Tuesday Sisterhood Meeting at the Church hall, which she rarely missed. No doubt it was a welcome break from home duties and kids, though all it consisted of was hymns, a prayer, tea and a talk from the minister or invited guest. I was reading, as usual. My sisters were washing and cleaning dolls' clothes. Suddenly there was an earsplitting scream. Phemia had mangled Betty's fingers along with the clothes. They were using the old red and green painted mangle with wooden rollers which was used for drying out the washing. Phemia had the presence of mind to reverse the handle immediately, but there seemed to be an awful lot of blood, and Betty was howling her head off. I wrapped a clean handkerchief round her fingers. None of the neighbours were at home when I knocked, so I ran to the church, half a mile away. My mother was just coming out of the door. Breaking it gently, I gasped 'Betty's mangled her fingers!' She turned white and ran off. I followed at a walk. It must have been a relief to find that only the fingertips had been caught, but the middle one had been burst open, and needed a stitch at the casualty department at the Royal Infirmary.

Though I was not at home at the time, I was blamed for another near catastrophe. From somewhere I had collected an ancient bicycle pump, and in a spirit of scientific enquiry found that I could suck smoke into it from the coal fire. By tapping the end of the handle, you could produce a series of perfect smoke rings. This provided us with hours of entertainment, all the more enjoyable because we were strictly forbidden to *play* with the fire. Stoking it up with another shovelful of coal was all right, but no more. On this occasion a blind lady, Madge Neave, who now and then was invited to tea with us, was baby-sitting with Charlie while my mother was shopping and we others were out at play. She was just able to distinguish light from dark. Suddenly there was a hiss and flare, and she dropped her knitting and screamed. Charlie had borrowed my pump to make rings himself, and the celluloid casing had caught fire. Fortunately he dropped it on the hearth stone, so no damage was done. I got a worse telling off than he did.

When we finally moved to Salisbury Square, we felt we had taken a step up in the world. It wasn't really a square, just an ancient stone-built tenement, with an alarming crack from the eaves nearly to the ground on the end gable. But it looked out on a pleasant little square park with grass, trees, and flower beds. It was railed all round and closed to the public, but was a pretty green oasis to enjoy on a summer evening. At the beginning of the war, all railings were

44

requisitioned, taken down and carted away. Bomb shelters were dug in the turf, and vandals hacked at the trees till only one or two battered survivors showed a green leaf. Even after the war the site remained a scene of devastation. The garden was never reinstated and all the houses in that area were eventually demolished in slum clearances. When I last visited the street, there was a wonderful view of Salisbury Crags and the park which before had always been blocked by mouldering tenements.

There was an entrance to the park only a few minutes walk from the house, and I used to imagine the valley between us and the Crags as it must have been a thousand years ago, thickly forested and with a stream running along the bottom. This aspect of the place could have been much the same in the days of the Laird of Dumbiedykes and Jeanie Deans. Her reputed cottage was only five minutes away, near James Clark School. The famous Wells O' Wearie, of the song, would be about a mile further, near Duddingston Loch, a bird sanctuary for many years.

Edinburgh is fortunate in its possession of King's Park (Queen's Park now), with its miniature mountain, Arthur's Seat; an old volcanic stump, like the Castle Rock. It contains three lochs. One, St Margaret's had boats for hire when I was small. The Salisbury Crags are a world famous geological phenomenon, and Holyrood Palace and Abbey adjoin one corner. It is not like the average tailored municipal park, with railings, clipped hedges and formal flower beds. *Our* grass was meant to be walked on.

Though the park was so close, it did not satisfy my longing for open spaces, though I spent many happy hours there. When I was sixteen, I got a bicycle; I saved up half the cost, and my parents added the rest. At last I was free to get out into the real country, and most weekends I explored all round the area outside the city. During the longer holiday breaks I would venture further afield, taking my own little tent and camping equipment. Later, Charlie also got a bike and we would go together.

One of my first long trips alone was down to the Border country. I pitched my tent beside a nameless burn in the heather covered hills somewhere near St Mary's Loch. Early in the morning I woke to the sound of the rushing stream. A thick white mist hung about the heathery knowes, and somewhere nearby, a cock grouse shouted 'Go beck! Beck-beck-beck!' The world was newly created, and there was silence. Plenty to hear, but never the faintest echo of human voice or technology. It could have been fifty thousand years ago. This I knew was genuine re-creation. It gave me great satisfaction to know I was now free to go anywhere I wished, carrying my own shelter and food, and prepared to cope with any problem that might arise.

THE very earliest memory I have is being held up at arms length by a soldier in khaki. I was very near the ceiling, looking down at the gaslight. It was in the kitchen, at night. I heard the hiss of the gas and felt the waves of heat rising from the light. I was scared, feeling terribly insecure, as though I could be dropped at any second. There seemed to be a crowd of other soldiers in the room, but I can't recall my parents, though they must have been present. Perhaps I cried. I do remember the fright. I had always thought this happened during the war, but my mother said they still entertained Anzacs as late as 1919, so I could have been three years old. At four I would have remembered more clearly.

The next few episodes certainly happened before I went to school, and I think they are in correct chronological order. My parents holidayed one or two summers at a farm near Stirling, with people named Teuch. I remember very clearly feeding grass shoots to a huge white chicken behind a wire netting fence. Its eyes were level with mine, and it looked straight at me, pecking with a hard yellow beak at the grass in my fingers. It had a glistening red comb and wattles, and scaly yellow legs. I was glad it couldn't get out. Across the dusty white road, straight and level both ways into the far hazy blue distance and empty as far as you could see, was an open gate leading into a vast grassy field, so big I couldn't see the far side. The sun was hot. Cowpats lay everywhere, dried out old ones with a papery skin, and fresh wet new ones with a moving cover of dung flies, yellow enamelled, with dark jewelled patterns. It you crept up quietly they didn't take flight, and you could study them closely — the glassy veined wings, the black and yellow mask with waving antennae. But jump at them and they dispersed in a flash with a satisfying roaring buzz.

Probably it was the same farm. I was taken up the grassy field by some older children; I see them only vaguely. But someone partly opened the lid of the well to let me see inside. I felt the cool damp grass on my bare knees, smelt the moist air. This well was a concrete tank maybe six feet square, and nearly full. Inside it was dark, cool-shadowed, but a thin shaft of sunlight fell through the clear, still water. I saw golden motes suspended, drifting in barely perceptible motion.

It could only have been here too that I was given a ride in a goat cart, drawn by a white nanny goat. These older children were also there, and the goat was led about the farmyard by a girl in a white pinafore. I wasn't too happy to be introduced to the goat, with those huge dangerous looking horns, but once I was safely in the cart all was well.

Then I was on one of the pleasure steamers that plied the River Forth, either the *Fair Maid of Perth* or the *William Muir*. These steamers had huge paddle wheels on each side, ponderous, wonderful, powerful, beautiful and romantic. Down in the engine room, which was open to the public, I saw the vast polished steel piston rods which drove the paddle wheels. They shone like silver, plunging irresistibly back and forth. The atmosphere in this hot and crowded hall smelt of hot oil and salt, and all around echoed the hiss, rumble and roar of the engines and the churning waves outside. I was dressed as a miniature sea captain, with captain's cap and a reefer coat with brass buttons. It was a grey day, blustery, and a huge swell made the ship rise and fall alarmingly. I could see no land, so we must have been well out in the middle of the Firth. I would have been scared, but my parents held me tightly so I could look over the side. Suddenly, seemingly only thirty yards or so away and overtaking us going seaward was a dark shape. A conning tower, decks below awash, and waves creaming back in its wake. I remember the lettering on the side of the conning tower — K22. Quite recently I read about a submarine, U147, which had sunk with all hands. It was later salvaged and re-commissioned, as K22!

My mother was going to collect materials from the wholesaler for my father, and had left me with him in the shop. I was bedded down on an old coat, with another to cover me, under the bench where he did his watch repairs. It was a strange place to sleep, but I felt warm and protected. Just above my head was the gas meter, which with its ticking, whirring and clanking should have kept me awake. Just behind my father's stool was the open coal fire, with its own tinkling, hissing and crackling. Dozens of clocks ticked, loud and soft, quick and slow, and at the hour there was a medley of gongs and bells and chimes, then comparative peace again. And there were intriguing smells; leathery smells, acid smells, oily smells, dusty, woody, and metallic smells. But I slept.

For some time my mother had been unwell. This morning she was still in bed, but from nowhere she had got me a baby brother as well as the two little sisters I already had. Our auntie (actually a great-aunt) was staying with us, and gave us cabbage soup that day. This had been made from the cabbage my brother had arrived in. Nobody explained how you managed to avoid cutting the baby when you chopped up the cabbage, and for a long time we watched with trepidation every time we saw a cabbage cut up to make broth. My mother had all her children except Betty at home. Most working class women did, unless complications were expected. There were no family allowances, free milk, orange juice or medicines, no baby clinics. Like many working class mothers on inadequate diets, she lost all her teeth when I was born.

Goldston was the tailor who had a shop in Nicolson Street. I had been taken there to get a blue serge sailor suit; blouse, shorts and hat. I was intrigued by the white square 'bib' which tied round the chest in lieu of a shirt. The square collar had the traditional three white stripes round the edge. The name on the cap was 'H.M.S. Invincible'. What gave me most pride though, was the white cord lanyard with bosun's whistle attached. The one which came with the suit was a wooden one, but later this was replaced by a silver one with a pea inside.

Goldston's was one of the few shops it was fun to wait in. They had a fantastic Heath Robinson system for sending your money to the cashier and getting the receipt back. All over the shop were gantries and guide rails. The money was put in a cylindrical metal container, slammed into a holder, and shot up to the overhead guide rails at the pull of a lever; then it zigzagged all the way to the cashiers kiosk to be processed. If the shop was busy there was a highly satisfactory clang, clatter, bang and whizz going on all the time.

Next door was the chemist, Boots, with a huge gold mortar and pestle sign suspended outside. Inside was plenty to look at. Best of all were three beautiful fluid-filled bottles in the window, like giant jewels, sapphire, ruby and emerald. There were glass display cabinets and a weighing machine, seats for the customers, and all round the walls tiers and tiers of varnished boxes with gold lettering on the front bearing mystic Latin phrases like 'SOD.CIT.'. Obviously there was enough medicine there to cure all of Edinburgh. Whatever you bought there was treated with reverence. It was neatly wrapped in white paper and sealed with red sealing wax. There was an eternally burning little gas flame behind the counter for melting the wax.

I was crying in the street. My bare knees were red and swollen, and the joints were stiff and painful. My mother took me into the shop just beside the pend, two steps down at the front door. This shop sold blinds; linen blinds, venetian blinds, coloured blinds, all sorts, and was owned by two nice ladies, the Misses Patterson. One of them heated her hands at the fire and rubbed my knees until the pain abated.

In the middle of the dining table in the farmhouse kitchen was a fly trap. It was a glass bowl about twelve inches across, half full of water, covered with a shaped glass top with a hole in the middle. The flies flew through the hole, couldn't find their way out, fell into the water and drowned. Modern technology provided us with the flypaper, a strip of stickum covered paper about a foot long which was hung in a strategic position. When it was black with dead flies it was burned.

OUR church in College Street beside the university was a pretty functional edifice. It was quite big, had a large organ behind the pulpit and a raised area in front for the choir and organist. A gallery ran round the other three sides, supported by cast iron Corinthian pillars. When I was very young, the semicircle of the apse behind the organ was covered by a religious mural, divided into several panels. I was too young to recognise the figures and incidents depicted. The general colour scheme was sombre; dull red walls and gold trimmings, and acres of near-black varnished pews. Later a brighter modern colour scheme was introduced which seemed less depressing. But they could not change our one stained glass window, a representation of a horribly sissified Christ by some undistinguished Victorian artist. I never ever experienced any truly religious feeling in this church. Would it have been different in some fine old Gothic cathedral, or even some ancient and honestly built old country kirk?

As soon as we were old enough, five or six, we had to attend Sunday School. This I don't believe any of us enjoyed. Apart from having to dress up in our uncomfortable Sunday clothes and shoes, we had to learn passages from the Bible by heart, and we were examined on 'The Shorter Catechism'. 'What is the Chief End of Man?' No — not his head. 'Man's Chief End is to Glorify God, and to Enjoy Him forever.' For us infants, there were some compensations. We got a coloured text every Sunday, with flowery borders and swags, and sugary Biblical characters. We sat on long wooden forms, trying to look suitably solemn and reverent. Hanging on the wall was a large coloured poster with a picture of God, with a stern expression, flowing white beard and hair, looking down through a cloud. Something like a gone-to-seed, off-duty Santa Claus.

God had a voice of thunder, and struck bad people dead with a bolt of lightning. This worried a lot of us during the occasional thunderstorm, but after surviving a few I had to conclude the lightning was striking people more sinful than I, probably in the next street. And if He knew everything, why wasn't I dead already?

The teachers kept telling us Jesus died so we could be forgiven our sins. What sins? I couldn't remember any, unless it was the time I didn't eat up my crust. And why was God always lurking up there in

49

the clouds, spying on us? Didn't he trust us? Did he *expect* us to sin? And he was ready to make a note in His book, and send us all to Hell when we died. But He was a God of love, they told us, and had Jesus crucified so we'd all be saved. This never impressed me as really a *loving* thing to do to your only Son. And when we started reading the Old Testament, God seemed quite an unlovable entity. Very confusing.

As we grew older, we split into groups, boys or girls, and took Bible study after the normal church service, and had different teachers for a year or two. They were all nice, earnest, well-meaning folks. We were set to learn by heart for the following Sunday passages from the Bible, or a psalm or hymn. As we had more than enough memorising to do for school during the week, I resented this as an unfair extra imposition. Also, most of it was deadly uninteresting in content. No one told us there were bits here and there which were *really* interesting and decidedly un-holy, but we found them eventually. One baffling phrase seemed to imply that angels or gentlemen always carried on conversations with a lady from a chair outside her room.

Though Sunday School failed to turn me into an orthodox Christian, I did appreciate the annual prize-giving, when we got books as prizes. Fortunately they were not religious books. Some of the ones I won were *The Coral Island, Nat the Naturalist,* and *The Gorilla Hunters,* all by Ballantyne, and most enjoyable yarns. Nowadays we realise that it wasn't such a good idea to safari through the jungles shooting everything on sight, but then it was accepted as a sport, or even profession, and demonstrated superlative skill and courage on the part of the white (of course) hunter. Everybody knew that lions, tigers, gorillas, elephants, rhinos and whales would attack anyone on sight. Vicious beasts! (Does anyone remember a cigarette ad series — Nature in the Raw is seldom Mild — illustrated with pictures of ravening wild animals? Now we find that almost *any* wild animal is prepared to be friendly with humans; tigers, lions, leopards, killer whales, gorillas and wolves. Even the African elephant has proved to be as intelligent and tractable as the Asian species. In my youth they were supposed to be untamable.)

On Friday evenings at seven we went to the Band of Hope. On joining, we solemnly signed the Pledge, which meant we promised never to touch Strong Drink. I wonder if anyone kept that promise? Well, at that age, it wasn't too difficult. There was an alphabetic poem we had to learn, 'A is for Alcohol, Man's deadly Foe; B is for Bottle, which leads to much Woe' — mercifully I have forgotten the rest. The meeting consisted of rousing hymns like *Onward Christian Soldiers* and *Dare to be a Daniel,* with an uplifting lecture and prayers. Very

50

occasionally, there was something more exciting, like a lantern lecture, but what really kept us going was the promise of the Christmas party. All 'pledge' cards were fully stamped in the weeks before Christmas.

Other church organisations were the Boys' Brigade and the Guides, with their junior branches, the Life Boys and the Brownies. My brother and sisters joined these, but I managed to resist. About the age of eleven, I and the others were forced to join the Children's Choir. Up till then it had been a flourishing affair with at times more than a hundred members, but now with decreasing numbers of children in the congregation, it was declining. Mr Foggo, the church organist, had run it for many years, organising every year a highly successful *Kinderspiel*. (I don't think anyone knew this was a German word, or its meaning.) When we joined, the intention was to produce a play, *The Nodding Mandarin*. Charlie was given star rating; all he had to do was sit cross-legged and nod. He became quite good at it. But the choir numbers continued to decrease, and Foggo reluctantly disbanded us after only six weeks. Personally I was delighted. I hated singing solo, and it was a wasted hour during which I could have been doing more interesting things.

When I was fifteen and old enough, I officially 'joined the Kirk', and had my first communion. When I ate the bread and drank the wine, perhaps I would experience some great revelation. But no; I drank the wine and it was delicious, but a thimbleful was not enough to produce the mildest euphoria. The bread needed butter or jam on it. So I attended church on Sundays, but only because of a sense of duty and because my mother was hurt if I jibbed. I would endure the services of an hour and a half or more, trying not to sleep through the sermons. The Rev. David Mair was a most estimable man and a true Christian, but only very rarely did his sermons raise any interest in me. When they did, there was usually some point I should have liked to argue with him. But no one interrupts a sermon.

Does it not seem odd that so many religions postulate, or even promise, a Heaven which the soul attains after the death of the body, and yet even the most fervent believer will go to any lengths to remain alive, even in the most miserable circumstances? There may be a Heaven and a Hell; as an agnostic, I'll believe it when I see it. Meantime I shall hang on to existence as long as possible. If it becomes unbearably painful I shall take steps to end it. But the more I experience, the more I see of the world and the universe, the more fascinated I become. As I write, I am aware of discomfort in greater or less degree, but so far this has been a negligible factor in the equation against living. I am interested in today, I can hardly wait to see what will happen tomorrow, and I want to know everything about yesterday.

As Teilhard de Chardin remarks, all our research into history, archaeology, geology, astrophysics, mathematics or whatever, is an attempt to 'remember' yesterday and to integrate Consciousness, past, present and future. Consciousness of the present moment can be expanded to include the instant of creation, and its end. 'The present time' can mean this year, this century, this thousand years and so on. The phenomenon of Man has just occurred. How significant is this in the cosmic context? Interesting, indubitably, but significant? Man is the first animal to become conscious of consciousness.

Every Christmas we looked forward to the Church soirée. We always went up to the gallery for this, and occupied a front pew. There were songs by the choir and individuals, musical selections, recitations. Half-way through tea was brought round, and we opened our bags of buns and sandwiches. We would get an orange on the way out. But the highlight of the evening was the magic lantern show, when all the lights were put out and the brightly coloured pictures were projected on the huge white screen erected in front of the pulpit. Some of the pictures could even be made to *move;* ships at sea, camels in the desert, fish in the water. Then there were black and white slides of scenes photographed at the annual Sunday School picnic and the BB's camp. When one year genuine moving pictures arrived, we had black and white cartoons — *Felix the Cat* and *Bonzo the Dog.* These got tremendous applause.

The annual picnic was the peak of our year. It was held in faraway, exotic places like Davidson's Mains Park, Juniper Green or Ratho. At first we went by charabanc. We called them 'sherrybangs'. Four or five of these monsters would line up in Chambers Street, and we'd all pile in. They were open motor vehicles, with high running boards along the side, up which you climbed to your seat. These were bench seats running the full width of the charabanc, and seated from six to eight or more. Each row had its own door. At the back was a folded hood which could be unfolded if it rained, and pulled with difficulty all the way to the front. In later years we went by train, and exciting though this was, it didn't quite have the family flavour of the old sherrybang.

Arrived at our destination, we'd spill out over the green grass, enjoying the space to run about like puppies turned loose after being tied up for a week. As town dwellers born and bred, we usually had to look both ways first, and never run into the street. Wooden forms were brought on the lorry which transported Mr Paton, our caretaker, and his field kitchen. These were for the use of any adults who wouldn't sit on the grass. Soon the games and races were in full swing. There was rounders, a game everyone could join in. For the little ones, there were gentler games, like Tig or Ring-o-Roses. For the older boys and adults there was five-a-side football. There were races for every age group from infants to grannies, with the usual variations — Sack race, Egg and Spoon race, Three-legged race and so on. There would be a great Prizegiving at the end. When I was five I was entered for a race. I came in a very late last, and knew I couldn't possibly get a prize. But some time later my Sunday School teacher came to me and said, 'Congratulations, George! Here's your prize!' It was a glossy yellow rubber ball, stencilled with brightly coloured patterns, which I loved on sight, and treasured for years. I still couldn't understand why I deserved to get it though. It was then my mother confessed *she* had given it because I'd gone in for the race and finished the course. In later years, I do remember entering for other races, but even with many yards start, I never had a chance.

The picnic lunch was in paper bags full of sandwiches and buns, and there were hot pies from the field kitchen, and gallons of tea. This we drank from our tinny, a tin mug slung over our shoulders on a piece of tape or string. Once you had your tinny slung in the morning, you knew nothing could stop the outing.

Local landlords I suspect were not overjoyed at the prospect of a picnic adjoining their land. Some of us tots climbed through a fence once at Davidson's Mains, and had a wonderful time playing in a field of very tall grass. It was higher than our heads and bright green. We found we could make paths through it, with tunnels and little secret rooms. Perfect for hide and seek. Finally one of the grown-ups spotted us and hauled us out, much against our will. It was a wheatfield of course, not grass, but nobody had told us. Probably if it *had* been grass, they would not have stopped us, being unaware that hay could be ruined just as easily.

The following year, at the same place, we got over a wall into the woods. This again was a marvellous place to play at stalking, hide and seek and house building. We knew nobody could argue about ruining crops. This wasn't a field, and the trees obviously were growing wild. There was a thick, rustling carpet of beech leaves, a lot of under-growth, and lots of fallen twigs and branches for building and props. There were intriguing hollows and dens everywhere. We made a native hut, and had all got inside when there was a mad bellowing and crashing in the near distance, like an elephant amok. It approached rapidly and we cowered in terror. Children were fleeing in all directions, and through the leaves we saw a large tweed-clad man with a furious red face, waving a ferocious looking stick. Thankfully, he passed within a yard or two and didn't spot us, and when he stamped off into the distance, we quickly made ourselves scarce. Probably we scared every one of his pheasants into the next county.

Going home was an anti-climax, but eased by the fun of riding in the charabanc or train. Usually we seemed to get a sunny or at least a dry day, but once the rain came down just after we'd arrived at the field. After half an hour standing under the trees for shelter, we found that rain *does* penetrate even the thickest leaf cover. It was obviously on for the day, so we trooped back to the local church hall, opened for us in an emergency. That picnic was not a success.

MY MOTHER was determined that we boys should pull our weight in the family, and we had to do our share of housework as well as the girls. When *she* was young, boys were not expected to do menial things like washing dishes, cleaning shoes, polishing cutlery or sweeping floors, and she and her sisters were always slaving after them. Though Charlie and I were not wholly delighted with this arrangement, especially as most of our friends looked on sisters as slaves, it did pay off in later life. We were capable of managing for ourselves in an emergency. At the age of nine or ten I could cook the Sunday breakfast, and as the others became old enough they shared in the chores. Camping was good training too, where everyone has to pull together.

I still played quite happily with relations and neighbours, but strangers were a different matter. The first year or so at school, I was physically much on a par with the other children, but then I started to grow much more slowly. Like a flock of chickens, children tend to peck to death any one that looks different. In the school playground, when I was baited, my own classmates tended to defend me. They knew and accepted me. But outside school it could be hell. I was regularly mocked and jeered at, and not being a fighter, I would go home in tears. Often I avoided going out just to avoid confrontations. 'They're only words. Say, sticks and stones may break my bones, but words will never hurt me!' But words can hurt worse than sticks and stones. My father also had to cope with jeering children, though adults within range would usually step in to reprimand them, at least in our neighbourhood where he was much respected.

Once a lad of thirteen or fourteen who should have known better baited him by lurching along in step behind him, getting closer and closer as he became more brave with no reaction from his victim. My father bided his time, then stopped without warning and swung a stinging slap to the side of the face. The lad made off, howling for his dad. A woman across the street called, 'Mr Thomson, I saw all that. If

54

there's any trouble, let me know!' Though the lad was a head taller, he obviously had no idea of the power of adult muscle packed into a limited area, or he would have remained well out of reach.

My father was always disappointed by my lack of aggression when provoked, and once or twice when I was very small tried to teach me how to fight, but all in vain. My nose would bleed copiously at the slightest touch; in fact, it could bleed without warning at any time, and once started was difficult to stop. I should have known that bullies cannot stand pain themselves, and if I had been prepared to give *some* back, life could have been easier.

In the twenties, horse cabs still plied for hire. There was a cab rank on the north side of Princes Street, near Waverley Station. Though we all would have loved a trip in one, they were far too expensive. Very occasionally we travelled in motor taxicabs though. When we were all too young to carry suitcases or parcels on the trams on our way to the station for our annual holiday, my mother would order one. We felt very grand piling into the taxi in front of the pend, with our neighbours looking on enviously. I did not learn for many years that Edinburgh's taxi fleet was unique. Every one was a Rolls-Royce.

Before we were old enough to go camping, we were now and then treated to a picnic in the Park, the Meadows, or best of all, Portobello Beach. That was then the highlight of our summer. It was still a popular holiday resort then. A great part of the enjoyment was the journey there. It was about three miles away, and we had to change trams at the General Post Office. We were used to electric trams, but here we changed to a *cable* car. It was even a different colour, dark green, instead of yellow and red. It had an open top deck, so you could sit on the slatted wooden seats enjoying the rush of air, the rock and sway and grind.

A tram journey always seemed enjoyable, even if it was only a short distance. When I was first old enough to take notice of them, they were just being converted from cable to electricity, and in many places the slotted centre rail for the cable remained between the tracks. Some stayed for many years, long after the last cable car had gone. The earliest trams I remember were all double-deckers, and many had open upper decks. At first the seats were long wooden benches the full length of the passenger area, with loops hanging from an overhead rail for standing passengers to hold on to.

Our favourite seat was at the front, where we could watch the driver through the glass. As on the early taxis and motorcars, the driver had no protection from the elements. Only in the later models did he have the luxury of a glass windscreen. Edinburgh trams had no advertisements outside, but there were many inside on a narrow strip above the opposite seats running the length of the car. 'Meet Me at Maules', 'Corstorphine Zoo', 'King's Theatre' and many others. If we had any choice, we went upstairs to a compartment at the very front, above the driver. Here you get the best effects of the speed and motion. Being so high up the sway and plunge were exaggerated. The top deck was for smokers; downstairs it was 'No Smoking'.

The driver wound a brass handle to control the electric motor, and another for the brake. He stamped on an iron pedal to sound the bell warning of the tram's approach. In emergency he could work another lever which dropped a sort of cowcatcher under the front of the tram, to catch bodies which otherwise had no chance. I never actually saw one used in earnest, but often enough they seemed to slip anyway, and they would drop with a tremendous clatter on the cobblestones. Then the driver had to get out to replace it. He had to change the points manually too, with an iron key carried beside the driving position, until automatic switches were introduced. It was the conductor's job to change round the contact wheel at the end of a long pole when the tram was turned at the terminus. It was always worth watching to see the shower of sputtering blue sparks as he manoeuvred the wheel on to the overhead live wire. The conductor had a black leather pouch for money, and a ticket-punching machine slung on his chest, along with a rack of multi-coloured tickets. These strips of card had a printed list of stops, and he punched a hole ('ching!') opposite the stop you wanted. Later, tickets were reduced to a flimsy strip of paper, printed with the necessary information as it was wound out. One of my uncles, Andrew Sommerville, worked as a conductor on the Edinburgh trams.

The tram showed to best advantage at night, with all its lights blazing, careering along the steel rails clanging and grinding, showering blue sparks from the overhead wires. The double bend at the top of the Mound was the best place to observe the phenomenon, and to experience it as a passenger inside. The judder and waggle at the sharp turns were almost equivalent to the Cakewalk at the Fun Fair.

Passengers were not supposed to ring the bell warning the driver to stop, but if the conductor was upstairs you either rang or jumped off. Boarding or leaving a tram between stops was also forbidden, but if it stopped due to traffic conditions and it was more convenient, you did it anyway. Average distances cost only a penny for an adult fare; longer journeys more by halfpenny stages to threepence, which took you from terminus to terminus. Twopence took you completely round the Marchmont Circle, and our mother sometimes took us for a pleasure trip.

Our cable tram would grind to a halt at Bath Street, and with mounting excitement we would see the blue of the sea at the foot of the hill. All the way down were enticing shops selling wooden spades, and tin pails with brightly coloured pictures on the sides. Wealthy people bought their children metal bladed spades, but we were happy with ours. In those shops you could also buy souvenirs and garish saucy postcards, which only needed a halfpenny stamp. As you neared the beach, the sand on the pavement grew thicker and grittier under your shoes, and the smell of salt and seaweed grew stronger. The first thing on the beach was to take off our shoes and socks and get into the water for a paddle.

In Portobello's heyday, there was a pier, which I can only just remember. It had gone by the days of our picnics, but the sand of the beach was still level with the promenade. When I visited the place many years later, there was a ten-foot drop to wet, seaweedy stones below. On sunny days, hundreds of people went to the beach, and all along the prom were entertainments — cafes, photographers, holiday hotels, chip shops, ice-cream parlours, fortune tellers, Punch and Judy shows, and sometimes a man who built real castles of sand and sand sculptures. Passersby would throw pennies in his hat.

At the west end of the prom there was even a permanent fairground, with side shows and a helter-skelter, and even a figure-8 railway. We patronised this Eldorado, when we felt wealthy, after we were old enough to make the journey on our own. At the other end was Joppa, which was much less commercialised, and had a rather stony beach. Here was a group of ancient red pantiled buildings which we were told was Joppa Salt Pans, now unused. Further on still was Musselburgh, all rocks and mussels. We didn't much like going there, and if we did, our picnic was on the Race Course rather than the beach.

On the beach, children up to the age of ten or eleven went bathing quite unremarkably in the nude. Swimsuits for children were only just beginning to become fashionable. Having experienced those cold, wet and gritty garments, I'm sure it was much more comfortable when you could do without. And much cheaper. I suspect present prudishness is fostered by makers of swimsuits, who would otherwise be out of business. By the time I was twelve, it was not permissible for a child to swim naked. Certainly not girls, and though occasionally a boy broke the rules, even that was not quite decent. Looked at logically, undressing to swim or go to bed would seem the rational thing to do.

OUR Saturday penny pocket money was on occasion augmented by an extra penny for the children's Saturday afternoon matinée at the La Scala Picture House. This we really enjoyed. We queued up for an hour before the doors opened, and once inside there was another half hour before the show started. We passed that time by playing guessing games, using the ads on the highly coloured safety curtain, and dodging the orange peel thrown from the gallery above. Occasionally the manager was called to throw out some trouble-maker, but few went so far as to risk missing the pictures. When the rose-coloured gas lights round the auditorium finally dimmed, and the safety curtain rose with a rattle, a tremendous cheer would go up, followed by an expectant silence. The films were black and white and silent. Musical accompaniment was supplied by a long-suffering pianist on a jangling piano. It was easy to see why the films were called 'the flickers'.

During the interval sweets and ices were on sale to the more financially solvent of us. We would look on enviously — 'Give us a lick!' During the show, an usherette would walk up and down the aisles at intervals, spraying a scented deodorant which we would inhale luxuriously whenever some spray reached us. Breaks in the film would occur, often at the best part. The villain's face would freeze in mid-snarl, slowly curling up and distorting, while the audience stamped, booed, yelled and whistled. How we loved Charlie Chaplin, Buster Keaton, Mary Pickford, Laurel and Hardy, Our Gang, and best of all the cowboy films!

There was also the 'Aibey in the Pleezince' (the Abbey Cinema in the Pleasance). This was the archetypal fleapit. I think I was only in it once, though it cost only a halfpenny against the La Scala's penny. The seats were backless wooden forms. We were warned not to go there in case we picked up beasties! The Pleasance ran through the worst slums in the city, and though the name suggests it was once a salubrious thoroughfare, people avoided it if possible.

It may have been partly through the cinemas as well as the schools that periodical epidemics of contagious disease swept through the school children of the city. Mumps, measles and whooping cough were taken care of at home, but scarlet fever and diphtheria were diseases that demanded hospitalisation. A special 'Yellow Fever Coach' would come around and collect the victims from their homes. I would watch the increasing number of empty places in

58

my classroom, and wonder who would be next. At last one of the family would go down with fever, then another, then another, to be wrapped in a red blanket and taken away. Somehow, each time I escaped scot free. Inexplicable, since we were all in such close contact all the time. But I was glad I didn't have to go into hospital. It meant I was in quarantine and had to stay off school for several weeks during each epidemic, as the contact period for incubation overlapped the first and last to contract the disease. I did catch the milder diseases like mumps and chickenpox.

Perhaps it was for reasons of public health that many familiar pieces of street furniture disappeared. Horse troughs were once common in many streets, where you could stand and wonder at the gallons of water being sucked up by thirsty horses. Once or twice I saw a few 'mennins' (sticklebacks) in the local trough. Probably they had been liberated from their captors' jeelyjars, deliberately or inadvertently while re-filling the jar. I wondered if a horse would notice one going down.

Then there were the 'Gents', mostly from the Victorian era. Ours must have been one of the few cities where a diabetic could happily undertake a long walk. Many were of cast-iron construction painted Corporation green, on the lines of the Parisian *pissoir*, and open to the sky, but more were of stone or brick. Now your diabetic must have a car.

Lamentably too, the ubiquitous iron drinking fountain has also gone. At one time nearly every street had one; ours was in front of our tenement. Apart from their normal use, they were a boon when for whatever reason the water to the houses was cut-off, when queues would form with buckets and kettles. Apart from the freestanding iron fountains, some were built into the walls of buildings, and there was one splendid pink granite monument at the entrance to the Park, with water spouts all round it supplied with iron cups on chains.

BEGGARS were part of the street scene, standing mutely in the gutter holding a cap or tin cup to receive the odd penny before being moved on by the local bobby. Some were old soldiers, wearing a row of medals on their ragged coats. Occasionally there was a knock at our door and some old tramp would beg a piece of bread. But not all were genuinely hungry; we would find sandwiches thrown in a corner of the stairs after they had gone. What they wanted was money which would be spent in the nearest pub. A step above beggars were the street performers; some were not bad, like the line of ex-service men who walked along the gutter playing various instruments. Some were less than expert, like one or two fiddlers or bagpipers we knew.

There were performers on the spoons, bones or 'moothie' (harmonica). One specialised in dancing dolls. He carried a chair around on which he could sit and make articulated wooden dolls dance on a springy piece of plank, while he produced his own music with a harmonica mounted on a frame in front of his mouth. The one-man bands fascinated us too. How could they possibly work all those instruments at once? Bells, whistles, hooters, trumpets, drums, moothies and cymbals!

Singers liked to perform in our back court, where there was less noise to compete with, and the police might pass them by. Once a year we saw a diabolo expert, hurling the spinning diabolo as high as our tenement roofs, catching it again and performing impossible feats. Then there were the pavement artists. Sometimes they would use the same pitch in turn, but mostly they had their own set of paving stones at some favoured spot, where they spent a day before moving elsewhere. The best one had a pitch near the Royal Infirmary who used pastels to draw directly on the stone. He could draw quite sophisticated baroque borders round his pictures, and used a variety of subjects from scenery to bunches of roses, all very realistic and beautifully shaded. But he was an exception. Most were poor draughtsmen and worse colourists. The even less professional displayed pathetic chalk drawings on cardboard, possibly drawn by someone else. At least when it rained *they* could pack up their stock and save it for another day. If the rain was not too heavy, the genuine artist covered his masterpieces with cloth till it went off again, when he would repair any spots and carry on.

Long after electric lighting had been installed in the main streets, gas was still used in the rest of the city. One of our free entertainments was to watch the lamp lighter at dusk. He carried a long pole with a gauze-protected flame at the end (oil powered?), with which he pushed up a little trap door at the foot of the lamp to turn on the gas and light the mantle. In the morning he would turn them *off* again. But modernisation deprived us of this enjoyment. They fitted clockwork contraptions which lighted the gas automatically, and we only occasionally saw the lamplighter with a ladder which he propped against the lamp post crossbar, and climbed up to wind the mechanism. Lamp posts were used as gymnastic props. Boys climbed up to swing from the crossbar. Girls tied ropes round them and swung around. They were also used as markers in street games.

60

Another free entertainment, which palled unexpectedly quickly, came when traffic lights were installed at the end of the street. For the first few days we hung out of the window, enjoying the lights, red, amber, green, and speculating how they knew when to change. They were like the fairy lights on Christmas trees, especially at night.

MY FIRST school was Drummond Street Infant School. Your first teacher went with you through each grade until you were old enough to go to South Bridge Elementary. By good luck or planning, the schools were adjoining. They were separated by a high stone wall with a small green door which the infants regarded with the reverence due to the Pearly Gates. Behind that door, opened only once a year for the elect (as far as we knew), lay the exalted realm where you became a 'Big Yin'. Until then you were a baby.

Miss Eales was tall, grey-haired, pleasant faced, with a quiet voice. She always wore a grey or lavender coloured smock. She must have been in her early fifties. I was good at drawing, and was always among those who were called out to have their efforts admired by the rest of the class. Most of my freely chosen subjects were animals — lion, ostrich, giraffe, canary and so on — but I also drew ships with impossibly high tiers of decks and dozens of funnels belching smoke. The more smoke and funnels, the more powerful the ship. Other details were added *ad lib*. Ventilators, anchor, portholes, and most important on a modern vessel, the wireless aerial. Battleships were top heavy with guns. Any spaces were filled with waves and seagulls.

These masterpieces were drawn on our slates with slate pencil. Sometimes they were preserved on the window sill for a week, propped up between the sprouting hyacinth bulbs and bean shoots. We had to provide our own damp rags for cleaning the slates, carried in an Oxo tin in our satchels. Those with dry rags moistened them illicitly with spit. Wealthy children had sponges. As we did all our other work on the slate, we were issued with replacements while our own slates were in the art gallery. At the very beginning, instead of slates we were given blackboards, thick card painted black, rounded at the edges and corners with constant use. We used white chalk on these, and had thick felt dusters for cleaning.

Competition was encouraged. The idea that equal opportunity meant equal achievement by equal talents had not yet been invented. It was accepted that children were more, or less able than average.

Luck of the draw. The brighter ones were encouraged to do more, the others were expected to do the best they were capable of. Miss Eales encouraged competition by awarding every Friday a Dux Medal of solid silver (we thought), which was worn all the following week by the proud recipient. Dux of course only meant top of the class until we reached the top class, when it was truly top of the school. I could hold it for several weeks at a time, but there was always a challenger to take it away.

Physical training then was called 'Physical Jerks', and most of it was done sitting at our desks. Some classrooms seated three or four at one long desk, so there were too few aisles to accommodate the whole class standing up. Some classrooms were built up in five or six tiers to the highest row at the back of the room, so that the teacher could clearly see those furthest away. Since classes numbered fifty or more, discipline had to be good. Our drill exercises obviously had to be mainly head, arm and body movements. One painful incident sticks in my mind. A new teacher noticed I hadn't got my arms straight up over my head, and 'helped' them up to the required position. My shoulder joints have to dislocate to do this. She did apologise afterwards. Several times since, my arms have been straightened, each time with a lack of appreciation on my part.

Around the mid-twenties, the education authorities were thinking about introducing free milk. Some schools were to get milk daily, others a biscuit, and the control group would get nothing. We of course were delighted at the prospect of a free bottle of milk. But guess which school was in the control group? *And* we had to put up with the extra medical inspections while getting nothing in return. Obviously the results decided the doctors that there were benefits for those who got milk, but five years later we still hadn't seen any.

Once a week in Infant School we had a modelling lesson. A dollop of clay was dumped on a board in front of us. We had no modelling tools, only our fingers, and we brought our own bib-aprons to protect our clothing. We sat without touching the clay until everyone had a piece. But we were not allowed to chose our own subjects, and we all had to make the same object, an uninspiring bird's nest. This was a round lump with a hollow in the middle to contain the four or five eggs. There was a large glass-fronted case at the end of the assembly hall. On the shelves were examples of the best bird's nests made over the years. But of more interest to us were the natural history exhibits, stuffed birds and animals, with a baby elephant for a centre piece. Whether this was genuine or a model, I can't say, thought it *was* four feet high. We never saw this case opened, nor were the exhibits ever used.

Boys and girls were strictly segregated, with different entrance doors, and they had to use separate playgrounds. In the classroom, boys sat on one side of the room, girls on the other. The boys' playground at South Bridge I can describe — the girls' I never saw. At three or four places along the walls, ledges of stone were inset. These were for sharpening slatepen, and in some places were worn nearly back to wall level. The school bell was on a little turret, rung by a long bell rope, unlike the Infants' bell, which was a large highly polished brass hand bell, wielded by the teacher on duty. The Infants School was a handsome red sandstone edifice, with four yellow electric lights in each classroom. We vied for the exciting job of switching these on on dark winter afternoons, clicking the huge brass-fluted switches. There was a shelter at the end of the playground for rainy days, with a pair of ancient 'henner-bars' on which the athletes displayed their prowess. Off this shelter was the echoing and malodorous 'pee-hoose'.

Though we had no contact outside the classroom, at South Bridge I was in love with Mary Morrison, a cheerful little girl with bobbed black hair, black eyes and rosy cheeks. I also liked a little Jewish girl, Anna Dorfmann. She was more serious, and was among the three or four of us who shared the top place in the class. That was as near as I ever got to having a childhood sweetheart. I worshipped them from afar. Since we never had school parties and were forbidden to ask friends home to tea because we couldn't afford it (and conversely couldn't accept the invitations we got) we never met socially. I couldn't even meet anyone on the way from school, as I had to collect my sisters and brother and see them safely home.

Only one Christmas party was ever given — the one for school leavers. It was free, so nearly everybody went. As a great concession, the top classes were given dancing lessons after school for several weeks before Christmas. I and half my class were too scared to attend — you actually had to dance with girls — and in consequence endured the party as wallflowers, a depressing experience.

At South Bridge we had three different teachers, one after the other. This arrangement seemed unnatural after having only one teacher during all our previous school life. The first was Miss McLennan, I imagine in her early twenties. Once during a drawing lesson she complimented me on my charming choice of colours for a simple pattern. Little did she know that pale green and lilac were the only two I could get my hands on. What I really wanted were bright reds, oranges, blues and yellows. She kept all the crayons in a box on her desk, and it was first come first served. I couldn't push in fast enough to have any choice.

The classrooms in the schools seemed vast, and ultra modern, because they all had electric light. There was seating for sixty or more

63

children at the old oak desks, with either two or four seats side by side. At the front of each place was a slot for the slate, and a little hole with a brass lid to hold the inkwell. Heating was an open coal fire which the teacher periodically stoked up, using an old glove or piece of paper to keep her hands clean. A high fire guard ensured that pupils could not get too close. Sometimes some of us would come in soaked to the skin on a cold, wet winter day, and the teacher would allow us to dry off in front of the fire.

Some teachers kept a conical dunce's cap for occasional use, when the victim would have to wear it, standing in a corner facing the wall, for maybe half an hour. Usually there would be vases or jam jars on the windowsills, with flowers or twigs in season. Favourites were pussy willows and sticky-budded horse chestnuts, which we might get to draw in an art lesson. Daffodils and hyacinths were grown in water vases holding a single bulb, which we watched week by week as the white roots grew longer and longer into a tangled mass, and a flower triumphantly burst through the bunch of green leaves on top.

Classroom walls usually held a selection of our drawings and a few educational pictures or posters. These might change from time to time, but there were two permanent fixtures — a huge linen-backed map of the world, with vast expanses of pink which we knew represented the British Empire, and a long yellowing varnished scroll with the Tonic Sol-fa printed on it. Between and to each side of the eight basic notes were extra half or quarter notes which we never seemed to use. I never really enjoyed music lessons. Learning a new song was all right, but it was usually preceded by boring sessions on reading the notes and deciding whether they were breves or demi-semiquavers. Chanting 'Ta! Ta! Taffa-tiffy Ta'! seemed to have little to do with music.

At South Bridge, we lined up in twos in the playground, then marched to our classrooms to the martial sound of Souza marches played by one of the teachers on a piano on one of the stair landings. We seemed to hear *Blaze Away* more than any of the others. If there was a hold up for any reason, we had to keep time, marching on the spot.

Miss Currie was a grey-haired motherly lady of around fifty. She was an excellent teacher, and I think it was in her class I started to learn how to learn. Strict by today's standards, unlike young Miss McLennan (though I don't recall *she* ever had any disciplinary problems), she was very fair and also knew when to relax. Sometimes on Friday afternoons, if we'd been specially good all week, she would sit and peel several Jaffa oranges, carefully removing every trace of pith ('It's indigestible'), then handed out one segment to each of us. We had to wait for the word of command before eating it. Another

Friday treat was her readings of Kipling's *Just So* stories, where I first heard of the Elephant's Child, and the great, grey-green and greasy Limpopo River, all set about with Fever Trees.

Daddy Wilkie had the qualifying class. He had a rusty Livingstone-type moustache, a gold watch and chain, and walked with a bad limp because of a club foot. Oddly enough, I never thought of him by his nickname, though most of the others did. I felt a sort of affinity with him. Perhaps because he was disabled he could better understand my thinking and attitude towards life. He was quite strict when he had to be, and was the terror of bullies. In his room he always kept a supply of books and 'Children's Newspapers', and anyone who finished a lesson ahead of the rest was free to read any of these until the others were done. Here was my first introduction to the excellent *National Geographic Magazine*, with its yellow and black border and list of contents on the front cover. This was my first real taste of exotic, strange and faraway places like Egypt and the Nile, Africa and South America. It was a great incentive to work fast so as to get more time for reading 'for fun', which I imagine was his intention.

At the end of each year, we had to take home our record cards for our parents' signature. Each year they were a different colour. Attendance and conduct were assessed as well as the individual subjects. Usually I had several 'Ex' marks (for excellent), and some 'VGs'. If I got a mere 'G', I felt I was not doing well enough. The only subject I ever failed in was History, in my last year at secondary school. The teacher was Miss Bonniman, and she made history even more boring than football or politics. It was not entirely her fault; History then was the memorising of endless lists of dates, kings and queens, battles, ancient treaties and dead politics. School books took an incredibly blinkered and biassed look at events, and started with only the most perfunctory notice of ancient civilisations, if indeed they mentioned them at all. The Romans deserved mention only when they occupied Britain. Our own history before 55 B.C. was lost in haze and myth. *Real* History is the history of the universe; all possible events and places, embracing every imaginable subject. History which covers a few hundred years out of billions is worthless.

My record card results were not undiluted joy to the rest of our family, or to our relations. As each became old enough to follow me through the school, the teachers would say, 'I hope you'll be as good as George!' They must have found it exasperating, especially my cousin who had the same name.

During the period I spent in Wilkie's class, Phemia and I had every afternoon off school, in order to attend the Sunlight Treatment Clinic at the Sick Children's Hospital. He gave me extra homework so I could keep up with the rest of the class, since the qualifying exam

65

was most important, equivalent to the 11-plus in later years. In the actual examination, I came second. My best friend, Donald Ferguson, scored 94%, while I only reached 92%. The highest mark qualified one for a scholarship to Boroughmuir High School, and I had hoped to get it. Still, I was pleased for Donald. He had been my best friend all through my schooldays. He was the biggest lad in our Infant class, and he was still the biggest when we parted. Very early on, he appointed himself my protector, and many a time frightened off bullies who would have made my life a misery.

Instead of the fee-paying High School, I went to James Clark Secondary, near King's Park. One had to choose between the technical and commercial courses. I was expected to take the latter, which prepared you for office jobs – white collar, respected and respectable. The technical course was for the plebs, the hewers and carriers, the coarser types. Needless to say, it was not stated so plainly as that. Nevertheless, we all understood very well what the difference was, as any child will today, no matter what fancy term is created to designate dim, normal, or bright.

The teachers and advisers did their best to steer me into the commercial course, but the idea of office work repelled me even then, and I could not accept that office work would be more plentiful than manual when I left school. As it turned out, the cream of the technical intake got a pretty good academic grounding anyway, fortunately for me, fifteen years after I left school, when I proposed to take the university prelims after only six months study. We had to work hard, with two hours of homework every night. I was pretty conscientious about doing it all, but if you dodged it or found it too difficult, like the poor lad who was bottom of our 'A' class, then you were punished. The tawse was in regular use then.

In the English class, we ploughed through *Macbeth, The Merchant of Venice* and *Midsummer Night's Dream*. Cromarty was an excellent teacher, but I was sickened of Shakespeare for many years. Had we read them for fun, no doubt we would have enjoyed them, but with all the parsing, analysis and compulsory memorising of long passages, Shakespeare was killed stone dead. The same with poetry. We learned a poem by heart, and dissected it for construction and meaning. Skimping on homework meant trouble, so these subjects took on the aspect of forced labour and remained distasteful long after we left school.

During the first few months at this school, I was still attending the Sunlight Clinic. Some of my schoolmates were curious to know if you had to take off *all* your clothes, and were there girls there too. I was quite unable to regale them with sexually titillating anecdotes. After embarrassment the first one or two times, Phemia and I quite

66

enjoyed the clinic. We undressed in an ante-room, got into a red dressing gown and wooden sandals, then clopped into the sun room, collecting a pair of green goggles on the way. The nurse would find us a place in the semi-circle of wooden forms facing the lamp. At half-time we turned round the other way. On a cold showery winter's day it was sheer bliss to bask in warm sunshine for thirty minutes or more, and we all acquired beautiful tans. Boys and girls were mixed indiscriminately, and I don't remember any of us being upset about being naked. We accepted it all quite matter-of-factly.

As an old hand I even learned how to readjust the lamps when the carbon elements were in danger of sputtering out, as occasionally happened when the nurse was otherwise occupied. Only once was there friction, when a new boy and his sister joined the group. They were a very posh-spoken pair, and he, particularly, objected to mixing flank to flank with the common herd. His method of obtaining more *lebensraum* was to pinch his neighbour — anywhere — very effective when your victim is nude. Normally even I would move over, but one day the benches were so crowded that evasion was impossible. He pinched and pinched, until finally the worm turned. I got him by the throat and held him at arm's length, while he howled for his mummy. Soon the nurse came and sorted him out, having listened to the accounts of the other long-suffering victims. She put him properly in his place, and he never troubled anyone again. I had quite surprised myself, as he was much taller than I, and I never expected him to crack at the first retaliation. But I was not popular either with him or his mother thereafter.

Each family group was necessarily thrown together in the ante-room, and usually the mothers became quite friendly. After our daily toasting, the nurse sprayed us cool with a tepid spray, and we were dried off with paper towels. We became fast friends with Amy and Margaret Stevenson and their mother. They were ten-year-old twins with blue eyes and blonde hair, Amy's straight and Margaret's curly; delightful children, cheerful and friendly. We would walk home across the Meadows together. They also were very posh-spoken, but being English they couldn't help it. Amy was lively and mischievous, and I liked her. Margaret was quiet and shy, but secretly I loved *her*. They had an elder sister, Lily. Our mothers seemed to think she and I might become friendly, and tried to edge us toward each other. But though she was very nice too, fifteen was far too old and mature for me, and no doubt thirteen was far too young for her. Margaret was the one for me, and I was sad when they had to move back to England.

For a long time we had weekly blood tests. Though we didn't enjoy them, at first they were not particularly dreaded. We would go to a room at the end of the corridor, where we got up on an examination couch and blood was taken from one arm or the other. But one series of jags was definitely painful. These were to collect samples of marrow. I know this now, but we were not told they were anything different from the usual blood test. The samples were obtained by pushing the needle of a large syringe into the base of the humerus via the inside of the elbow joint. This took a long and painful time, but we had been brainwashed into believing we were being very courageous in co-operating with the doctors, and not howling our heads off. While I underwent this protracted torture, I was allowed to wind the handle of a small hand centrifuge beside the couch, the equivalent of biting on the bullet. The worse it hurt, the harder I wound the handle. This business left me with quite a large and pain-ful lump and bruise for weeks after. The lump remained for months after treatment was stopped, and the area stayed sore under pressure.

The sunlight treatment was stopped not long after my thirteenth birth-day. During the two years I was attending the clinic, I never had a cold or cough. Whether I owed this to the sunray lamps, the daily shower or the daily spoonful of virol which came with the treatment, I do not know. Whether it did any good in any other direction is problematical, but I know I was very sorry to miss my daily dose of sunshine.

Many papers and magazines ran painting competitions for children, and entering these I could win the occasional postal order for anything from 2/6d to 7/6d. When I was thirteen I sent in an entry to a nation-wide competition sponsored by Toblerone chocolate. I got the first prize — £10! This was a tremendous amount of money when few people had even seen a £5 note. It came at a time when the family finances were very low. We all needed new clothes and shoes, and there just was not the money to buy them.

The morning the letter arrived there was great excitement. The others had all hoped I would win *something*, perhaps a consolation prize. I was allowed to open the envelope myself. I'd never seen a cheque before, let alone one for £10, and I got a great boost to the ego as it was passed reverently round the breakfast table. My delighted parents said I could have the day off school in celebration. That morning my mother and I went up to see Mr Oldham, the headmaster, and explain why I had not come in. He too was very pleased, and in the middle of the congratulations my art teacher, Gordon MacDonald, came in with some papers. Oldham said, 'Here, take a look at this!' He took the letter with attached cheque and made to leave the room. 'Come back here — I'd like to do that myself!' said Oldham. Gordon too was very chuffed that one of his pupils had been so lucky.

Later we went to the bank to cash the cheque. More congratula-tions. The afternoon was spent going round the shops, buying all the things we needed. I didn't want anything extra, but my mother thought I should have something to keep as a souvenir. So we went to the art shop at Greyfriar's Bobby, where Renée Simm sold us a box of oil paints at the exorbitant price of 15 shillings. (I saw Renée recently, and she remembers that day.) There was 7/6d left, and I said she should have something too. So she bought a leather handbag with a coloured design in relief on the front, which she treasured for many years. I never again won anything of that magnitude, but I could always win a few postal orders during the year.

My reputation as an artist went sky high with my classmates after this coup. The doctors had recommended that I be excused PT, or drill as it was termed then. Boys used the Drill Hall not far from the school, as the gym in the school was mainly reserved for the girls. This suited me nicely — I found PT and team games immensely boring. But I had to go there with the class, and along with the other dodgers, I was made to do arithmetic instead. This was the teacher's method of putting pressure on me to join the rest of the class, instead of 'coming the old soldier'. (He was an ex-army sergeant, and looked it.)

One day at the beginning of our acquaintanceship, he queried the doctor's advice against PT, and sneered 'Huh! Infantile paralysis!' My mother was incensed at this and went up to school to remonstrate. The drill teacher apologised, but no doubt he had no clear idea of what infantile paralysis really was. I have often wondered since whether exercise would have done all that much harm. Presumably the idea was to prevent undue wear and tear on the joints while they were still growing. That was a slow process; at fifteen I was still only four feet, 11½ inches, and it took another five years to reach five feet. Anyway, the result was that I was allowed to take art during the PT periods.

About half our class elected to leave school at the legal age of fourteen but in 1931 jobs were hard to find. The rest of us listened to our teachers' advice to stay one more year, taking the Higher Dayschool Leaving Certificate, which supposedly gave us a better chance on leaving school. So we all worked diligently for another year. It made no difference whatsoever, and 1932 was worse. I won good grades in the examination, and was top of the school in Art. Also momentarily, joint top in English. Mr Cromarty drew me aside when the results were finally given. At first evaluation, I had come equal first in English, but the girl who shared it was in the commercial course, and to give her an undivided first, which would be useful when she applied for a job in journalism, they'd reduced my score by half a mark to 98½%. This was decided by the weight of what they felt was an unnecessary comma. I wonder whether she *did* get that job. Cromarty pointed out that he was not supposed to tell me about this bit of wangling, and asked me to keep it dark; but he felt I was entitled to know. I appreciated his thoughtfulness.

Now there was pressure on us to stay yet another year. The next hurdle would be the Junior Commercial Certificate, almost guaranteed to get you a job. I actually started taking extra lessons for this, adapted from the commercial course, but I failed that exam and by summer, decided I'd better get out and try for something, no matter what. For the previous year and a half, I should have been bringing in *some* sort of wage to augment my father's meagre earnings, and I felt like a parasite. A few of the more robust lads got jobs as delivery boys, taking groceries around on carrier bikes. The rest of us signed on at the Junior Employment Exchange, where I can't remember anyone actually being given a job. We received no dole or any other money. If you had been in a job previously, you were entitled to £1 a week for thirteen weeks, when it stopped. There was a device called 'Poor Relief'; if the authorities classified you as really deserving you were granted public assistance — if you passed the means test. This was the most resented stricture ever imposed on the unemployed. In effect, it meant that if there was any object in your possession which could be sold to obtain food or rent money, then no help would be offered.

During our last six months at school, we had been taken round a variety of factories and workshops, to give us a glimpse of what our future might hold. We visited an icemaking plant, saw the *Evening News* being printed, got a slug with our name on it from the linotype operator, and watched our guide run his finger through a tank of molten type metal. None of us took up his invitation to try it. We also went round a plant producing heavy vehicles, and spent an afternoon at Nelson's Printing Works. At Redpath Brown's heavy engineering works, gloomy, full of noise, flames and smoke, we came to the steam hammer. The operator called for the smallest boy to climb up beside him. He showed me how the lever was operated, and with a series of tremendous earthshaking thumps I flattened a foot-thick chunk of red hot iron. 'Nobody will dare bully you after that!' he grinned.

But still it seemed half the country was unemployed. I joined the dole queues, hundreds of men waiting for hours in queues that never seemed to move. Once, years later, in one of those dreary halls, after waiting interminably for my name to be called, I complained about the useless wait. (I was not eligible for dole money.) The counter clerk, secure and pompous in his unassailable petty authority and

70

sure of his own superiority — *he* had a job — snapped, 'What are you moaning about? You've got nothing else to do anyway!'

RARELY, a potential job was advertised in the papers. 'Ticket-writer's apprentice' sounded a possibility. At the interview I was asked to fill in an outlined 'C' with red poster paint, as fast as possible. This I did promptly and neatly, and thought I'd made a good impression. But I had no chance against a girl graduate from the Art College who did get the job. The only other job I saw advertised was for an architect's apprentice. My letter of application was one of five accepted out of a total of 96. (Nearly a hundred people after one job!) My English was reasonably good and my writing legible, though it was based on Vere Foster exemplars, not a form that I, as a calligrapher would now recommend.

When I entered the waiting room, two husky looking six footers were already there. They looked to be in their early twenties, and probably were graduates of the Architecture School of the Art College. The interviewer took one look at me and pointed out that I couldn't even reach the top edge of a drafting board, which was true. He did congratulate me on my letter though. He had expected to meet someone as mature as the other applicants.

By the autumn of 1932, it seemed I would *never* get a job. I wondered about the possibility of getting further qualifications which might enable me to make some sort of living in commercial art, Art being the one talent which seemed to offer any hope at all. But we discovered that the yearly fee at the Art College was £16, and this vast sum was out of the question. Expenses for materials would add a substantial amount extra. As student grants were unheard of, I felt it would be unfair to expect my father to support me for the four-year duration of the course, which he would have to do even if all expenses were paid.

One Wednesday my mother and I went to the Synod Hall for an interview with an official of the Education Authority, which had put an ad. in the papers saying that deserving cases could be given scholarships for further education. A middle-aged lady assessor looking like a promoted clerkess took down our details on printed forms. She had the air of finding the whole business distasteful and boring, and hearing that I aspired to become a commercial artist, pointed out that the Art College could not accept me unless I had the Higher Leaving Certificate. And even if by some wild chance I did qualify, 'Do you think you'll ever be worth your salt?' We obviously had ideas above our station. Who ever heard of a member of the working class becoming an artist! So we were refused. I imagine she then went off for a cup of coffee, glowing with satisfaction that she had well and truly done her job — saving the taxpayers' money.

We now thought there was no way through the difficulty, but the Rev. David Mair heard our story and vowed to find some way. He carried out some research behind the scenes, and finally told us he had got me an interview with the principal of the Art College. I don't know how he engineered this, but I shall be forever grateful. The principal was Hubert Wellington. He was tall, wearing an impeccable grey suit, and had a sandy blonde goatee. Only artists dared to wear beards. His accent and manner were as impeccable as the suit. I was quite overawed by his boardroom, which could have swallowed our whole house six times over. It contained a huge oval table covered in dark green leather, an acre in extent. His desk was at the far end of the room in front of a huge fireplace, so I had to walk about half a mile to get there, feeling smaller and smaller the further I went. I still wore short trousers, and must have looked like a ten year old to him. (I had no difficulty in travelling for half fare on trams and buses — one of the few advantages of small stature.) He did his best to put me at ease, an impossible task in the circumstances, and looked over the collection of drawings and paintings I had brought.

The result was that I got a scholarship from the Andrew Grant Bequest which paid my first year's fees. I started evening classes in October because I could not be admitted to the day courses until I was sixteen, which was in December. I should not really have qualified to enter until I had reached the age of eighteen, when students normally took their Highers. Some of my classmates were four years older than I. This requirement was waived in my case. The first year was to be probationary. If my progress was unsatisfactory I would not be allowed to continue.

Now I started wearing long trousers and changed my hairstyle from the schoolboy quiff I'd worn until then. I didn't *feel* any older, but at least I didn't look so obviously juvenile. When I saw the standard of work produced by the evening class students, it was obvious I had a lot to learn, and I worked hard. By the time I was admitted to the day course in January, I felt I could at least keep up with these older students. That first morning I got my timetable in the College office, and was told to report to the instructor in the main design room upstairs. I found the room. 'Mr Smith?' I enquired. But I'd started on the wrong foot. 'Smythe!' he grated. I had no idea he made it rhyme with 'scythe'.

Professor Wellington and Victor Rushforth, the vice-principal and registrar, both tried to persuade me to take a diploma course, with a view to becoming a teacher. But I simply could not imagine myself ever having the courage to stand in front of a class of forty children — forty pairs of eyes! It would be better, I thought, to learn anything that would be useful in the commercial art line — illustrating, posters, book jackets, whatever. So they constructed a special course for me, making it clear that I would not be eligible for a diploma at the end of it. Already I had heard that prospective employers were unimpressed by diplomas; all they cared about was whether you could do the job. This I discovered later to be true. But a prospective teacher was not accepted at teacher training colleges *without* the diploma.

My timetable combined subjects from the three diploma courses — drawing and painting, sculpture, and design. The School of Architecture was virtually a separate College under the same roof, so nothing was included from that department. During the first two years, I took all the subjects specified for the general course, which all students had to take. After passing all exams you could specialise in the next two years. I was delighted to discover that day students could attend all the evening classes free, and I fitted in all the extra subjects I could. In addition, it was permissible to work between four and seven, when no classes were available. So most of the time, I could work from nine in the morning to nine at night, with an hour lunch break.

We had to sign a class register morning and afternoon. Ten minutes' grace was allowed, then a blue line was drawn across the page, and any name below it was officially late. This was a black mark on your record, and I was reprimanded several times, but someone must have remarked that I was putting in a whole lot of extra time, and nothing serious, like cancelling my fees, happened. Occasionally I was late in the mornings, having overslept, but the afternoons were difficult. It took twenty minutes to walk home and twenty back again. That left only twenty minutes to eat. I had no money to spend at the college restaurant, not even for a cup of coffee at the morning break. Between four and seven I had an apple and raisins or a biscuit, which served until I got home. Sandy Hall, the head janitor, was responsible for drawing the blue line, and many a time when he saw me appear, just too late, at the end of the corridor, he would leave a space for me.

By the end of the first year, I must have done well enough. The Andrew Grant scholarship was renewed for each succeeding year. The cost of materials was unexpectedly high, and was a constant drain on my meagre resources. Happily my name appeared regularly on the list of those students awarded prizes each term for good work. I suspect some of the tutors noticed my problem and tried to help.

73

These awards were drafts on the college shop, which allowed me to buy another few pounds worth of materials. I could not have managed without these unexpected bonuses, and the occasional art competition brought in another pound or two. Each Christmas I could count on three guineas from Jenners' Christmas poster competition, when ten posters were chosen.

Nevertheless, I always felt inhibited about using materials, and it felt as though I were drawing on pound notes. When I should have applied paint freely, as in oils, I couldn't help thinking, 'there goes 7 shillings worth of flake white!' Though I was self-supporting in materials and fees, by the end of my college years I was the only non-contributor to the family finances. The others had all managed to get jobs of some sort. They had their own money; embarrassingly, I had to depend for pocket money on my father's generosity.

There was a very pleasant working atmosphere at the college. Under the guidance of Hubert Wellington, the principal, an easy relationship between staff and students was maintained, with mutual respect. On the whole, we students accepted the authority of our teachers, recognising the standing and skills of what was really an outstanding group of artists.

When I returned to the college in 1950, it was different. There was a feeling that the staff were not secure in their posts, some sense of political jockeying, and Robert Lyon, the principal, gave me the impression that he was acting a part he could not really fill adequately. This I think was illustrated best when he appeared at the Christmas Revels one year, dressed in the white and gold dress uniform of a Fleet Commodore.

Fitting in extra evening class subject meant I missed bits of the lecture courses compulsory for diploma students, but I managed extra time on different nights when I need not have attended. During the two year general course I passed all the exams comfortably. In life drawing and sculpture, I usually had marks in the upper percentile. Alexander Carrick, head of sculpture, wanted me to make that my main subject. Had I been independently rich, I could well have followed this branch of art. Principal Wellington thought I should take drawing and painting, on the grounds that good commercial art entailed good draughtsmanship and colour handling. I know now he was absolutely right, and were I starting over again, that is the course I would take. But just then I was not so sure, and it seemed that a knowledge of printing processes and preparing work for reproduction might be better in the end. So my main efforts were aimed at design, though I did fit in more than the normal amount of drawing and painting.

My main subject in the design course was to be writing and illuminating, which was taught by Irene Sutton (who later married

74

Hubert Wellington). She was a dedicated, enthusiastic and highly skilled calligrapher, and we were fortunate to work under her guidance. She had learned the craft from Edward Johnston, who revived the art of broad pen writing in the early years of this century. His book *Writing and Illuminating and Lettering* is still a must for any student of calligraphy, and I feel privileged to have been taught by one of his first students. In the thirties he was still alive. Scribes who attain Irene Wellington's standard have every reason to congratulate themselves.

It was through her interest and encouragement that I fixed on lettering as my first subject. It seemed too that a thorough grounding in calligraphy would be useful when I left college, as so many ads used at least some hand drawn lettering. I enjoyed writing, though I could see I had a long way to go. Irene used to say it took twenty years to make a master scribe. The orientals say it takes forty. Though I qualify on both counts, I still have a lot to learn. Life is really too short to allow one to become truly a master of any art.

During my last two years, I undertook quite an ambitious project, a book of animals, written on vellum, with linocut illustrations, and bound in goatskin vellum. Though I just managed to finish it before I left college, I had not had time to bind it, and without access to the college equipment, there seemed no way I could complete the job. But Irene offered me the use of her own bookbinding presses, and helped me through the process. This entailed going to her home each week for some time and spending the afternoon working. She even provided tea. Since time is the craftsman's most precious commodity, I really appreciated her generous assistance. We kept in touch over the years, and I owe a lot to her encouragement and always constructive criticism.

Irene Wellington died in 1984 at the age of eighty. In her closing years she was unable to pursue her craft, and latterly could not answer my letters, though I kept her up to date with my own projects. I believe she had as much influence on this century's calligraphy as her mentor Edward Johnston, developing her own unique style and furthering his teaching. She was universally loved and respected by anyone who met her, as attested in her illustrated biography by Heather Child, Heather Collins, Anne Hechle and Donald Jackson, *More Than Fine Writing* (Pelham Books Ltd.). In this book are shown many fine examples of her work, some of which I remember from the thirties. I especially recall the sunny afternoon when she brought to the college the Diary printed on pages 72–75. A joy and an inspiration, though at the time I felt that work of this amazing quality would forever be beyond my capabilities.

My interest in animals led me to take animal drawing as a special subject. J. Murray Thomson was an excellent teacher and a first-class draughtsman and painter, very down-to-earth. He got me a season ticket to the zoo as an 'associate fellow'. This allowed me in on Sunday mornings, when I could work without having to cope with the public, not allowed in until the afternoon. In the summer I often went between four and seven, and became friendly with the keepers. One of them gave me the chance to enter a cage containing four lions, and I still have the sketchbook with their portraits. Well, yes. They *were* only a few weeks old.

Most drawing and painting students felt, erroneously, that animal drawing was a lesser skill, and few attended the class. They would claim that anyone good at life drawing could draw animals too. But painting a carefully posed and motionless human model needs a lot less concentration than painting animals. Successful representation of an animal requires real concentration and an adequate knowledge of its anatomy. Some knowledge of habits and habitat is also desirable. Some years later Thomson told me I was one of the best students he ever had. Knowing how inadequate I really was with animals, I feel he must have had a depressingly poor lot of students to work with. When we were sorting out a pile of drawings and paintings, selecting work for my final show, he singled out the painting of a lamb. 'That's very good!' he said. I pointed out that it would be — he had shown me how a few finishing touches would bring it to life. It was his touch that made it outstanding.

David Foggie, David and Henry Allison, William Gillies, William McTaggart, Adam B. Thomson, Donald Moodie, Eugene Carolan and John Maxwell were some of the talented artists on the college staff. Though we students appreciated their worth, our attention would tend to flag at the end of a long day drawing a not very attractive model we had studied scores of times before. We still had to learn that a masterpiece is the product of the artist, not his subject matter. Contrary to popular belief, life models are rarely physically attractive. I remember once we had a new model, a really beautiful girl. None of the male students turned out a worth while drawing that day, and we never saw her again. It's easier to concentrate on *drawing* when there are no distractions.

The senior model was old Mancini. He was still working in the 1950s, looking more mummified than ever. Occasionally he would drop off to sleep, and when the rest break came would sit there without moving. We'd wonder if this time he was really dead. It was difficult to tell. He told us that as a young man he was the model for Jesus in Leigh Hunt's *Light of the World*.

One hot afternoon some of us tried to revive our flagging interest by doing some Picasso/Cubist drawings from the model, using a lot of flat charcoal work. Great! We were producing masterpieces every five minutes. Then Foggie came around to check our work. 'Don't expect me to waste time criticising this rubbish!' he snorted, 'Let me know when you make a drawing!' And he was right. We had to work very hard indeed at learning how to draw, and knew we had far to go. For instance, we had to pass exams on muscular and skeletal anatomy, essential if our drawings were to have any integrity. Some years ago I was invited to teach some life drawing at an American college I found that the students were encouraged to 'express' themselves, using any medium they chose, but they had received no basic training in drawing what they knew and could see. We at least had sound elementary knowledge and skills to build upon. Expression came much later.

Book illustration was taught by J. Mason Trotter, a hunchback and even shorter than myself. But he was a superb draughtsman and watercolourist in the super-realistic mode now returned to fashion. Attempting the photographic (and failing) was a splendid way to find out just how far short one's knowledge and capabilities fell of even competence in art. He lived with a certain panache. He wore a large floppy black hat, a bow tie, a flowing black cape and carried a black cane. I met him once after I'd left college, and by then he'd also grown a classic black beard.

Commercial art (contradictory term!) was taught by Archie Imrie. Bow tie, checked suits, small moustache, verging on dapper. He was a pleasant bloke, and most people liked him. But I am bound to say I learned very little from him about the kind of commercial art which earns you a living. There was too much bias in his teaching towards poster design and similar prestigious work. Lithography though was one useful art I picked up through his classes. Typography, which should have been a joint subject, was taught by Johnson Walker, and I learned a lot in the 'typo room'.

Once or twice I had short vacation scholarships which enabled me to work in the art studios of works like MacLagan and Cumming, an Edinburgh printer. Archie was one of the top artists here. Tom Curr was head of the studio, and did weekly cartoons for the local papers which were highly regarded. A lot of the work was hack — jam labels, illustrations for cheap magazines. No glamorous posters, *Vogue* covers or Ritz menus, such as one might have expected after Archie's classes.

Alexander Carrick and Andrew Dodds taught sculpture. For most of us, this was only clay work; stone and wood were for advanced students. But I did learn how to make moulds and plaster casts. My last exam there called for a reproduction of a classic plaster head. My effort was preserved (very few ever were), and on my second stint fifteen years later I was gratified to see it still there up on one of the shelves. Some years later I saw a head by Andrew Dodds in the Royal Scottish Academy. He had borrowed my surface-finishing technique — justifiable as I was not making my living as a sculptor. I feel now my method is too mannered, but it was quite novel and inventive at the time, and suicidal to use for the first time in a crucial exam. I passed comfortably though.

I employed my modelling expertise in the animal drawing studio, and did studies of goats, pigeons and so on. Carrick wanted me to specialise in sculpture, but though I enjoyed it, I had to refuse. Even with the minimum of competition, the handful of sculpture students who made it their career found things difficult. Norman Forrest, who graduated a year or two earlier, had become an assistant in the department. I enjoyed the matey atmosphere here, where the janitor would have his tea and sandwiches with the head of department, sitting on the clay bins beside the pug mill.

AT the end of my fourth year, I had a nasty sense of anti-climax. The diploma exams were over. I had not been allowed to take any exams after the second year because I was not going into teaching. Jobs were still difficult to find. One morning I was summoned to an interview with Wellington, as I thought, to say farewell. He asked if I had any prospects in view, and I had to say no. Then how would I feel about a further year at college? Again, he assured me, all fees would be paid; and this would really be the equivalent of a post-diploma year, which only a handful of students could normally hope for. I asked the family if they minded waiting yet another year before I could help financially, but they all thought I should seize the chance.

Some of my friends had failed the exam and had to stay on another year. The usual quota, four to each school, had been awarded a post-dip year, for which one was entitled to an 'Endorsement', an extra qualification (equivalent to Honours) which enabled an Art graduate to become a headmaster in due course, if he so wished. So I was not entirely isolated in a new situation, and in any case had friends among the newer students. The students who had passed and been accepted by Moray House Training College would call in periodically with horrific tales of what was in store for us.

That summer I was awarded another vacation scholarship to

78

London. I stayed at the YMCA at Tottenham Court Road, a depressing barracks of a place. I tried their 'porridge' the first morning. It was repulsive; no salt, and the consistency of pouring custard. London depressed me. It was dirty and claustrophobic and noisy. One day I walked to the centre of Hyde Park, hoping to find a little peace, but all around was the roar of traffic, and the air felt over-used by the millions of people. I discovered with horror that the water supply from the Thames was used several times before it reached my area. Every building seemed grimy and dingy. Some years ago I saw London from the air. How different! It looked clean and pleasant, and the buildings now seemed fresh and new looking.

As a student in those pre-war days, I had permits and letters of introduction which allowed me to visit and study in various museums and galleries, and I made good use of my time. Any metropolis has to be a splendid place for research and cultural pursuits, but I felt uncomfortable all the time I was there.

All the following year I worked away happily, but as the diploma exams approached, again I felt anti-climax. I'd had no goal to aim at, unlike the others preparing their diploma shows. In the end I was asked to put a show together anyway, though I had not done the prescribed projects which allowed the assessors to compare one student's work with another's. My work was a hodge-podge of different disciplines — sculpture, design and drawing and painting. Space was found for me in an obscure corner in the 'House Painting' studio. No one, I thought, would even be able to find it, and I felt it was all a waste of time, as I wanted to get on with a dozen different things while the college facilities were still available to me. Later I heard that the assessors *had* visited my show along with the rest, and I assumed it was just out of curiosity. Meantime I was back at work. Most students eased off during the last month, but there was always a nucleus of enthusiasts who kept on to the very last day. The problem was finding a room to work in when so many studios were in use as temporary exhibition halls.

One morning I was working away as usual when a friend, Bob Balderstone, came up in some excitement to tell me my name was on the prize list for a travelling scholarship, worth £100! I took this to be a practical joke, and refused to go down to the notice board, even when two more people told me the same thing. I knew these scholarships were only awarded to people who had the diploma. But they insisted I should go and see for myself, which I did, feeling a fool for being conned. But my name *was* there. I was sure there had been some mistake, and went to check at the college office. It was true. This award gave me a great psychological boost just when it was needed, but being completely unprepared, I had no idea what to do with it, or where to go. Apparently I had a very free choice, but I was expected to give the college a preliminary timetable showing what I hoped to accomplish, and to send regular reports during my journey. Any work done during this period had to be assessed by the college, which had first claim on anything they wanted.

Now was my chance to see some of the places I had read about. I had always wanted to travel. A lump sum of £100 was something inconceivable to my family, or indeed to any of our friends. A school teacher's average wage was around £4 weekly. I could not imagine ever laying hands on so much money again, and was determined to make the most of it. On reflection, I felt I could cover more ground more cheaply if I travelled by bicycle, rather than rail. (Only millionaires could fly.) Youth Hostels charged only a shilling a night, and all European countries had them. Some students used the money to travel to Paris or Rome first class, living in style for only a few weeks; I wanted more time, and comfort was the last item on my list.

S O, I worked out an intinerary and presented it to the principal. He and Rushforth tried to dissuade me. No one had attempted this mode of travel before, though one student had once gone on a motor cycle, and then only for a few weeks, not the unspecified number of months I proposed. They asked who was going with me, and were taken aback when I said I would do it alone. They said it would be dangerous. In the end they agreed, but they thought after a few days' hard pedalling I would admit defeat, in which case, they told me, it would be no disgrace to curtail my tour and continue by train.

In the thirties, travel outside Britain was very expensive and restricted only to the wealthy. Places like Biarritz, Monte Carlo, Cannes, Florence, Rome, Venice, St Moritz and Lucerne were known to us through the newsreels as resorts frequented by the idle rich, and we knew the only way *we* could ever see them was to win a football pool, about as likely as flying to the moon! NASA was in the distant future. Places further afield had not been developed, or were unfashionable. When I visited the Côte d'Azur, St Tropez was a simple fishing village, unspoilt. Majorca, Greece, Palestine, Egypt, Tunisia, Algeria, Hawaii, Indonesia, Australia, South America, were more for explorers than holiday-makers. My projected journey was the equivalent of someone today setting off to cycle single-handed from Buenos Ayres to Tierra del Fuego.

My intention was to cycle to London, thence to Dover, ferry to Calais, then on to Paris, where I could spend a month or so visiting the Paris Exposition, the Louvre, Bibliotheque National and various museums. Then I would go on to Florence, Rome, Germany — as far as my funds would stretch, with an open date for my return.

When I was sixteen, I had bought a bicycle. I paid half, my parents the rest. It cost around £3. I knew a drop-handle racing type bike would be uncomfortable for long distance touring, so I took £5 off my scholarship money to buy a New Hudson, with standard handlebars, along with a one-piece pair of canvas carrier bags to carry my kit. These were really meant for use on tandems, but were relatively capacious. I knew better than to cycle long distances wearing a rucksack. But they made the bike tail heavy when fully loaded.

That summer I joined the Scottish Youth Hostels Association, and went on a two-week tour of Scotland, with the intention of getting fit, and also to discover if I really did have the nerve to attempt the real journey. To work out a realistic itinerary, I had to discover how many miles I could expect to travel each day.

Hostel life I found difficult to adapt to. I had always been shy of meeting new people in new situations, and I found it difficult to sleep in a noisy dormitory. But I knew I had to adjust or give up the tour. These were the early pioneering days of the SYHA, and arguably the best, when everyone pulled together to make it a success. Hikers tended to scoff at cyclists as sissy, and hitch-hiking was for the lowest of the low, only to be countenanced in the direst straits. Like a broken leg. But hostellers were a cheerful lot. They greeted one another on the highways, and anyone in trouble on the road could count on help.

You could leave all your gear at a hostel and nothing would be stolen, and there were no locks. Roads were relatively free of motor traffic, and hiking and cycling more enjoyable. Most Scottish roads were two lane highways; second class roads tended to be narrow and winding. My road to the north led through Perth and Dunkeld on the way to my first hostel at Birnam. Though it was the main road to the north, it was narrow, undulating, twisting but beautiful. Now it's a major motorway, with only fragments of the old road still showing to one side or the other, like bleached whalebone relics on a lonely beach.

The tour took two weeks, and I reached as far as Ullapool. I calculated I could cover between forty and fifty miles a day without undue fatigue. Now I sent for the continental YH *Handbooks*, and worked out a provisional route. The first hints of a possible war were in the air, and I felt I should visit these countries and cities before they

81

were destroyed, perhaps for ever. It would be enlightening too, to judge for myself whether all they said about frog, wurst and spaghetti eaters was true. Hitler and Mussolini seemed the likeliest instigators of a serious war, but no one had any clear idea of when it might start. My guess was it might take ten years yet, or it might be averted altogether. Ample time for me to complete my Grand Tour and return home. Perhaps if I could make the money spin out, I could take a whole year. I could never expect to travel abroad again. Maybe I would be able to afford it if I ever could command a salary of £10 a week, but that would be in ten or twenty years' time, if at all.

When I admitted to the principal that I could speak no foreign languages, he urged me all the more strongly that I should accompany someone who could. But I knew I would find it easier to travel at my own speed, which was slower than most; I could stop any time and place I chose, and I could change my itinerary without consulting anyone else. And I thought I could learn the essential phrases fairly quickly if I were alone — I'd *have* to. I bought three Woolworths miniature dictionaries at sixpence each: French, German and Italian. They served me very well. My pronunciations were all wrong, but I learned rapidly, and could at least make myself understood. You can go a long way if you can say 'How much?', 'Too dear!', 'Yes' and 'No', and of course 'Please' and 'Thank you'.

It was my intention to make the tour during the winter months, spending January and February in the south of France and 'sunny' Italy. All the travel brochures promised sun and warmth in these areas. Now I know better. On the Côte d'Azur, they told me it was their worst winter for fifty years, and it rained for two solid weeks in Rome. The weather was little different from home, and since then I have noted winters where these sunny climes have suffered ice and snow, when there was none in Scotland. For an art student, 1937 was a specially good year to visit Paris, as the Exposition offered enormous interest to artists. It was remaining open for the rest of the year, so I set off in October, with the intention of reaching Paris by the beginning of November.

I WAVED goodbye to the family and pushed my grossly over-laden bike up Brown Street. The panniers weighed between fifty and sixty pounds, and the steering was exceptionally light. Within ten minutes of starting, I had an accident. I wondered if this was a sign that I should turn back before it was too late. About twenty yards ahead, a man stepped on the road without looking. No problem — I was moving quite slowly, and he'd be across the street before I reached the spot. He looked right and saw me coming. I steered to go to his left. He stepped back. I steered right. This happened about six times, until at a standstill, my front wheel touched him, and I fell off. The pedal crank was bent, and could not be turned, but fortunately there was a cycle shop not far away, and there it was levered back into position. Had I been tall enough to touch the ground without dismounting, all would have been well, but I always had to get off when I stopped.

On the first day of my Continental Grand Tour, I covered over seventy miles, far more than I had intended, and arrived at Carbisdale Youth Hostel. October was well past the holiday season, and only one other lad was there, a hiker. We chatted with the warden over our evening meal, and he told us some of the history of the Castle. 'We have a ghost', he said. 'She lives in the White Lady's Tower.' This had at first been used as a dormitory, but after some hostellers had been terrified by the apparition, it was now only used as a store room.

I said I'd always wanted to see a real ghost, and the hiker was of the same mind. 'How about letting us sleep there tonight?' The warden agreed, provided we understood it was entirely at our own risk. It was after 10 when we prepared to go to the Tower, long after the time when people were supposed to have arrived at the hostel, when a girl hiker came in. Regretfully the warden told us we would now be unable to use the tower, as it was in the women's part of the hostel. So I still have not encountered a ghost.

Staying overnight at hostels, usually empty because of the lateness of the season, I made my way to London. From here to Dover was over ninety miles, and I intended to camp halfway, as there were no hostels. But I cycled on and on. There was no countryside! All the way the road was lined with buildings, like an endless suburbia with occasional citified clots. I cycled on in the dark to arrive exhausted at Dover around 11 at night. I was so tired I could not sleep at first, still watching the lit patch of tarmac in front of me endlessly slipping under my front wheel.

Next morning I took the ferry to Calais. Knowing how easily I got seasick, I had chosen the shortest route, and also took some pills for motion sickness. The ferry was the biggest ship I'd ever been on, but even so it heaved quite a lot in a heavy sea. But the pills worked. After passing through customs I made my way to Boulogne where there was a hostel. It was daunting to find everyone speaking an incomprehensible language, and every sign unreadable. I had to remember to use the other side of the road too. The directions in my

French hostels handbook were beyond me. I stopped and asked a young boy, 'Ou est l'Auberge de la Jeunesse? Rue Angellier?' trying various pronunciations, mostly wrong. But at last he understood, and directed me along the path over some waste ground by a railway. The first hurdle taken; my Woolworths dictionary was justifying the expense.

The hostel was concrete, huge and depressing. It must originally have been a barracks or a jail. It was cold, I was the only hosteller, and all was strange and alien. I found a washroom, but no lavatories, only the usual porcelain stalls of any urinal. At last it dawned on me that this *was* the lavatory. There were two corrugated foot rests, and a much larger drain than would have been necessary underneath them. No one, ever, had suggested there would be differences between French toilets and ours. I felt their standards were fifty years behind ours.

Standards of behaviour too were different. Anyone caught short walking, cycling, or driving along a country road could it seemed stop and have a pee without offending tender susceptibilities. And it took me a long time to get used to the presence of the old ladies who sat knitting at the entrance to public conveniences with a saucer in front of them for the obligatory tip. Even at the Paris Exposition, where everything was ultra-modern, the toilets had the same entrance, *Hommes* on one side, *Dames* on the other. Inside was a handrail down the centre of the salon; one side was the *pissoir*, the other a set of cubicles with doors. In France and Italy, when there were no specially built *pissoirs*, sometimes the 'convenience' was simply a tarred corner in an angle of a building. Ladies I presumed practised superhuman endurance.

Late that night I heard someone enter the cell next to mine, but when I left next morning he was still asleep. Some miles along the road I heard a shout behind me — in English! This was the late arrival. He introduced himself as Bob Griggs, a student from Ohio, also doing a cycle tour of the Continent. He had started from Amsterdam, where he bought his bike, and was heading for Italy. He could speak French, took me into several shops in the next village, and cleared up several problems for me in the way of pronunciation and how to haggle. I was never happy about the latter though, and preferred just to pay the asking price.

In the evening we stopped at the Hotel Tête de Boeuf, an ancient inn in Abbeville, and far more expensive than my budget allowed for, but there were no hostels in the area. Bob suggested a celebratory bottle of wine with our meal. The smallest bottle available was a full litre. The food was beautifully but daintily served, and not nearly enough for two hungry cyclists. We ate everything on our plates, including globe antichokes, which I dislike. More than half the wine remained, and as we'd paid for it, we proceeded to finish it, hoping it would help to fill the remaining space. Though it was expensive, to me it tasted vinegary. Somehow I got my share down, and opted to go to bed early. It was only approaching ten. But when I rose, I saw the doorway was sliding from side to side. Aiming at what I calculated to be the true position, I managed through at first go, and climbed to my room. I expected to go out like a light when I hit the mattress, but the expensive French cuisine took its toll, and I was deathly sick for two hours and lost it all.

Next morning we set off together, but my slow natural speed obviously was holding Bob back. All he carried was a small saddlebag, only a fraction of the size of mine. About midday, he invited me to join him in a visit to Chartres, where he had been invited to visit Chagall's studio. He was sure I'd be welcomed as a fellow artist. But I felt I would be regarded as a gatecrasher if I arrived without precious warning, and I thought I had to keep to my itinerary. This decision I've regretted ever since. For such an opportunity, the college would have been delighted to allow a small adjustment. So we wished each other luck and parted.

Late at night I entered Paris by the Porte St Denis. I managed to convey to a helpful *gendarme* that I was looking for a room *pas trop cher*, and he directed me to a house at 17 Rue du Sommerard (even today it sounds exotic!) Here I got a tiny attic room at the very top of the building which cost only the equivalent of a shilling a day, and this was my home for the next month. It was near the Cluny Metro station, which was convenient for reaching any place I wanted to go. But no meals were served and I had to eat out. The worst part of this was having to get up and go out into the cold without breakfast. But there was a bistro not far away, and the French coffee and brioche suited me very well. I'd been warned by my friends that tea would be unobtainable and I should get used to the taste of coffee. George Kelly and Roger Poole, fellow students in typography, started this process by supplying cups of Nescafé brewed on the typo room gas ring. The real thing tasted far better, and I enjoyed it.

My vision of Paris had been based on paintings and travel brochures, and I was unprepared for the reality, cold, wet, dull and windy, just like home. It *was* November, but I expected more warmth being so far south. A great deal of time was spent at the Paris Expo, for which I had a student's season ticket. The Trocadero art galleries had been specially built for this occasion, and housed a unique collection of art work. The Eiffel Tower was right in the middle of the exhibition area, with various booths underneath. One specialised in the newly invented milk shake, and I enjoyed many a hot drink there after a chilly trek round the grounds. Notable were the vast and imposing Russian and American pavilions, built facing each other. On top of the latter was a resplendent American eagle, while a huge metal sculpture of two workers brandished at it the hammer and sickle of the Soviets. The inside of the Russian pavilion was less imposing, just a vast, bleak hall which dwarfed the exhibits on the floor. The British pavilion was an embarrassingly modest affair. Each country had its own more or less elaborate pavilion.

There was also a huge entertainments park, one of the main attractions being an immensely high tower from which the foolhardy could make tethered parachute jumps. As there was an additional charge, I never sampled the amusements. I *did* pay to go up the Eiffel Tower, though. The top part was closed for the winter, but even from halfway up there was a panoramic view of the city, and looking down on the Expo I felt I was really quite high enough.

The Arc de Triomphe, Champs Elysées, Luxembourg Gardens and Vincennes Zoo in the Bois de Boulogne were all places I had read about and now had the chance to visit. With my student's pass, I could enter many museums and libraries free or at a reduced rate. The Louvre, with the Mona Lisa and Winged Victory, had to be first, and thereafter my time was very fully occupied.

Not long after I arrived, the College sent me Bill Gear's address, and I went to visit him. He had been in Paris for several weeks by now, and was quite at home. Also he could speak French. He was living in an old shop in squalid surroundings, but it was cheap and therefore acceptable to a student. He had a gas ring for cooking, and was quite self-contained with plenty of working space. He took me by bus to the Latin Quarter, Montmartre, where we had a splendid lunch in an artist's cafe. It only cost pennies and was mainly spaghetti, and filling. The cafe was a long room with a cooking range at one side, a long trestle table, and benches down each side. There were some weird characters among the arty clientele. Later he turned me over to Joe Forrester, also on a scholarship. Joe had taken the other approach to the proper use of a post-grad grant. He had taken a really plush apartment in the fashionable Rue de Rivoli. Naturally he didn't expect to stay so long in the City of Light, but he too was working hard.

No one would visit Paris without visiting the Folies Bergère or Moulin Rouge, but I found that the prices charged for one admission would have financed me for another week. It would be a pity to cut out a visit to Rome for the cost of one night's entertainment in Paris. For the same reason I did not visit the expensive restaurants, and if I had, probably I would have been refused admission. Perhaps I was not exactly scruffy, but no doubt I was near the borderline.

86

M Y INTENTION had been to cycle all the way, but now on working out comparative costs, I found it would actually be cheaper to travel by train to Toulon, rather than spend two weeks cycling there. Besides, it was now very cold and wet, and I still had some residual faith in the travel brochures — it was after all, a very long way further south. 'Côte d'Azur', 'Sunny Mediterranean' and so on. The train arrived after dark, and I pushed my bike out of the station to find I really *had* arrived at the fabulous South. It was all true! There were three fully grown palm trees in a garden plot directly opposite the entrance.

Hubert Wellington knew this area, and had urged me to visit St Tropez, a picturesque little fishing village not far along the coast. I had stopped overnight in Toulon, but St Tropez was an easy run next day. There were no hostels here, but I found the Hotel Helvetia on the town square which was almost as cheap. M. Grieshaber, the Swiss proprietor, and his wife made me welcome. I was the only guest. I had morning and evening meals, and they made a packed lunch for when I was out exploring and sketching. There were no libraries or art galleries, so I was quite glad to be able to relax for a while and do my own work. Passing time in the evenings was a problem. The dining room was lit by a dim bulb, just enough for the locals playing checkers, but not enough to read by. One side of the room was occupied by the bar, with a mightily impressive collection of bottles of all sizes, colours and shapes. The light in my room was worse. The light barely illuminated the floor underneath, and flickered unsteadily. The local power station was probably a donkey on a treadmill.

Otherwise, it was a very peaceful and pleasant place to stay. One morning I looked out to find the square covered in snow. *Snow!?* But on closer inspection it was only a thick layer of hail. On some of my forays round the village I had found four-foot-long curtains of icicles hanging from wayside rocks. So much for your Sunny Mediterranean. But they said I had chosen to visit during their coldest winter for fifty years. St Tropez today I understand is a very different sort of place, quite unimaginable in those distant days.

A week or two later I moved on to Cannes, where a hostel remained open over the winter, and here I stayed over Christmas. Cannes was a fabulous place I never expected to see. The hostel was perched well up on the hills behind the town, with a marvellous view of this haunt of the filthy rich. All around, the area was brightened by many mimosa trees, with lush green leaves and cascades of brilliant yellow blossoms. These were just coming into season, when the flowers were a major export of the region. Occasionally there had been some quite pleasant sunny days, and Christmas day was hot enough at midday for the warden's children to play nude in the warm sun. In the grounds of one hotel there was even a banana plant with a bunch of little green fruits, but I doubt whether they ever ripened.

From my Cannes base, I visited Monte Carlo several times. I pushed my bike all the way uphill to see the world-famous casino close up. It was closed for the winter, but at a minimum stake of ten francs I would not have tried to break the bank anyway. On one occasion I had gone as usual by the coast road, and when I came to return found it closed, with heavy waves breaking over it. I had to return by the Moyen Corniche road, which meant a hard climb with the bike, but not so hard as the Haute Corniche, which was higher still. At Éze, a hamlet impossibly wedged on a cliff outcrop, I stopped to do a watercolour. The vegetation all along the coast — palms, aloes, and the mimosas just breaking into flower — all suggested a warm climate, but I still needed all my winter woollies.

It was at the Cannes hostel that I met Bill Cowley, a Yorkshire student, who was on a walking tour, and we have kept in touch ever since. He subsequently became a District Commissioner in India, and not long after the war invited me to go out there to paint. All I had to do was find the fare, and I could stay with him free. The fare was out of my reach, but I wish now I had tried to get it somehow. I know now I could have earned enough at least for the return fare. After the Partition, he returned to run his own farm in Yorkshire. He was the founder of the Lyke Wake Walk over the moors. He and his wife, grandparents now, are still fit enough for a spell of hill climbing in the Highlands.

My next stop was the Mentone hostel. Mentone was a pleasant and peaceful little town, with its own quota of palms, cacti and aloes, and even in one pocket-sized park a grove of orange trees hanging with golden fruit. There were two visitors in the hostel when I arrived. One was French, and he left the following day. The other was John Griffiths, a retired Welsh teacher of seventy from Mansfield, who spent his entire winters there. He dabbled in watercolour sketching, and I was able to give him some useful hints. He knew the surrounding neighbourhood, and showed me some paintable spots. The first Sunday, he took me along to the Scots Kirk and introduced me to the minister, Fred Hall and his wife. There was a large enough colony of retired Scots living there to support the church.

Why did I voluntarily attend church? After Christmas I had another attack of homesickness, and needed to hear people speaking in a language I could understand. The Halls made me very welcome, and I was invited up to their house twice a week for an evening meal. I was able to repay their hospitality by designing a pulpit lamp and other church furniture. Their son Ken was twelve years old, and his hobby was making model warships, which he did very well. He was working on his latest, a 'Pocket Battleship', one of the two sunk by us during the war. When I last heard of him, he was a surgeon in a Scottish hospital. I corresponded with the Halls until their deaths some years ago.

Bill Cowley now arrived and spent two days before moving on again, when I walked along with him to Ventimiglia, the border with Italy, and waved him off. He promised to leave me a note at the hostel in Munich, which I expected to reach in a few months time. My stay in Mentone might have been prolonged more than a few weeks, but I knew extra time here would have to be deducted from the end of my tour. Still hopefully looking for sunshine and warmth, I looked for ways to speed my advance southwards. Someone suggested I could do this *and* save money by taking a border to border train through Italy. The journey could be broken at some selected town for quite a long period. This I found was indeed true, and the rail ticket was remarkably cheap. I made my first stop Florence. Surely this would be warmer, and no student of art could possibly omit the city from even a curtailed itinerary. The railway passed through Pisa, and on the far side of a green field, I saw the Leaning Tower, looking every bit as impossible as in its photographs.

Contrary to expectations, I found Italian rather easier to understand than French, and my Woolworths dictionary again proved its worth. I stayed at the Pensione Bristol, paying rather more than allowed for in my budget, but I reasoned that I had saved enough by using the train to justify the extra expense. It was a cheap room, and that was because it looked out only on to a very small courtyard, almost a ventilation well. But you could just see the top of the Duomo over the roofs. It was best to keep the window shut. Just beside it was a broken and overflowing drain pipe which stank to high heaven. In summer it would have been intolerable even with the window closed.

With its museums and galleries, its architecture, history and situation, Florence is a city which needs years to assimilate and appreciate, rather than just a few weeks. I tried to visit all the places I had heard of, and covered miles each day walking from one location to the next. There were paintable views at every turning. Inevitably I ended up with cultural indigestion. There was just too much to see and do, from Michaelangelo's 'David' to the Ponte Vecchia, the River

Arno, the Duomo and Baptistery, the Pitti Palace. The weather remained cold and watercolours took forever to dry out in the open air, but Florence was a very pleasant place, built on a human scale.

From here I cycled on to Rome, stopping on the way at Siena and Viterbo. It was dark when I reached Siena, and the *campanile* and *piazza* were floodlit in pale blue-green, looking like some splendid stage set for an Italian opera. Down an alley I found a little *albergo*, 'il Tre Donzelle', where I had a decent filling meal. These run-down little places catered for less genteel apetites than the big expensive hotels. In Viterbo I found a really scruffy one, the grandiloquently titled 'Albergo Aquila d'Oro'. The owner was a greyhaired old crone, who said I could have a room for one lira. She showed me up to the room, then waited. She had to have the money in advance. When I paid over my lira, she looked closely at it, bit it, and then pinged it on the marble table top. Fortunately it was genuine. Though the place was falling to pieces, again the food was good. It was charged extra to the room, but also very cheap.

Peacefully cycling along one sunny day, enjoying the scenery, I nearly fell off my bike at a shotgun blast beside my ear. A hunter rose from behind the bushes at the verge, and twenty yards ahead a small songbird fluttered in the grass. I knew they were caught for food in France and Italy, but this seemed an expensive way to get a dinner. One shell per mouthful, if indeed there *is* a mouthful of meat on a sparrow.

ROME to me had always seemed remote and unattainable, a great and splendid city, the centre of the ancient world, but intangible as a mirage. But there I was, cycling on a modern road round the Colosseum, which close up seemed more massive even than photographs had suggested. Much of the stonework looked every minute of its two thousand years. History seemed to emanate from every pore.

During my two weeks in the city I stayed at a *pensione* filled with Germans. It was by my standards an expensive place, and meals in their dining room were pretty formal, but it was pleasant enough. After the evening meal, the Germans would sit around the radio, listening to Hitler and applauding the more raucous parts of his speeches. I remember one rolling phrase — *ein hundert tausend millionen*. Sounds a lot more in German. These Germans kept to themselves as obviously of higher social status than I, and I never

RUBBLE
PLUMB
SOFFIT
CLunch
LEDGE
PIER
mandREL

Acrostic 10, 'Builder', 27½" × 18½"; 1978.

IMPRESS
SORT
QUOIN
FONT
REGISTER
STET
KERF

Acrostic 4, 'Printer', 27½″ × 18½″; 1976.

'The Lord's Prayer', 17½″ × 17½″; 1951.

It may be of interest to record here that the specimens of writing shown in the centre panel below were collected mainly from

CALLIG

Aids to memory of all kinds, the knot in the handkerchief or the marking of ways by the blazing of trees or painting with strips of colour, belong to the mnemonic or preliminary stages of writing. So do the notched stick, or tally, as an aid to counting, and the quipu, the series of knotted cords used as a method of writing by the ancient Peruvians. More developed early forms of writing are paintings and drawings, such as the Neolithic and Paleolithic cave paintings. At a comparable stage of development are the more recent paintings on buffalo hide by the Red Indians. But only when the pictorial signs become constantly recurring symbols, that is to say, ideograms, can we speak of true writing. Such is the writing of the Codices of the Mayas. These ideograms are highly simplified versions of natural forms, which reproduce the meanings of the words. Every kind of developed ideographic writing eventually has-

THE WORD CALLIGRAPHY IS FRO
BEAUTIFUL WRITING. THE CENTI
OF THE ORIGINS OF WRITING, AN
ENT COUNTRIES AT DIFFERENT PE

By writing in general we mean deliberately fixed signs, which imply a meaning & can be read. All genuine writing is a convention & therefore intelligible only to the initiated. It is never the result of arbitrary inventions, but always the laborious achievement of many generations, often of many peoples, at last crystallized to a mutually accepted code. Even our shorthand can only be read by those who have learnt it. Any-

SOME EXAMPLES OF HIS

Below is an example of Egyptian demotic script of about 1500 BC written with a

Here is an interesting example of Etruscan lettering, 5 BC, from a stone inscription

The Greek letters below are of the third century B.C. The ones above are probably older

These are Roman capitals of the 4th century. They are the contemporaries of the Traja

The origins of the minuscule or small letter is seen in this sixth century Rom cur

Seventh century Anglo-Saxon hand which has much in common with the next

The half uncial is seen at its best in the Book of Kells variant, but is rather difficult

In this 9th century Roman may be seen the process of change from the half unc

Irish 10th century. The tenth century was a period of beautiful and legible han

Eleventh century Anglo-Saxon; a pleasant, legible round letter, still with half unc

found its pictures become abbreviated, petrifying to mere formulae, the original significance of which gradually becomes lost. The cuneiform writing of the ancient inhabitants of Mesopotamia was inscribed on clay tablets, and in its older forms there are still recognisable pictures. Like the Maya writing, the Hieroglyphics of the ancient Egyptians developed from painted pictures of great verisimilitude. These pictures gradually evolved into abstract shapes, which in the end could be written fairly nimbly with a reed nib, in the form called 'demotic'. The origins of European phonetic writing are still obscure, but Greek writing, the mother of the Latin alphabet, is generally assum

'Panel of Calligraphy', 28" × 42"; 1951.

The panel was prepared for the Edinburgh College of Art diploma exhibition of 1951 and was later shown in galleries in Zurich, London and Bristol.

RAPHY

THE GREEK καλλιγραφία AND MEANS

ANELS BELOW ILLUSTRATE SOME
E VARIED STYLES USED IN DIFFE
DS FROM THE VERY EARLIEST TIM
C PEN FORMED HANDS

a Slavonic script of the 12th century, forerunner of the present day Russian alphabet

ШКNHENZEБIЛZCOЛYHEЖO

from a Hebrew MSS date somewhere between the 11th and the 15th centuries

ןיךיריךךרunילbrwחישלויוחix

Lombardic initials shewn are representative of a class of very beautiful letters. 15th C

IOTIENSINARPVLVCDRE

century Spanish version of the widely used Gothic. A difficult hand to write

ntigas alfonso al lo compuso: johan

wly written book hands all have their rapid cursive counterparts—Spanish 16th C

nuctorizado que'c para el hombre testigo m

elandic 15th century hand has strong Gothic affinities, & a strong lively character

xu uf dome sangsga f ne'eitt hoge·Elé fige hi

lagolithic 14th century book hand is introduced as an interesting variation ss

ШХƆΜΙ·ΠΠƆJⱯⰋЬ⅄ⰋᕼⱯⱢ͈ⰎⰁΜΕΓΛΧⱨ

a very individual interpretation of the Gothic hand; 15th century N. Gothic see

egrediebatur baptizabantur abstum

16th century humanistic minuscules—one of the results of the Renaissance

lemus frater gessisti eqidum

h century Italic chancery hand, which is enjoying a revival at the present day

babbi alla mia Cancellares figlione se

---

infringement of the rules makes it a puzzle for everybody else, or at least more difficult to read. Four can be distinguished in the histories of most writings. First, the preliminary stages—mnemonic or memory signs— then the pictorial signs—pictographs, the signs for ideas—ideograms, and finally the signs for sounds—letters or ideograms. Writing in phonograms is not adapted to all languages: the Chinese remains in the stage of ideographic writing even today.

A genuine culture in writing would extend its influence even to the humbler applications. It cannot be saved for merely writing in ceremonial teachings such as is done in certain schools, used in some countries. All must spread, writing with respect.

with a broad, spatulate brush, which wrote like a broad-nibbed pen. From the capital form developed the pen written book hands, the quadrata, and the cursive rustic capitals. The freely written later Roman cursive gave rise to half uncials, which later developed into small letters or minuscules. The minuscule, it may be said, owes its very form to the broad-nibbed pen: and its creation about the turn of the seventh century marks the last great stage in the development of writing. The employment of the quill pen had a decisive share in particularly in fashioning the shapes of the forms of the minuscules in the age of Charlemagne. Our present day Roman print, its broken variants, the so-called Black-letter & German Fractur, are all derived from the minuscule with its deep insight into the necessities of letter formation. Our hand-writings are also derived from the same source

---

ed to be derived from the writing of the ancient Phoenician traders. The brilliant clarity of the old Greek alphabet is due to the contrast between straight lines, triangular and circular forms, which is more striking to the eye than any other contrast of forms. The inhabitants of southern Italy took over Greek writing before it had been completely developed, and added new letters to the alphabet. The Roman inscriptions of the classical period are the unsurpassed, perfect and timelessly beautiful archetypes of our writing in the narrower sense. On the Trajans column, the letters display a modulated alternation of thick and thin strokes which is due to their having been traced

Top: 'Ceud Mìle Fàilte', the Gaelic greeting, 'one hundred thousand welcomes', 13½″ × 13½″; 1973.

'Quem Pastores Laudavere', illustration for a Christmas card, 3½″ × 6″; 1986.

caife gaelach
irish coffee

1 double measure Irish whiskey · 1 cup strong, hot, black coffee · 1 tblsp double cream · 1 heaped tsp sugar

Warm a stemmed whiskey glass. Put in the sugar and add enough very hot coffee to dissolve it, and stir well. Top up with Irish whiskey to within one inch of the brim. Hold a teaspoon across the glass, curved side up, and pour the cold cream carefully over it, slowly, so that it floats on the surface of the coffee. The cream is not to be stirred in; the hot beverage is drunk THROUGH it.

Recipe and illustration for 'Irish Coffee' from *Traditional Irish Recipes*, Canongate Publishing, 1982.

Selection of designs from *Rubber Stamps and How to Make Them*,
Canongate Publishing, 1982.

Preliminary sketches of apes for the unpublished *Zoo Animals*, 1934.

STAGE
SCript
COSTUME
SPOT
PART

George L Thomson
acrostic 6 -
1977

Acrostic 6, 'Actor', 29½″ × 18½″; 1977.

BROSE
CRANACHAN
BANNOCKS
HOWTowdie
Cock-a-LEEKIE
HAGGIS
SCONES
CROWDIE

George L. Thomson
acrostic 7
77

Acrostic 7, 'Scotland', 29½" × 18½"; 1977.

succeeded in having a conversation with any of them, which I thought would help when I reached Germany. The hotel porter though was friendly and helpful, though he spoke no English and I understood only the barest essentials of Italian.

In the street one day I was stopped by a large policeman in 'fancy-dress' uniform of cocked hat, jackboots, whistle, baton and gun. He held forth with a flood of intimidating and incomprehensible Italian, but I had no idea what he wanted. I said, *No comprende!* Upon which he prodded me with his baton and pointed it at a nearby sign which said *Pedoni a sinistra.* Then it dawned on me. Everyone on my side of the street was walking towards me, and on the other side, in the opposite direction. Chastened, I slunk across the road and joined the law-abiding crowds on the far side.

Much of my time was spent studying in the museums and libraries, though I regret missing the Vatican library. They provided some respite, too, from the endless cold and rain. When I was leaving I told the porter in disgust, *Bella Roma!* Sunny Italy! *Piove! Piove! Piove!* Rain! He apologised for the atrocious weather, and pointed out that it was better in the summer. But further *south* he said, it was unusual to have a lot of rain. I was beginning to have my doubts.

The remains of Imperial Rome were endlessly fascinating, even in the wet. I was thrilled to see the actual Trojan's Column from which the plaster cast inscription in the Art College had originally come. I visited the Capitoline Hill and the Forum, Castel Saint Angelo and the unexpectedly insignificant Tiber, and the modern white marble memorial to Vittorio Emmanuele III, adorned with Mussolini's vast carved stone maps of the Roman Empire at different periods of history. I climbed up and down the Scala d'Espana. I visited the Colosseum. The floor of the arena was then intact, but it has since been excavated to show the chambers and passages beneath.

Now I was comparatively near, I was aiming at Naples, another travel brochure city; sunshine, Vesuvius, Pompeii, the Isle of Capri and the Blue Grotto, figs and grapes, eternal summer. Maybe? As I cycled along the Via Massimo, with vast and ancient tombs lining the road, the cold rain poured steadily down, until evening when I reached the little town of Frosinone. There was only one hotel, so I had no choice, and it cost four times as much as I wanted to pay. But it was off-season, so I expect I really got off lightly. It was a whitewashed modern cube of a building. The proprietor proudly showed me his guest book, signed by Mussolini, no less, and a galaxy of famous names like Charlie Chaplin and Mary Pickford. If it survived the war years, my name is still there among the stars.

Early next morning I set off for Naples. The rain eased off after an hour or so, an encouraging sign. Then at midday I came to a fork in the road. (This was the main road to Naples, remember.) It was the perfect Y-junction, nothing to indicate which was the main road, no signpost, no traffic. My map showed no side-road at all at this point. On closer inspection I noted that the macadam of the righthand fork was in much poorer condition, with potholes as far as I could see. Obviously the left-hand branch with the good surface was the one to take. Ten miles on I was up in the mountains, humping my bike up a steep series of cobbled steps, the main street of some obscure hamlet, and obviously designed for the use of pack mules rather than motor vehicles.

Even allowing for continental backwardness in road-building, it seemed this could not possibly be a main road. (Route Nationale No.1, which I followed to Paris, had been for most of the way an un-macadamed dirt road.) An ancient resident sitting at his front door directed me back to the main road by a short cut, a footpath through the fields. I should have gone back the way I came, for it was impossible to ride my bike for much of the way. It was pouring again, and when at last I did regain the road, I had concluded that sunny Naples was a delusion, and cold and wet, I turned back in the direction of Rome.

There I spent three more days visiting some of the places I had not been able to fit in before, then took the train to the frontier, at the Brenner Pass. This had become famous as the meeting place for Hitler and Mussolini. Since the weather everywhere I had gone so far had been indistinguishable from a Scottish winter. I mistakenly assumed the rest of my journey would be much the same.

I T WAS around twelve and pitch black when the train arrived at Brennero. The officials tried to prevent me getting off. They could not believe anyone would *want* to visit the place after midnight in the winter. I pointed out that my ticket was only valid to this station, and I was not going to pay extra to go on to Innsbruck. At last I got on my bike and prepared to cycle on in the dark. But I had not reckoned with the Customs. They refused point blank to allow me through, and to discourage me, indicated the snow-covered road. I had cycled on snow before, I said, but still they refused. They kept my passport, so I had no option. They allowed me to sleep on a bench in the Customs hall. It was a cold, uncomfortable night, with the lights on all the time. In the grey light of early morning, they very kindly gave me a cup of coffee before I started, but clearly they thought I was mad to even consider cycling any further.

On the Austrian side, the officials obviously had the same views, but at last they allowed me through. After pushing the bike most of the twenty-five miles to Innsbruck I began to understand their reasons. There was about six inches of hard packed snow all the way on the road, possible to cycle on while the night's hoar frost still provided some sort of grip, but very slippery later in the day when the sun came out. Here and there I found I could cycle in the six-inch-wide ruts where the snow had melted, sometimes for several hundred yards at a time. The snow-covered mountains, the fir trees and the chalets were just like the travelogue pictures, beautiful but cold.

Halfway down, I ate a cold lunch at the roadside, but I was glad to get on the move again. About four in the afternoon the valley ahead opened up and I could see Innsbruck. Hundreds of skiers dotted the slopes between me and the town. What they thought of a cyclist approaching from the Brenner I can't imagine. The town streets were cleared of snow, and I made for the youth hostel. It was closed for the winter, but it was part of a hotel, so I got a room. It was small and unheated, though there was a huge tiled stove in the centre. I took off my sodden, freezing socks and hung them in a wardrobe to dry. I forgot to take them out next day.

In the bar-restaurant that evening, I was adopted by an Austrian who spoke English. Well, just enough to make earthy remarks about the barmaid, who had a good idea of what he was saying, and I could see she had his measure. The place was typically Tyrolean; the decor, the barmaids' traditional costumes, the beer steins, the singing, even the zither player. Had I been a drinker I could have had a good time. My friend stood me a beer, but I could only finish half of it. I can only enjoy beer on very hot days. I was very tired, made excuses and went early to bed. The barmaid never arrived, in spite of my friend's promises. I did need a hot water bottle. The room was icy, and instead of blankets there was a foot-thick feather duvet. Though this could have kept me quite warm, there was no way to prevent a draught down my neck every time the quilt sprang up. This happened each time I dropped off and lost my grip.

Perhaps I should have stopped for a winter holiday of a week or two. I could have learned to ski. Skis cost only the equivalent of sixteen shillings a pair, and had I known I would not be able to take my Austrian schillings out of the country, I certainly would have spent them there. But there were no institutions where I could have pursued my studies, and it was far too cold to paint outside, though subjects abounded. At the station, I bought a cheap student's through ticket for Germany, from border to border, as I had done in Italy. I suspected, rightly, that most of Germany would also be snow-covered, if it was as thick as this in Austria.

At the German border, the train stopped for Customs at a little station. I wanted to change my schillings into marks, and was directed to the official money-changer. He was an immensely fat man, sitting at a tiny table on a tiny folding chair, almost invisible under his bulk. He wore a flashy military uniform, with braid, medals, ribbons and lanyards, jackboots and a Nazi-type high-peaked cap. He also wore a revolver. When he saw my schillings, he became quite abusive and kept waving me off. I had to give up, as the train was ready to leave. I found this red faced stand-in for Goering was a common type among German officials, and never grew to love them. Even when I got home, Thomas Cook's refused to reimburse me.

Ah, but it was during this stop that I was introduced to *wurst and brotchen*, one of Germany's better inventions. Delicious! On sub-sequent occasions, I always grabbed the chance of having another. They were sold from little carts like ice-cream carts, except that the containers had fires under them.

Munich was my first German city. I arrived after dark. It was raining and cold. I had to cycle several miles to the hostel, a vast and palatial building, where I found the expected letter from Bill Cowley. But there was no room for even one more hosteller. There was some sort of celebration going on in the town, and the hostel itself was like a beehive. As I realised very much later, all this activity was the result of the *Anschluss*; Hitler had marched into Austria just after I had left. I was directed to a satellite hostel some four miles away through wet and deserted streets. Here I met close-up for the first time members of Hitler's Jugend. Blond, seven feet tall, physically magnificent, arrogant. They knew they were members of the 'master race'. None of them spoke English, and I am sure they felt that if I was a sample of the opposition, then the war (still in the future) was a foregone conclusion.

Drab, grey, sprawling and industrialised, Munich seemed to have little that would encourage me to stay. Also I had been receiving increasingly agitated letters from the college urging me to return at once, or avoid travel in Germany; or at least curtail my remaining time. From the train windows, I had seen that snow was covering most of the country we passed through, and it seemed best not to stop at any other cities I had hoped to include, like Dresden, but to go straight to Berlin.

The Munich train drew in at an elevated station, the *Anhalter Bahnhof*, and the only exit was down a long flight of steps to street

94

level. I carried my bike and pack down separately. An information kiosk reluctantly gave me an address in *Friedrichstrasse* which would provide cheap lodging. It was quite a small flat, inhabited by an old couple with their daughter of about thirty, who could speak a few words of English. Though I never found out for sure, I think they were Jewish. There was a subdued, claustrophobic atmosphere, an uncomfortable feeling, in the house. The daughter avoided any reference to politics, and only went out to do the shopping. The old people I never saw go out at all. They seemed grateful for the small sum I paid them at the end of each week. I fear those nice, ordinary people met the same fate as most other Berlin Jews during the following months and years.

On my first day, I saw flags and bunting everywhere and sensed a sort of holiday atmosphere, but I was a long way from finding out why. In a letter home I said I thought it might be a special welcome for me — maybe Hitler had heard I was coming. Certainly I did get the impression that Germany was preparing for war. Nazi swastika banners were everywhere, and uniforms abounded, not least those of the Brownshirts. I can still see the guards in front of the *Reichskanzlerei* in the *Unter den Linden*, impossibly spick and span and gleaming, goosestepping back and forth like jack-booted robots.

On the other side of the street was the huge wooden statue of Hindenburg, with scaffolding and walkways built round it. It cost one mark to hammer an iron nail into it, to help the Nazi funds. More guns, less butter. Apart from the tense atmosphere, Berlin was an attractive city, a pleasant place to walk in. Also the weather had improved slightly; no snow, but cold and sunny. Several of the better days I spent drawing animals at the splendid Berlin Zoo, and the museums and libraries appeared little affected by Nazism, though Hitler banned the Impressionists and modern art as decadent. Perhaps I would have spent more than two weeks in Berlin, but an urgent letter from the college made me start off in the direction of home, though I was reluctant to agree to their suggestion that I take the train all the way.

From Berlin I took the train to Osnabruck, the station nearest the Dutch frontier where my ticket ran out. There were a lot of Brownshirts in the town, complete with brass band, preparing for some kind of parade. After sending down roots after staying in one place for more than a week, I would always start off with a mixture of reluctance and anticipation, but after a few hours' cycling, I would start to enjoy it again. And the sun was shining. It would not be impossible, I think, to adapt to the nomadic life of gypsies or circus people.

The warden of the first Dutch hostel was Car Dyck, who was an artist and spoke good English. He was interested in my sketches and notes, and fascinated by the story of my travels. He hoped one day to visit and exhibit in London. I wonder whether he made it before the war started.

So, via Deventer, Apeldoorn (where the Kaiser lived after the first world war), through Amersfoort to Amsterdam and Rotterdam. During the weeks I spent in Holland, I grew to like the Dutch. They were home-like people, their houses were like ours, and even the language was familiar, though I had been unable to find a Dutch-English dictionary in Woolworths. Many words were identical with braid Scots, and with my newly acquired smattering of German, I got on very well. As we had been taught at school, Holland was *flat*. Perfect for cyclists. I had never imagined so many, especially in the evenings when people were making their way home from work. By now I could claim to be an experienced cyclist, but compared to them I was a novice. They did things with and on their bikes that I could never attempt. The one drawback to the long straight roads was having to cycle against the wind. Since the prevailing winds came from the west, where I was heading, I got the impression that Holland was all uphill to the North Sea. Once or twice, cycling into the teeth of a gale, I would get off and push the bike for a mile or two to get a rest.

Every Dutch town was neat and tidy, and no litter could be seen anywhere, which pleased me. Also they seemed compact, human places to live in, not too sprawling or industrialised. I enjoyed the canals and the trailer trams. Many of the paintings in the world-famous art galleries showed scenes little changed from the originals even now.

Making my way along the side of a canal one afternoon in Amsterdam, I was stopped by two large men in raincoats and felt hats, obviously policemen. They asked to see my papers. Since they spoke no English, communication was difficult. They went on and on in hectoring tones, but at last gave up, returning my passport, and I guessed from their growls warning me just to watch it and not do it again, whatever it was. Long after I returned home, a local newspaper dramatised the incident with the headline, 'Scots student arrested as spy!'

Via Breda I went on to Antwerp, Ghent and Bruges. Belgium too I liked, a compact little country. But here for the first time I became aware of the animosity between the French and Dutch speaking segments of the community, much sharper than Scots-English rivalries. With its canals, Bruges was very like a Dutch town. I could have spent a long time painting here, but the weather was still cold. Thankfully, there had been no more snow.

With some reluctance, but also some sense of relief, I cycled the last lap via Dunkirk to Calais. Dunkirk I remember as a nondescript little town, and certainly I had no premonition of its later fame, when friends of mine would be killed or taken prisoner, and where John Thomson, the youngest of my uncles, would also die. His body was never found.

The Customs officer at Dover was amazed at the duration and extent of my journey, but put his chalked 'X' on my bags and wished me luck. I had promised to visit my aunt, Jessie Luke, in Yeovil before I made my way home again, and three days later arrived at her little cottage at the foot of Ham Hill in Somerset. Aunt Jessie had been the district nurse here for many years, and was well liked and respected by the locals, who loved her Scottish accent. To us, when she visited Edinburgh during her holidays, she sounded completely and irretrievably English. She made me very welcome, and I had a well-earned rest of three weeks, with plenty of good food.

BACK in Edinburgh I reported to the Art College, where they confessed they had been really worried at several points of my tour. War had seemed a definite possibility, and I had passed through several sensitive areas where I could very easily have been picked up and interned for the duration. But they were delighted to see me back, and my work seemed to have been satisfactory. I had established a record in duration, and had been the first to attempt a tour by bicycle. Including the sections covered by train, I had covered 7,500 miles in seven months, and I had averaged forty-four miles a day when cycling.

On my return I had several interviews with Professor Wellington and Rushforth, and confessed I was still rather doubtful of my ability to earn a living. They felt that after this epic journey, I should not need to be scared of anything at all. But to prove their confidence that I could succeed, they offered to finance me at the rate of £5 weekly for ten years, if I would undertake to pay them half my salary thereafter. I should have accepted — they would both have been considerably out of pocket, but I would not have gone hungry so often. Rushforth was good enough to buy some of my tour watercolours, which eased my immediate financial situation, though I still had around £30 of the scholarship money left.

Now I had to think seriously about making a living. Work in commercial art or related graphics was only to be had down south — meaning London. Any art work needed in Scotland was done by the very few artists already employed. My final gift from the College was

97

a month's working scholarship with the *Radio Times*. The editorial staff, surprisingly small, worked all together in a tiny office in the BBC's annexe in Langham Place. Maurice Gorman was the editor, and the vice-editor Graham and two girls each had a table. Another was found for me to work on. I was still painfully shy, but they were all very kind to me, and the time passed pleasantly and profitably, in the sense that I learned quite a lot about production and deadlines. I did drawings and lettering which were used in each week's paper, but I felt a very raw beginner. For some of the drawings I should have searched for references, rather than depend on my own memory, but I was afraid to ask for time off to visit a library or museum, which would certainly have been granted without a moment's hesitation. I felt I should be able to draw anything I was asked to from the information in my own head; which of course is impossible.

It was most enlightening to see the original drawings by artists like Eric Fraser, Reinganum, Clixby Watson and Sheriffs, and to compare them with the printed results. I learned a lot about reductions and tints and line blocks. Once I was allowed to follow one of my own illustrations from the office, through all the processes to the finished line block, and then the final printing of the *Radio Times* at Waterston's. Looking back, I cannot claim that my drawings were inspired, but they were at least good enough to be printed each week. When I had finished my sponsored month, I was flattered and encouraged when Gorman continued to commission drawings. Since *Radio Times* paid generously for art work, I was grateful. In the year before the war, paper was being rationed more and more strictly. Advertising was drastically cut, and with it the necessity for advertising artists. Publishers cut back, especially on illustrated books, and very few commissions came my way, though I covered many miles travelling round the agencies with my portfolio. Without the almost weekly cheque from the *Radio Times*, I could not have remained in London. A newly started commercial art studio, Brockhurst's, took me on at £3 weekly, but they had to pay off their artists one by one. I lasted three months, and they folded shortly afterwards due to lack of business. I was to have been their lettering and animal specialist.

I had been in London for a few months when I met Jack Hannan, who had been at Edinburgh Art College in the year behind mine. He was working as a commercial artist, and beginning to find a reasonable amount of work. He lived in a basement not far from my lodgings, not the sort of place I would have preferred as he had to work by artificial light even during the day, but he was quite happy to do so. I saw him several times again when we were both back in Edinburgh. We kept in touch until the first year of the war. He was in

98

the Naval Reserve and had been called to man one of the barges near the Forth bridge; there was a flotilla of them carrying tethered barrage balloons to protect the bridge from enemy air attack. He told me it was quite a safe and easy job, and during the summer it did appear to be so; but within six months he was dead, killed during an air raid which was never mentioned in the papers or on the radio.

Pre-war London was supposed to be an exciting and stimulating place to live in, and really it was probably the centre of the world then, politically and in business. The only other capital city which presented any real challenge was New York. To be a success there was to be a success everywhere. But this reputation, held for so many years, resulted in New York becoming a vast urban sprawl too big as a human environment, and it is much worse now in that respect. Man was not designed to live in caves in the centre of square miles of sterile rocky canyons, with no physical contact with the world of nature, and where wild animals and plants and open space are in the realms of myth or fiction. Or it could be that I am unable to adapt. Maybe the human race of the future is *meant* to live in such artificial and crowded conditions, and interaction with the world of nature will be through ancient films showing what the earth once looked like. Certainly of recent years things seem to be going that way, and it could be that the planet will become one vast city, with some flat open spaces producing one or two staple crops and no wild life at all. It may be this development will be necessary to force the race to concentrate on the evolution of the powers of the mind as opposed to physical evolution. The south of England and around London was already urbanised pre-war, and is even more heavily over-built today, along with centres of population all over the world. I believe the human psyche is badly traumatised by life crowded in over-large cities, and this accounts for the rise in crime everywhere.

Edinburgh was once a city for human beings to live in, small enough so that it was possible to walk to the furthest suburbs comfortably, with open spaces, green, to serve as lungs. Now like most other cities, it grows larger and larger, and no one seems to know how to stop the cancer.

There was a surfeit of places of entertainment in London — but for the great majority of them you needed money, of which I had very little to spare. I very occasionally went to the cinema, but otherwise I depended on books from the local library. At weekends I went for walks, usually in the parks for a sight of greenery. The museums and art galleries filled much of my spare time, South Kensington being my favourite. If I had no commission to work on during the week, I spent my days toting my art portfolio round the many studios and publishing houses, with little result, as already the rationing restrictions on paper were beginning to bite, and most firms were reducing their output. I know very many people would actually *choose* to live in the metropolis. I was glad to leave. If I were to sum up in one word how I felt about London, it would be 'suffocating'.

Even at Hampstead Heath — open country to Londoners! — the hum and roar of traffic still vibrated through the air. One Sunday I set out to walk in a straight line across the city from east to west. I walking along *one street for eight miles* — High Holborn, Oxford Street, Great Western Road; nothing but buildings. Claustrophobic.

Most of my earnings had to go on rent. Lodgers were expected to eat out, but could use the gas ring provided there were no cooking smells. I became expert at living on very little food. I made a quarter pound packet of tea last three months. Eggs at the local big store cost a halfpenny each. They were small like bantam's eggs, but round, and stamped 'Egyptian'. I discovered after a while that they were crocodile eggs, though needless to say, the store never advertised them as such. But they were perfectly good eggs, and I continued to use them. I used a lot of the Scot's staple, porridge, cheap and filling, and various other foodstuffs could be had very cheaply from time to time. Nevertheless, when I returned to Edinburgh, my weight was down to seven stone four pounds, a stone less than normal.

M Y RETURN to Edinburgh was decided for me by the international situation. Everything now indicated the strong possibility of war. Hitler had walked into the Sudetenland, Austria and Czechoslovakia, and now was threatening Poland; it seemed he could annex any country he chose with impunity. No major nation wanted to risk taking on the Wehrmacht. Prime Minister Neville Chamberlain's policy of 'appeasement' was increasingly suspect. It seemed he would submit to *any* demand of Hitler's.

In Britain at least there was a strong feeling against war. The 1914–18 conflict was supposed to be the war to end war, and now they wanted to start all over again. Many of us had had faith in the League of Nations, but it had lost all credibility by then, as country after country was invaded and they stood by and did nothing. Had the League owned a bigger stick than anyone else, they might have been listened to with some respect.

Personally I was a pacifist. I believed in peace at *almost* any price, and thought interminable argument better than shooting. Now I feel if a bully strikes me, I should strike back. If Britain at last were to

100

stand up to Hitler and say 'Enough!', we could expect to be pretty badly beaten up before we could hope to rally enough to repel him. Defeating the Nazis seemed too much to expect. We believed that all our major cities would be bombed flat in a matter of weeks, or maybe a month or two, and I thought if I had to die, I'd rather be at home. The general impression was that we were not as prepared for war as Germany, but that we could soon build up an adequate defence force. Very few had the slightest inkling of how totally unprepared we were. Most of the time Churchill's warnings were dismissed as scaremongering, but how right he was. We were virtually defenceless, and had Germany invaded during the first few weeks, we would have indeed been fighting on the beaches — 'with broken bottles' as Churchill said *sotto voce* after one of his famous speeches. ('We will never surrender.') Chamberlain's piece of paper — 'Peace in our time' — had at least gained us a year's respite, during which some basic preparations had been made. Very quietly, because I remember no hints in the media.

On Sunday the third of September, 1939, we were in our holiday hut at Pettycur, listening to our little portable radio. (Weighing eleven pounds, and the size of a small suitcase. Now we have matchbox sized transistors.) An important announcement was to be made at 11 a.m. Chamberlain's voice came, — 'at war with Germany'. There was some relief that the waiting was over, but a sense of foreboding and unreality too, as if war was unthinkable on such a beautiful sunny day. The holiday camp was soon closed, and we were not allowed back until the end of the war. (On our return we found the acres of sand covered with hundreds of wooden poles set in concrete bases, erected to smash any German planes or gliders which might attempt to land there.) A stick of seven bombs landed in a field at Burntisland some months later, and the craters are still visible. My first assistant art teacher, Margaret Sutherland, remembered running along the street as a little girl, with a German plane machine-gunning her personally, as she thought.

During the few months preceding the war, everyone was issued with a gas mask. This official precaution seemed to make it all the more inevitable. The masks were carried everywhere you went, in a cardboard box slung over the shoulder with string. Little children who might be scared of the regulation issue were given 'Mickey Mouse' masks, and for babies there were cot masks with a perspex window, and a pump for air which someone had to keep working. We all carried electric hand torches at night in the blackout, always to be pointed downwards. Public transport was blacked out, all the windows painted over, only a few lights inside, and those a dim blue. Light masks were compulsory on all vehicles, even bicycles. A grid allowed a minimum of light to reach the ground immediately in front of the wheels. Windows everywhere were criss-crossed with sticky tape to minimise the effect of bomb blast. Blackout curtains were compulsory. If the slightest chink of light showed after dark, a patrolling A.R.P. (Air Raid Precautions) officer would shout, 'Put out that light!' Offices and public buildings had their entrances and lower windows protected by walls of sandbags. My brother and I and most of the lads in our street volunteered to fill sandbags during the day or two before the third of September, for the protection of the Deaconess Hospital at the top of our street. Air raid shelters, large and small, had been dug everywhere, even in the middle of the Brown Street garden, which was quite ruined.

At the very beginning of the war when invasion seemed imminent, the Local Defence Volunteers were formed. This was the L.D.V., soon to become the Home Guard. Few weapons were available, and they drilled with shovels or broomsticks. They did get tin helmets, but the only uniform was a yellow armband printed with 'L.D.V'. We also had Civil Defence (C.D.) concerned with A.R.P. These wardens had dark blue uniforms and helmets, and went out at night to ensure that the blackout was total.

Each tenement was expected to do its own firefighting, as in the event of an air raid, the fire services would be otherwise engaged. We were supplied with buckets of sand and water, and an official stirrup pump. One day the volunteers in our street were called to take part in an anti-fire exercise. An incendiary bomb was lit in a local air raid shelter, and we crawled through dense white smoke past the flaring bomb and out the other end. We were drilled in the use of sand and water in extinguishing the blaze. It was imperative only to *spray* the bomb with water, otherwise it would explode. Hurling a bucket of water on it produced a bang and dozens of smaller fires all around. Burning bombs inside a building were to be picked up on a long-handled shovel and carried or thrown into the street. As we lived on the top storey, it was our responsibility to deal with any bombs which landed on our tenement. It was expected they would break through the slates and land on the rafters, so we had to explore the area under our roof so we would know where to go. Charlie and I and the two Forrest boys next door would be the fire-fighting team when it happened. Happily we never needed to put our skills to the test.

There were periodical air raid warnings, but Edinburgh was comparatively unscathed, and very little bomb damage was reported. But every time we heard the ululation of the sirens, we wondered if it was now our turn. The sound of the German bombers was quite distinctive. Instead of the steady drone of ours, they had a fluctuating beat. We would put out the lights and look out of the window at the

102

waving searchlights, listening for the distant 'Thump-thump-thump-thump' of the anti-aircraft guns. Actually we were supposed to keep as far away from the windows as possible, for fear of flying splinters. There were dugout bomb shelters for everyone in the street, but not everyone used them. If the sirens sounded in the early hours of a frosty winter morning, it took a real effort to get out of a warm bed and go down five flights of stairs to sit in a dark and freezing brick tomb. We boys had to stay aloft anyway to deal with incendiaries, and most families elected to stay and take their chances.

Blackout was strictly enforced. Even street lights were replaced by dim blue glows that barely showed the ground below. The darkness of the city at night was depressing. Life was claustrophobic, with rationing, censorship and restriction of movement. No one could travel from his immediate neighbourhood without an official permit.

We had all seen the newsreels showing Hitler's vast martial arrays, rallies with thousands of robot-like goose-stepping soldiers, hundreds of tanks and guns. Though film of Mussolini did not show the same terrifying might, he still appeared formidable enough. With these two joined together against Britain and France, it seemed our chances were slim. When Russia joined them, it seemed all we could do was go down fighting. Then Japan also took a hand, against all logic; how could they ally with a régime dedicated to the idea of the superiority of blond, blue-eyed *Herrenvolk*? America believed in isolationism, and it seemed would not lift a finger to save us from annihilation. So it was a considerable relief to hear of the moth-balled cruisers which were 'lent' to us at a critical moment, and 'lend-lease' seemed to indicate that we might get some real help before it was too late. The bombing of Pearl Harbour decided the waverers in USA, as it became obvious that *no* country was to be considered safe, whether or not they practised non-intervention or isolation.

On my return to Edinburgh, I had got a job of sorts with B. C. Young, an advertising agent. The pay was only £2 a week, but there was really very little work, owing to the increasing pressure on newspapers to cut advertising to the bone. They were eventually reduced to four pages. Any advertising was prestige publicity only — most goods were unobtainable anyway. B. C. Young was a character, always very nattily dressed, wearing, of all things, *spats*. I'd never seen these things on a living person, and thought they had gone out with Jeeves and Bertie Wooster. He had a large, glossy, salmon pink car, costing to run the equivalent of the combined salaries for a year of his tame artist and secretary-typist. Miss Pringle apparently did most of the work, and had been with him for years. He was forty-odd, pink and balding, but seemed in pretty good condition. He had never married, and tried to convey an aura of the bachelor gay (in its original connotation). He was a hypochondriac, and kept an array of patent medicines, some of which he advertised and could get as free samples. When he felt his vital powers had been seriously depleted, he would go to a health farm for a week or two. He would return looking like death, but claiming now to be in bounding health. He tried to convert Miss Pringle and me to his beliefs, but we never could have afforded it. This job only lasted a few months. So little work came in that my pay was cut to £1 a week, for two days' work. It was during this first year of the war that I exhibited two paintings at the Royal Scottish Academy in Edinburgh. Though the fees were large in relation to my income, I thought I might just possibly make a sale, and also it seemed it was time I made a bid to show my work regularly — the only way to get one's name recognised. This would have been the logical procedure in normal times. But at no time during the following years could I afford exhibition fees, and the next time I exhibited at the Mound Galleries was in the fifties, when I was elected a professional member of the Society of Scottish Artists.

Shortly afterwards I received my calling up papers. Not long before this, I had called in at the R.A.F. recruiting office. A volunteer could usually choose the service he wanted, and I had no wish to join the army or navy. I never could walk long distances — ten miles in one day was my record; and I got seasick very easily. But the officer in charge took one look at me and said he could not accept me. He even refused to let me fill in a form. 'But', I protested, 'Douglas Bader's still allowed to fly, and he's lost his legs!' The officer stayed adamant. So now I reported at the specified centre for my medical. There was a long line of perhaps a dozen doctors which each candidate had to pass. The doctor at the first table took my papers, and I answered all the questions suitably. It seemed I was 'in'. I passed on to the next stage. The doctor there took one look at me, called the rest of his colleagues and went into a huddle. I was told I could go home, classified as '4-D'. But apart from the occasional rheumatic twinge, I was as fit then as ever I was to be, after my long continental tour. The intellectual capacity of a prospective recruit was completely irrelevant. Or perhaps one of the later doctors in the line sifted out the 'brains'.

Apart from the ignominy of being classed a reject, I was quite pleased to be out of it. I had no desire to kill anyone, for whatever reason. Most of the people I had met on my journey were nice, plain, ordinary folk trying to live an honest, decent sort of life without hurting anyone else. How could I drop bombs on them? If I could have been sure I could wipe out the Nazis, the Gestapo and S.S., the politicians, the manipulators, then I would have had little compunc-

104

tion. In any war, ordinary, nice people are conned into believing that somehow the other side, 'the enemy', have suddenly become evil and sub-human. It helps if the media can invent some derogatory term for them — Huns, Krauts, Frogs, Wops, Japs, Gooks or Argies.

It was recently revealed in Tom Bowers' *Blind Eye to Murder* (Andre Deutsch, 1981) that the great majority of Nazi war criminals were not only pardoned and released, but actually encouraged to set up new businesses, with the help of vast money loans. This was in the immediate post-war period, when the Board of Trade was putting every possible obstacle in the way of our struggling art shop business, and finally closing it down. If my partners and others in the same position had been aware of these facts at the time, there could have been real bloody revolution at home. The very people and organisations we had suffered five years of war and privation to destroy were being given not simply preferential treatment, but active monetary help, from *our* Government!

When I was very young, I believed true communism, sharing, could be the beginning of real civilisation. Having seen the results of political communism, I'm not so sure now. Any culture which has to build a wall to keep its happy citizens at home would seem to be not quite perfect. The manipulators at the top of each great state deal quite happily with each other, even though their political programmes are diametrically opposed. To a politician, today's friend is tomorrow's enemy, and vice versa. Many of us were enthusiastic about the League of Nations. At last, it seemed, men would come together and iron out their differences by discussion and rational agreement, using the billions spent on war sensibly. But it failed to prevent the Spanish Civil War or Mussolini's invasion of Abyssinia. Today's United Nations seems to do more good in limited ways, but is also powerless to stop the invasion of one country by another. Humanity's greatest vice is greed. Eliminate covetousness and the millennium is at hand.

Food, clothing, sweets and petrol were all rationed. Since we had no car, petrol rationing did not affect us directly. With six ration books, my mother managed the clothing side better than some. Though we never saw any, parachute silk was in great demand for making underwear and wedding gowns. Our American allies were exceedingly popular as the sole source of nylons. Papers printed articles showing how to make clothing from unrationed materials like dishcloths. Magazines and newspapers were shadows of their pre-war selves, and a lot of the paper was recycled, grey and unattractive.

Pre-war white bread tasted of nothing, but now millers had to leave everything in the flour, and the 'national loaf' was far better. There was a scarcity of anything to put *on* the bread. Margarine was more plentiful than butter, but unfortunately, I could tell the difference. The whole week's butter ration was just enough for one bap, and that was how I used mine, putting up with marge for the rest of the week. Potatoes were now good for us, not fattening as formerly. So 'Potato Pete' told us. Cakes used such unlikely ingredients as carrots, but with one egg a week and scarce sugar, not many were made. I cut down my sugar by half, and Charlie cut it out altogether, as our parents both liked more than the official ration. Now having a sweet tooth anyway, I gave away most of my sweet coupons. Children were always pleased to have them. Meat and cheese came measured in ounces, about enough for one sandwich. From America came spam, a real delicacy, also dried eggs and powdered milk, and we were glad to have them. Imported fruits like oranges, pineapples and bananas vanished completely. Ice-cream was a memory. Children who were offered bananas at the war's end did not know what to do with them.

TRAIN journeys were highly uncomfortable. Stations were dark, with dim blue signs and notices. 'S' for shelter, 50, 300 persons or whatever. There were two tiny blue lights in each compartment when you finally boarded the train. They were not nearly bright enough to read by. I hardly ever managed to get a seat anyway; even the corridors were crammed to capacity, and it was wise to have an up-ended suitcase to sit on during a long journey. Service was erratic, and unscheduled stops and delays had to be accepted with no more explanation than the universal 'Don't you know there's a war on?'

The entertainments available were cinemas and dance halls, and a few theatres. At the beginning these had all been closed. But after dark, most people remained at home and made their own entertainment. The radio was indispensable. Everyone listened to the news at six, especially during the Battle of Britain. The announcers never *quite* got around to 'German planes down, 54; British planes down, 3; German battleships, 2; —', but they came close. There was no doubt that Churchill's speeches had considerable influence on morale. So too did radio entertainment, especially 'ITMA', with Tommy Handley. Its catch phrases were heard everywhere — 'Can I do you now, sir?', 'Don't forget the diver!', 'This is Funf speakink!' Everyone looked forward to *Monday Night at Seven*, even when it was changed to 'Eight'. *Workers' Playtime,* a light music programme, was welcome at first, but latterly became boring. Serious music and plays were much appreciated.

Also classed as entertainment was listening to 'Lord Haw-Haw', speaking in English from Germany. Even his more convincing attempts at propaganda were nullified by his affected 'upper-class' accent. Hitler could hardly have chosen a voice more likely to be ridiculed. His supercilious delivery guaranteed that his hearers would be antagonistic.

Long-term entertainment was also available to those of us with longer memories, from our own Ministry of Information. At the outset of war, when Stalin joined forces with Hitler, we were told that the Russians were a rabble of bloodthirsty Cossacks in rags and furs, with a few pikes and sabres, and lots of horses because they had no motorised transport. An ignorant lot of peasants jumping on Hitler's bandwagon. Then Hitler attacked Russia, and overnight the Russians were our noble and high-minded allies, hard pressed, but fighting with skill and determination, using the most modern equipment to best advantage. And of course with the very best of intentions to the smaller surrounding nations they were striving so valiantly to protect. Similar entertainment can be enjoyed even today by anyone who takes the trouble to record what each political party promises *before* it is voted into power, and what it says when finally it is voted out again. Invariably it is the preceding party which got the country into the present mess, and most of the term in office has to be spent putting things right, so they have no time to put their own reforms into effect. The opposition always knows *exactly* what must be done to put the nation back on its feet, and of course is automatically re-elected. Fortunately for politicians, the memory of the public rarely stretches as far as two years.

A pastime adopted by many during the war was making models, ships, planes, tanks and so on. My choice was planes, and I started by making solid models, but found them less challenging. I progressed to flying models, not of real planes, but designed for flying. I made one or two elastic powered models, as petrol engines were far too expensive and demanded larger craft than I had space for. The geared prop from a 'FROG' (Flying Rise Off Ground), I found very useful, and I incorporated it in each successive experiment. My final masterpiece was a piece of original thinking. I reasoned that since the fuselage contributed nothing to the lifting power, I could dispense with it altogether. I built a simple rectangular machine, like a section out of the middle of a wing; just a flying aerofoil with a stabilising fin at the end. This invention flew beautifully with a very shallow glide angle, and was the most stable of all my models. Six months after I made it, on a Pathétone newsreel I saw a full scale version of it, a single-seater built by a Frenchman. Obviously really big planes could be built to the same design. I still wonder why it was never followed up. Every surface was a 'working' surface, no surplus weight just along for the ride, as with the sides of a fuselage.

In spite of the desperate state of the war, the depressing effects of the blackout and rationing, and the complete uncertainty of the future, December 1941 was the beginning of the happiest period of my life. Against all my resolutions and intentions and quite against reason, I fell in love. My parents had decided to have a silver wedding celebration, rationing and restrictions not withstanding. It was possible to get an attenuated feast of sorts, using unrationed foodstuffs, and caterers were allowed some meats which they could use on special occasions. They decided on the Cavendish Halls at Tollcross. All our friends and relations were invited, over 100 guests.

Since none of us could dance, we prepared by taking lessons from young Willie Guthrie. Once a week, we four, our cousins Betty and Isa, our teacher and his younger sister Eleanor gathered in our big room with my brother's gramophone and a pile of dance records. I bought Victor Sylvester's dance book, with its diagrams of footsteps in the snow, and with some of his strict tempo music, we felt we were really swinging. We marched solemnly around, counting, 'one, two, three, cross, chassée', or '*One*, two three, *One*, two three'. Soon we were confident we could cope with a real dance.

The celebration was to be on 31st December, and we started our practice at the end of October. Though Willie was some years younger than I, he had been going to the Palais de Danse in Fountainbridge for years, and we all envied his smooth confidence and matter-of-fact and masterly guiding of his partner. He was also a natty dresser. One evening the Guthries brought along a visitor, an attractive dark-haired girl, Phyllis, and introduced her as a cousin who lived in Leith. They wondered if she could join our practices, as she also wanted to learn how to dance. We were delighted to have one more.

The silver wedding was a great success, due partly to the contrast with normal drab wartime existence. We had bright lights, colour, music, warmth, good food and cheerful company. I had more-than my quota of dances with Phyllis, which ensured the success of the evening for me personally. When it was over, we all walked back home for supper in the early morning, through the blackout. Even the weather was with us that night. It was quite still, very frosty, and a 'Bombers' Moon' lit our way. There had been some snow, and the roads were icy and slippery, which gave us an excuse to link arms for safety.

Phyllis continued to visit each week, and at last I found the courage to ask her for a date. I was delighted when she agreed. I had expected a blunt refusal, because my physical attractions were nil, my job was only part-time, and there was no sign of any future career which could promise financial security. Whereas she was really pretty; dark brown eyes, black hair in the popular pageboy style and an attractive smile. She was rather taller than I, which really should have ruled her out as a possible partner. I was never attracted to tall — or fat — girls. But three inches seemed near enough. She could have had her choice of all the tall handsome young lads in uniform, but she had deigned to notice me.

It was odd. Ever since I was fourteen, I had been determined not to marry, and to me that meant no girlfriends. I knew achondroplasia was an inherited condition, and I was not going to risk passing it on to any child. The chances of finding a mate who would be happy without children seemed remote. So I built up the reputation of being a woman hater, quite contrary to all my natural inclinations. (Had homosexuality been out in the open then, I would have been horrified to think that this façade might lead people to think that I was one of them. Looking back, I believe it *did* mislead a good friend of mine, and it was a good few years later that I discovered he was one.) This posture was accepted by everyone who knew me. I had always felt that a little man with a large wife looked ridiculous; like comic seaside postcards; and I was determined in no circumstances to have anything to do with girls taller than myself.

In addition to all this, I had been thoroughly conditioned against involvement with the opposite sex from my earliest years. At christmas or other parties, I very soon found that girls avoided me as a partner. If forfeits were called for, they went to extreme lengths to keep out of my way, and if this was impossible, made it very clear that kissing me was not their cup of tea. Affection in our own family circle was to say the least undemonstrative. I never saw my parents kiss or embrace, except latterly once a year at Hogmanay. Nor did they kiss or hold us that I can remember, though they must have done when we were babies. Over the last few years when my mother introduced the New Year kiss, I was always first to receive it, being the 'Traditional First Foot'. For some reason, it had been decided I was a lucky 'first fit'. One year a neighbour had beaten me to it, and we had a terribly unlucky year after that; so at five to twelve each Hogmanay, I was pushed outside the door with a bottle of lemonade and a piece of coal, ordered to knock as soon as the clock chimed 12. The clock in the lobby was a grandfather clock, my father's pride and joy. And its chimes could be heard at the far end of our street.

Yes, it was odd. I had set myself up as a sitting target for ridicule from every direction, and I didn't care. I had dropped my protective shield, destroyed my carefully built reputation. I tried to rationalise. Why should I deny myself the pleasure of female company because of accidental deformity? And thousands worse off than I must have found happiness in marriage. Though marriage seemed financially out of the question for the foreseeable future, when it did become feasible, surely we would come to some agreement on the question of progeny. Had living together been socially acceptable, it would still have been impossible, as together we didn't earn enough to live on.

In the company of my girlfriend I was deliriously happy. I lived only for the few hours we could spend together on Wednesday and Sunday afternoons. We went to the cinema or the Palais, or on Sundays for a walk. Three nights I walked her home before I dared to kiss her goodnight, and not fancying myself as Clark Gable or Tyrone Power, I asked her permission first. It was a bungled and amateurish performance compared to the polished demonstrations we'd seen in films, and which I thought didn't seem too difficult to copy. But I was completely unprepared for the actual sensation — undiluted pleasure. Uniquely, *this* girl was not showing signs of repugnance. I surfaced for air, trying not to explode with sheer joy, and floated home ten feet tall, lips still tingling. So she did love me.

We got on remarkably well together. On the few occasions I was jeered at by the inevitable urchins, I loved her all the more when she said not to mind. While she would dare to appear in public with me, I felt human at last; equal to any normal man, because here was an obviously desirable and attractive girl who had chosen to associate with me. I admired her all the more for her courage. The whole family was supportive at that time, accepting that it was quite normal for me to have a girlfriend, even though she was six years younger. There was a drifting, dreamlike quality about these few weeks. I hoped they would never end.

Some lads of my acquaintance wanted to know how far I'd got. The implication was that you were subnormal if you stopped at a goodnight kiss. But I loved her so much I would have done nothing to harm her, or against her wishes. I was grateful for the minimal, by today's standards, goodnight kiss, or indeed any demonstration of affection. We may have been naive, but I was completely uninformed as to accepted erotic behaviour, and I had no reason to believe she was otherwise.

After some weeks, Phyllis started coming also to the Home Guard Whist Dance on Saturday nights. The Guthries had introduced us to this weekly function some time before we learned to dance. It was held in a Church Hall and was always well attended, with fifty tables. I was not really keen on whist, but it provided an agreeable night out. Week after week I got impossibly bad hands, so regularly that I got the reputation of being a Jonah, and any lady who was doing well bemoaned her luck at reaching my table, which would ruin her score.

I must have won more booby prizes than anyone else. They were usually packets of cigarettes, and this is what started me smoking. I was really not a bad player — I always played my cards for all they were worth, and on the few occasions when my luck turned, I actually won first prize for best score. Tea was supplied, and the ladies brought food for each table. Afterwards the floor was cleared for the dance, slippery powder was sprinkled on the floor, and the three-piece band struck up. The dance was an enjoyable affair, as everyone knew everybody else. Before I learned to dance, I always went home at this point, missing what could be the best part of the evening.

So now twice a week we could dance together. I counted the hours between. One Saturday I was to wait for Phyllis at the tram stop, bringing her dance shoes which she had forgotten the previous Wednesday. It was the end of March, dark, moonless and cold. I waited on that draughty corner while tram after dimly lit tram ground to a halt, then moaned away again without disgorging my love. Ten, twenty minutes, over an hour. I told myself there must be some good and mundane reason why she had been unable to come, but I knew with a dreadful and numbing certainty that this was the end. I walked and walked, anywhere, heavy with misery. The whole world for all eternity was dark. The stars above should have been winking out, one by one, for ever. And the 'observer' at the back of my skull sniggered nastily and said, 'Told you so! You knew this wasn't for you. And stop feeling so bloody sorry for yourself!' But I did.

Subsequently I found she had been seeing me all this time without the knowledge or consent of her parents. She had told them she was visiting the Guthries. Someone had seen us together and had passed on the news, and since her parents knew my father and had also seen me, they had forbidden her to have anything more to do with me. On hearing this, I thought as a forlorn hope that I might change their minds, and called on them one night. The father sat reading a newspaper and left most of the talking to his wife, who was ironing aggressively by the light of a single gas mantle. Phyllis sat on a seat at the far end of the fender, and I was grudgingly allowed to sit at the other end. Her mother talked over the thump of the iron. For one thing, I was far too old for her daughter. A young girl couldn't be allowed out alone with such an aged and experienced male. For another, I should know better than to get into a situation where I

111

might later marry. Wasn't my father that wee dwarf watchmaker? And she wasn't going to have freaks for grandchildren. And what sort of prospects had I anyway? I'd never get a decent job, the way I was.

It was impossible. I noticed Phyllis had another black eye, like the one three weeks previously, when she had walked into a door in the blackout — a fairly common accident. But it seemed her father had done it when they first found out, and she had not wanted to tell me. She had still kept our dates, defying them, but of course they found out again. How could I expose her to more of this treatment? I couldn't have her hurt any more. And so much of her mother's tirade was the truth. Sadly I said goodbye. I heard that six months later she had run away and married a soldier.

For a year after that I must have been very difficult to live with, snapping at everybody. Nothing would ease the pain, and I got heartily sick of the phrase, 'There's plenty more fish in the sea!' I knew this was my one and only chance, and I had lost it. Not that I didn't *try*. I was on the rebound, and after a few weeks started going to the Palais again. There was no other way to meet a new girl. But it was a grey, lonely, unfriendly place now. The usual response when I approached a girl was 'Nut dancin!' And it was utterly humiliating to see her go off with the next man who asked her. One girl did give me the occasional dance, and some time later I tried for a date. She then pointed out she was wearing a wedding ring; she took it off when she went to the Palais because then nobody would ask her to dance. This was the last straw. I never went back again.

Just after my doomed love affair, my mother and sisters used to visit a great-aunt every Sunday, and they prevailed on me to go along with them instead of glooming at home. Maybe I went because my great-aunt lived in the same street as Phyllis, and perhaps one day I might see her. I never did. But through this weekly visit I did meet someone who helped to salve my wounded ego. My great-aunt had two daughters. The husband of the married one had deserted her some years previously, leaving her to bring up five little girls, ranging from two to eleven years old. In spite of this, she was always cheerful and smiling. She was fair, rosy and plumpish, and loved her family, who were a likeable bunch. I could never understand why the man would want to leave them.

What happened was that Moira, the second youngest, fell in love with me at first sight. She was four, fair and freckled deliciously. She had candid grey eyes and her hair was combed back from a generous brow. And I loved her in return, though I would not admit it to myself. After all, I was going around with a lump of cold lead where my heart used to be. How could a little girl not much more than a

112

baby fill the aching void in my life? But the fact remains, there was a tremendous rapport between us, an affinity I never felt with anyone else. She seemed to understand on some deep level just what I needed, and radiated love and warmth to me. She would look into my eyes and hug or kiss me without reserve or excuse, sometimes to the outrage of her sisters, and she didn't care what they thought. To the adults, I had to give the impression that all this eternal love business was just in fun, but to Moira it was all deadly serious, and she knew I would never ridicule her. She would have done anything for me, and I her. Once when we were out walking they jokingly tested Moira out by suggesting she should come home and live with me. I knew what her answer would be, and off we went hand in hand. Then they had to explain that her Mum and sisters loved her very much, and would be very sad if she left them. So she told me that she would marry me when she was grown up, when she was fifteen.

Each Sunday I continued to visit. Three months before, if anyone had suggested I would waste every Sunday afternoon playing cards, dominoes and ludo with a family of little girls, I'd have told them they were daft. Once I even took them to the zoo, where we had a great time. They were *nice* kids, all of them. I have thought since that most probably I was a father substitute for them, which would explain their easy affection for me. But bless them all, and Moira especially; they helped me more than anyone at a time when I really needed it. When I had to leave Edinburgh, I lost touch with them.

Eighteen years later, I met Moira again at the great-aunt's house. She was tall, off hand, wore glasses, and a half-burned fag stuck to her lower lip. She looked grey, worn and tatty. Her scruffy little two-year-old old brat whined snot-nosed round her feet. Where was that wonderful affinity? I suspect she didn't even remember me.

I T WAS almost a relief when I lost my job with B. C. Young, and the Ministry of Labour directed me into 'war work'. I thought I might be good at instrument making, one of the categories offered, as I'd had some practice on clocks and watches in my father's shop. Needless to say, they had nothing to offer a professional artist calligrapher. Camouflage artists there were, all enlisted men, and there were the official war artists, who all seemed to be established names. The course I applied for had just been discontinued, so instead I was sent to Coatbridge Technical College for a three-month course in engineering inspection. Lodgings were paid for, and the trainees' allowance was double the amount of the dole. After training we could be sent anywhere.

There were fifteen of us in the class, and I was the youngest. The others' ages were from forty upwards. Our main instructor was Bremner, an old retired teacher in his mid-seventies. He was an impressive figure, over six feet tall. We found immediately that our mathematical abilities had all vanished apart from simple addition and multiplication. Even vulgar fractions had us floundering. But Bremner asured us that by the end of the three months we would again be coping with trigonometry and logarithms. He was right. It was quite amazing how fast we regained the forgotten skills.

Practical engineering was taught by a dour-looking, taciturn Scot, McArthur. But he knew his job, and after you got to know him — which wasn't easy — he revealed quite a sense of humour. He made each of us start by sawing off a six-inch length from a strip of mild steel still covered with a layer of blue furnace scale. We were ordered to file it flat and clear, using the files supplied. Easier said than done. The files were old and not only blunt, they were polished. After two days of hard, pointless work, I suggested to him that, in the well-worn phrase, there was a war on, and if he wanted any results before it finished, he would have to supply a new file. He saw the point, and slipped me a new one which I had to keep hidden. Maybe six of us managed to wangle a new file, but some of the rest were so ham-fisted they were still trying to file the thing flat at the end of the course, and they would of course have ruined a new file in minutes.

It took much longer to find out what we were supposed to be making, if anything, but at last he relented and disclosed that we were going to make a Multiple Gauge, worked by hand to within a thousandth of an inch. None of us believed this was possible, but I was pleasantly surprised to find in a week or two that I had a piece of steel squared off, and flat on both sides to within two thousandths of an inch. We had now to make different metal pieces, round, squared and angled, and make and fit test pieces into square, triangular and hexagonal holes accurately placed on the polished plate. A big Aiberdeen chiel and I were the only two to finish it all by the end of the course.

Bremner, besides teaching maths and theory, also taught the use of drawing instruments — T-square, setsquare, compasses and dividers. I had used these daily for years, and when he saw this, I was roped in to help some of the others who were particularly slow. My particular mate had been a bookie's clerk, and was good at maths. After some instruction, he coped adequately with the drawing instruments, but there were six or seven who never did get the hang of it. Their fingers were all thumbs and remained that way no matter how earnestly they tried.

On completing the course, we were directed all over the country, but were allowed some choice, within reason. Sick of living in lodgings, I felt I would be better living at home and contributing something to the family budget. Sent back to Edinburgh, I was told there were no vacancies for engineering inspectors, but I could have a job as a fitter with the Scottish Motor Traction Company in Fountainbridge. I did not realise that it was work which could have been done by an averagely intelligent chimpanzee, and within days I was bored rigid.

The S.M.T. was a war factory adapted from the bus station, and built tail assemblies for Lancasters and other large bombers. I was assigned a mate, and with a squad of women cut the sheets of aluminium, called skins, for the cladding of the tail planes, filed them smooth, then rivetted them to the skeleton frames already set up in vertical jigs. These sheets were delivered to us ready drilled with rivet holes. I had to measure half an inch from the holes, draw lines for the edges and trim off the surplus metal with a compressed-air driven nibbler. All the power for the many hand tools was supplied by an air compressor. Often water condensed in the lower pipes of the system, and everything went slower and slower until the drills and rivetting guns refused to work, when the water had to be drained off. Only the foremen were authorised to touch the drain cock, but as often as not they could not be found, and I learned how to do it myself. This bleeding off tended to lower the pressure in other parts of the factory, and it took some time to build up again. Several times I was reprimanded for this unofficial activity.

During an average twelve-hour shift, I and my mate were expected to finish four sets of skins, but once our charge hand asked us to work on through the night shift as well, as there was a 'flap' on. During that twenty-four hours, working flat out, we produced nineteen sets, and finished up dead on our feet. We found later we had created a record, but nobody even said 'Thanks', let alone 'Well done!'

In complete contrast, there were spells when there was nothing to do at all. Our charge hand warned us to look busy if any bosses were around. Not long after our marathon shift, all our section was taken off the skins and split up among other departments. On being assigned to 'Jig and Tool', I looked forward to something more challenging than measuring half an inch. Along with the others I was given a small hand-held jig. We took a foot-long aluminium strut from the pile on the bench, locked it in the jig, and filed off the sliver of metal sticking through the end. We did this for days and days.

115

With a powered hand drill and stone, the lot could have been done in an hour.

Only a few more weeks of this pace would have seen me carried out screaming, and I was perennially tired, but that November my father died, and I was granted 'compassionate release' so I could wind up his affairs. He had come home at seven as usual, and Charlie gave him a tow up the stairs. He walked in, sat down in his armchair, sighed and was gone. Although we all knew it could happen any time, we felt 'not just yet'. I called the doctor, who refused to come that night. Next day he explained it was best father had gone quickly. Had it been possible to revive him, he would only have been preserved for more months or years of dreadful agony; angina was one of the most painful maladies known. My mother was quite broken up, and missed him for years afterward.

The funeral was on a dull, damp November day, fittingly depressing. We were in the first of a line of cars following the hearse to the crematorium. We started off at a sedate and respectful pace, but soon speeded up, and after the service returned home at normal speed. This was when I recognised the finality of the proceedings. The world would go on quite comfortably without my father.

For several weeks we worked at making inventories in the shop, settling anything outstanding and returning customers' property. We found no unpaid bills, and everything had been kept in good order. But we had to check through boxes and drawers full of old watches, clocks and jewellery. Most of it we had to class as junk, but it would be worth a lot today. I think especially of some old watches with beautifully engraved or enamelled cases and dials. They didn't work, but as period pieces or props they would be very collectible now. We had an offer for the business — £10! We felt this was an insulting offer and would have waited for a better one, but my mother wanted to be rid of the shop as soon as possible. So for that paltry sum the buyer got all the stock, clocks, tools and equipment. He even insisted on having the 'goodwill' of the business, meaning none of us could open a shop to compete with him. Some years later we heard he had gone bankrupt. His repairs were not up to my father's standard. After we had paid a lawyer for the necessary legal business, the value of my father's estate, after a lifetime of hard and honest work, was £2 12s/6d.

POSSIBLY I could have gone back to the S.M.T. job, but I felt anything would be better than that, and I was directed instead to a job as an Engineering Inspector with Tecalemit at Brechin. Tecalemit was the trade name of a USA firm specialising in lubrication equipment — this was one of their UK factories. Lodgings were primitive. I had to share a bed with a lad from Stonehaven who had been directed to the same factory. The old couple who owned the house slept in the kitchen, we in the bedroom. There was only one gas light, the one in the kitchen. Cooking was done in a coal range, and we washed at the cold water sink. Baths were out of the question, and there were no public baths locally. Their lavatory was one of a row of W.C.s out at the back of the tenement, and to reach it you went out the front door, which opened directly on the street, and through an entry to the back yard.

At the factory I was more or less my own boss, and was in charge of all inspection of their entire output, which was all kinds of lubrication equipment from grease nipples to oil pump casings. I started out by failing a lot of casings because of misalignment of the cores, beyond the tolerances specified in the blueprints. Then it was gently put to me that such a large proportion of rejects would put the factory out of business; the things would work perfectly well with only a few flaws. I adjusted, failing only grossly out of line castings, or dangerously porous ones.

The factory had been an old linen mill, powered by a water wheel, which now drove different machinery. The place was permanently damp, and very cold. Within a few weeks I had to ask for a transfer owing to increasingly severe arthritis. This time I was sent to Rolls Royce, Glasgow. No jobs were now available for Engineering Inspectors, and I was classified as unskilled labour, forced to take anything that was offered. Along with a dozen others, I was given a test form to fill in. When they noticed I was an artist, they asked if I could perhaps draw machinery. I said of course I could draw anything, but I had to prove it by drawing some of their tools and pieces of engine. No problem. Now I was re-classified as a 'lithographic draughtsman', whatever that might be, and set to work in the drawing office. I was made assistant to a lad of seventeen who had been good at drawing at school, and was making three-dimensional drawings of pieces of machinery, up to cut-away sections of the Merlin engine. Rolls Royce specialised in adapting the

American Packard Merlin aero engine which was shipped across the Atlantic to Glasgow. His technique was self-taught, quite unsuited to depicting metal, but his immediate superiors knew no better, so he continued drawing pistons and cog wheels with a fussy, hairy pen line more suited to landscape etchings or woolly dogs.

A rival department later acquired its own tame artist, also just out of school with no art college experience, and they spared no expense in fitting him out with a splendid studio for his sole use, and even equipped him with a powered aerograph. He had no idea how to use it, and I was sent to teach him. This lad and my 'boss' each received about £10 weekly. I was paid £4. For my help in teaching I got no raise in wages, or even a small bonus. The head of this department once requisitioned my services for some days, and took me to Belper in Yorkshire, where another branch of Rolls Royce was stationed. In their drawing office I found a young draughtsman I had previously known at the Glasgow office. I was sworn in under the Official Secrets Act, then I was shown the workshops where they were building Whittle's first jet engine. Though at first glance it looked like a large copper boiler wreathed in a spaghetti-like tangle of tubing, I found this immensely exciting. I was right at the cutting edge of science and technology. Something *was* being done up front after all! I made drawings of the engine, and on my return made a simplified drawing explaining its working for the use of air force and engineering technicians. It was first explained to me by Toby Furman, a draughtsman engineer from Helsinki, so I would understand what I was doing. He was a likeable young man, but prickly about his origins. He probably had a higher I.Q. than anyone else in the factory.

My temporary boss and I put up in a typical old English country inn, and it was the proprietor who offered me a job after the war was over. As a jockey. He owned a stable of horses. But I've always felt horses are too high, and it's a long way down to the ground if you fall off. I thanked him but told him it was unlikely I'd take up his kind offer. This working break was most welcome after the monotony of war work.

Some time later the Finn, Toby Furman, asked if I could do a special job for him. A new two-speed, two-stage supercharger was to be added to the Merlin engine, and only one or two people could understand how it operated. He showed me the pile of blueprints which had baffled the drawing office, and explained to me how the thing worked. What he wanted was a cutaway view of the supercharger in perspective, with arrows showing the directions of the moving parts. This I did to his complete satisfaction, and copies were circulated to all departments. None of these highly skilled special jobs seemed to qualify me for any increase in my basic wage, and it was raised, to £8, only two weeks before I left. Engineering inspectors received £20 or more per week, as I discovered from one of the men who had taken the course with me, who I found in one of the workshops. That was big money. Looking back, I should have created a few waves.

I applied for release from Rolls Royce some weeks before V.J. Day, the end of the war. Work had been running down for some time, and there was no sense of urgency in the air, so I was permitted to leave without being directed into other war work.

I T was through this drawing office that I had my nearest contact with the world of entertainment. There were twenty draughtsmen in the department, mostly quite young. Jack Broadbent was the chief draughtsman. He was pleasant and hard working, and it was largely due to him that the office ran so well, though his immediate superior, Fox, was the nominal head. Some of the men I got to know quite well, and one day Ewan Fallon, the lad next to me, mentioned that Gordon Jackson, the now well-known actor, had been working at my drawing board only two weeks previously.

One of the older men introduced himself one day. He was of medium height, balding, about forty, and had a Hitler moustache. (Pre-war it was a toothbrush or Charlie Chaplin.) Nothing seemed to ruffle him, and he perpetually sucked on an ancient briar pipe. He introduced me to his wife, Pip, a tall blonde girl who had a job elsewhere in the factory, and soon I was invited to their home in Barrhead for a meal. They rented two rooms in a large mansion standing in two acres of ground, most of which was market garden. There was also a large heated greenhouse in which the owner grew tomatoes. As long-term tenants, one might have expected Ted and Pip to get tomatoes at a slightly reduced rate, but they were charged the full shop price.

Ted had the use, though, of a large part of the garden, and grew all sorts of vegetables. He it was who first introduced me to the use of compost, and on his garden it certainly produced results. He grew tree onions twice the size of any I have seen, and one day brought into the office a huge clump of mushrooms, bigger than his head. They were horse mushrooms, but none the less edible. I did a cartoon of him as a pixie, sitting on the biggest one, smoking his pipe.

119

That first meal with the Lindleys was a huge plate heaped with salad, since they were both vegetarians. I found it delicious and ate the lot, with some difficulty towards the end, I have to admit. I had been so long without fresh vegetables that I was probably starving for vitamins. Ted congratulated me on finishing my salad. It was a joke they played on all their visitors, most of whom admitted defeat half-way through. Quite often thereafter I would visit Barrhead, usually staying overnight. We would converse until the early hours of the morning on every subject under the sun. This was fine at a weekend, but during the week it was an effort to rise early and cycle several miles to work.

Ted seemed to be able to take days off whenever he felt like it, and was never reprimanded. I wondered about the tolerant attitude taken by everyone in the office, until one night he explained. He had been caught in the Coventry blitz, and barely escaped alive. He had had a complete nervous breakdown, and even now had nightmares of being surrounded by fire and exploding bombs, of running for his life along streets of flame with the walls of burning buildings collapsing on top of him. Ever since then he had been unable to sleep within the four walls of a house, and he and Pip had actually lived in a tent, summer and winter, up till only a few weeks before we met. Even now he would feel the building he was in beginning to fall on him, and would have to get out into the open. Once we went to the local cinema to see a film with Betty Grable and Don Ameche. Though he felt worst in a darkened building, he thought he would have another try at controlling his phobia. He stuck it out until half-way through the show, though we heard him fidgetting. His face was white and tense in the light of the screen. At last he got up and without a word, walked out. I thought we should go with him, but Pip said it was best to leave him. He would walk for hours until he had control again.

One night when we had settled down by the fire after our evening meal, Ted said they had something to tell me. He and Pip were *not* married. They were in fact 'living in sin', and they would quite understand if I were to walk out. Some others at the factory had discovered their 'guilty secret', and thereafter ostracised them. Ted's wife had left him, taking their son, after his breakdown. Pip had helped him back to sanity. I pointed out that obviously they didn't know *me* as well as they'd imagined, and that it made no difference whatsoever; I was still glad to have their friendship.

AFTER the war I kept in touch with the Lindleys, and when they had found a place to stay, they invited me to stay for some weeks. They had rented rooms in an isolated farmhouse called 'Ty-Plilip', in Angelsey, near Beaumaris. Now they had a baby son, Michael. At first I slept in a tiny bedroom at the top of the stairs, with a window at floor level, but I soon decided it was too stuffy indoors, and set up my tent at the foot of the garden. The farm was run by an old woman and her brother. They lived in the other part of the farmhouse. When I was introduced to them that first night, they seemed quite perturbed at the idea of my sleeping in the little bedroom, and I had the impression they didn't really want another stranger in the house. But when I put up my tent, they seemed even more agitated, and did their best to persuade me to stay *in* the house.

Now Ted explained that the farmhouse was haunted by the ghost of a deceased younger brother, who had hanged himself in the adjoining barn. This barn was used to store antique furniture, a money-earning ploy which they found more profitable than farming. They encountered the ghost all round the farm at any time of the day or night. One popular spot was the bedroom, which had been his. A favourite walk was along the foot of the garden — where I'd put my tent.

One day, Pip was in bed with a really bad attack of 'flu, and Ted had just gone off to work when a man came through the open door, wandered slowly across the room, then back again and out without saying a word. Pip, doped to the eyes with aspirin and only half awake, assumed this was some farmhand she had not met, and muzzily thought he had a nerve walking openly into their bedroom.

When Ted arrived home that evening she told him about the incident, and he immediately went to complain to the farmers. They asked what the man looked like. Pip described him, shortish, sandy hair and moustache, riding breeches and boots, check jacket. 'That's our brother!' they said. They had not mentioned the ghost in case their prospective tenants would be scared off, and were relieved to find that a ghost would have been an added incentive to stay here. Ted never saw the ghost, but Pip saw him several times afterwards. She never felt scared. He gave the impression of a sad, harmless little man with a lost air about him, certainly not someone to be frightened of. I was delighted. It seemed I now had a good chance of meeting a real ghost. Ted had not mentioned him previously so that if I *did* see

121

him, we could not say it was because I knew about him. But not once in all the weeks I stayed was there even the faintest hint of an apparition. In the pitchy darkness of my tent, I never felt even a slight prickling of the scalp.

For many years I have been interested in the possibility of extrasensory perception, though I have never personally experienced anything of that description. When I was a teacher I occasionally tested a class to see if it was possible to make telepathic contact, a phenomenon which I suspect has already been noted by others. With classes aged twelve and over, the results were no better than average, but with younger children, they were well above the predicted scores. First I tried the five Zener signs, and got what appeared to be significant results. Then I went beyond this. I made a series of twenty simple drawings, and asked the class to concentrate on each one as I tried to broadcast it. Ten out of thirty produced near approximations of a few of the drawings, but one was a direct hit — a pair of spectacles drawn in the same perspective as mine. The odds against this must be phenomenal. With practice, I am sure the scores would have improved, but I only had the younger children at long intervals, when some teacher was off sick.

Twice I have experienced the classic nightmare, as opposed to the simple frightening dream, and on neither occasion could I blame an indiscreet meal at a late hour. For those who have not experienced this, it is difficult to convey its horror. In both cases, I became aware, through my sleep, of a huge black (I intuitively knew it was black) shapeless Thing from six inches to one foot thick, which stealthily lowered itself on to my back. I am unable to sleep face upward, which is supposed to be the position most likely to engender a bad dream. The entity was large enough to cover the bed, like an over-sized duvet. Gradually I felt its weight increase until I could hardly breathe, and I was quite unable to move hand or foot, though I tried hard. By now I was trying desperately to wake up. A feeling of hair-prickling, intolerable menace and unutterable *evil* emanated from the Thing. It was definitely malevolent, I found I was literally suffocating, all the air pressed out of my lungs, and unable to draw a breath because of the dead weight above me.

At this point I made a last desperate effort, bouncing a foot off the mattress with a yell as I pushed the Thing away, and gasping for air. It seemed to recoil and I sensed it drifting upwards and dissipating. This was not the usual simple nightmare when you know you are dreaming, here you know you are asleep, but know with a dreadful certainty that it is a real Thing.

My friend Margaret Balfour has spent many years in the Middle and Far East, and when I mentioned this Black Horror, remarked that many Orientals would have recognised it. It is widely known as an evil spirit which waits until the soul is detached from the body in sleep, then attempts to take over the body for its own ends. While I was familiar with the idea of out-of-the-body experiences, this was the first time I had heard of this particular Thing. The Shamans of Siberia, North American Indians and others who communicate with the spirit world take stringent precautions to safeguard their bodies from these evil entities while they undertake astral projection.

When I was six or seven I had a nightmare I can still describe in every detail, because it was repeated many times on into my early teens. I was in a subterranean gallery, maybe a mine, quite brightly lit but without any visible source. This long straight corridor, about seven feet square, stretched on and on into the distance. Far away the light seemed brighter. I walked along, noticing with increasing terror that the stone walls were closing in on me, all in utter silence. Horrified, I felt them clamp me so that I was unable to move, then squeezing and squeezing in on me until I was enclosed in solid rock, squashed and compressed into a vertical needle shape. It didn't hurt, and oddly enough there was still light, and now there was sound also. The needle — me — was spinning on its axis at infinite speed, and the sound was like the singing in your ears in an utterly silent place. This part always continued for what seemed like eternity, and the terrible climax came when a vast, echoing voice filled the universe, calling in measured and awe-inspiring tones, 'GEORGE! — LAWRIE! — THOMSON!' It was, of course, the voice of God. Fright then took over and I would be allowed to wake up at last. This dream was all the more terrifying in that every time I found myself trapped in that horrible corridor, I knew in every detail what was going to happen to me, like a film seen a dozen times. And though I knew it was only a dream, I was helplessly unable to wake up until the very end.

Researches into the experience of death, as recounted by people who have 'died' and then been resuscitated, seem to agree on something similar to that dream, with a long tunnel showing light at the far end. But the 'dying' persons agree that there is a pervading sense of warmth, peace and happiness, not the helpless terror which I experienced. It is remarkable that after scores of repeats, when I knew the script backwards and knew I'd wake up none the worse at the end, still the edge of terror was never blunted.

Some early experiences might be classed as revelations. We were at camp at Pettycur, and I was about twelve. It was mid-morning, a wonderful summer day after a day of rain which had washed all dust out of the air, so that the sky was the deepest blue I had ever seen. Normally, no matter how bright the sun may be in Scotland, there is

123

always a softening effect due to suspended moisture, and of course, in the city unfiltered sunlight was unknown. This blue was the purest, cleanest air, up and up for miles, and the sun had cleared any last suspicion of haze. It was as if a pair of fogged spectacles had been wiped clean. I lay on my back on the warm turf, and in this fantastic light everything seemed fresh, bright and new.

As I gazed straight up into this blue beyond blue, I felt my consciousness expand from merely the bay of bright sand to the awareness of the crawling sea and the hills beyond it to the south. I knew the spidery railroad tracks and the roads spreading across the land, the cultivated fields and the wild places waiting. I felt life, the people I could hear, those further away in the local towns, and on the fringe of my own little perception, the thousands in Edinburgh and along the coasts and rivers. Then suddenly, I felt the curve of the earth; I felt its weight under my back, countless millions of tons; I felt its *round*ness, with its skin of life; I became aware of the sun as a star, off to one side, lighting up this side of the planet, with shadow on the night side. I understood the vastness of the earth, its teeming surface life, I felt it spin on its axis. But at the same time, I was aware of how very small the world was in relation to the sun, and how small even the sun was among the hosts of other stars. I felt bigger than the universe, and yet infinitesimally tiny. I found myself looking *down* into space, out beyond the atmosphere, and I wondered why gravity could hold me pinned to the ground, when by all the rules I should have been spun off the surface of this solid revolving sphere.

This state of super-awareness, a feeling of being intensely alive, lasted for perhaps half an hour. This, I imagine, is the 'high' which some people have to take drugs to achieve, or the state of religious ecstasy sought by the adept.

From time to time I still attain this threshold of perception, sometimes without trying, sometimes voluntarily. Perhaps my training as an artist bestows an advantage. An artist must observe his subject with the utmost intensity — a place, a person, a situation, an idea. Each has to be *seen*, felt, experienced, known to the last possible atom. The observer becomes the observed. You have heard the term, 'seeing the light'. This is perhaps as close as one can get to a description of the process. In 'high' conversation with friends early one morning, we agreed it was like seeing everything in a brilliant white light; nothing seemed impossible. In this state of hyper-vision, your mountain, tree, flower or grain of sand seems to be illuminated both outside and inside.

One such ecstatic vision remains with me from my early twenties. From the inside of our holiday hut one summer day, I could see through the doorway to the open end of a green tent about thirty

124

feet away. A young girl of about fourteen had just come up from a swim, and just inside the tent her mother took off her swimsuit and went to the back for a towel, leaving the girl facing outwards and unaware of observers. It was only a matter of seconds, but during that space of time I had a flashing revelation of absolute beauty so intense it was almost pain. That vision was Ishtar, Venus, Helen — the ultimate distillation of femininity, achingly beautiful. Light glowed around and from inside her. She was eternal grace and light and love.

This effect had been quite unpredictable to me. During my college years, I had made hundreds of drawings from the nude, trying to see truly, striving for the boundaries of the senses where a work of genius becomes possible. But all these hours of steady work seemed grey, drab and profitless compared with that one burst of glory. Had I captured that ineffable vision on canvas, it would have outshone Botticelli's 'Venus' and Goya's 'Maja', and any other work of the old masters. There is an odd thing; I have never experienced the same elevation of spirit from the contemplation of any human construction, whether painting, sculpture, architecture or music. But I recognise that in every true work of art, the originator has at least started with something like this flash of incandescent revelation.

With practice, I believe anyone could increase the number of these 'high spots'. Merely knowing they can be experienced tends to improve the quality of living. In a very small way, I tried to communicate this faculty of 'seeing' during my teaching career.

Once I camped overnight in the ruined village of Rieff, on the coast north of Ullapool. It was midsummer, and I spent a wakeful night in my little tent. The sun shone all night, and never set. Every hour or so I would look out and see that it had traversed another arc of its circle, but at its lowest it was still several diameters above the horizon. I had never actually seen this happen, and though I knew the Orkney and Shetland Isles were in the latitude of the midnight sun, I never heard of the phenomenon being observable quite a long way down the Scottish mainland.

Again I had an immediate sensation of the turning world. In choosing to camp in the village, rather than the more isolated spots around, I again had it in mind that I might encounter a local ghost clinging to the tumbled remains of what at one time must have been a very pleasant place to live in, surrounded by beautiful scenery; the sort of place anyone would enjoy re-visiting from the world beyond. But here, too, there was no hint of the supernatural.

Many youth hostels were very ancient buildings, from castles to cottages, and quite a number were reputed to be haunted. I never met a hosteller who had actually seen one, but some claimed to know

125

someone else who had. Some people I know are very sensitive to atmosphere. Probably most of us have had the experience of walking into a house and feeling immediately that this was not the sort of place we would choose to live in, or alternatively that it was a happy place and would welcome new tenants. My cottage is well over 150 years old, and must have had many previous owners, but so far none has attempted to communicate.

These experiences strengthen my convictions that the human mind has dimensions we are only just begining to explore, and capabilities far beyond anything imaginable by most of us today. I understand that recent researches prove that we only actually use a very small percentage of our brains. This is borne out by studies on a child who was born with a minimum of brain tissue, which was distributed like a shell up to one-inch thick round the inside of the skull. A light shone through one ear could be seen clearly through the other, the hollow space between filled with fluid. All previous experience would indicate this child would soon die, or grow up a vegetable. But the boy grew up normally, and at the time of the TV interview, had taken nine O-levels, and was looking forward to university. The hollow space inside the brain had grown fibrous tissue, thus stabilising the skull interior. Still, around 50 per cent of a normal brain was missing, including areas that were thought to be critical to normal development. This was not an isolated case. Several other children had similar deficiencies, missing parts from a normal brain, but again finding no difficulty in living a perfectly ordinary life.

Unless the recently postulated 'worm-holes' in a convoluted and folded universe turn out to be real, space travel beyond the solar system would seem to be impossible. Physical travel, that is. But what if we learn to use the full potential of our brains? Thought is instantaneous. We may be able to travel with our minds only. Think again: light travels 186,000 miles per second. But we tend to think in miles per hour, and when you work it out, light travels around 72,000,000 miles per hour. When you consider that the *nearest* star is four and a half light-*years* away (a light-year is the distance travelled by light in one year), that is an awful long way! And we talk about astronauts (those who navigate among the stars) or cosmonauts (those who navigate among the galaxies), when really we are tied to this planet, or optimistically, this solar system.

THOUGH paper was still stringently rationed, and advertising at a minimum, on my release from war work I started a studio in Thistle Street, Edinburgh, paying a rent of £1 a week. Perhaps if people knew I was available I might get work as business slowly returned to normal. I struggled on for a year, and at the end I had earned only just enough to pay the rent. The landlord, Butterworth, then offered to waive the rent if I produced a poster for him every week, depicting various scenic views of Scotland. This generous offer I had to decline. each poster would have called for a good deal of time and research, and £1 for so much work was very stingy even then. I closed shop.

One day in the street I met an old schoolmate, McWilliam, who, not long out of the services, was trying to run a small art shop with his brother and a friend. I was not at all keen, but he persuaded me to go into partnership with him as a co-director. I pointed out that with *four* people to pay, profits would have to be at least £20 per week. No problem; they already had a china-painting commission worth £60, and with my expertise could accept even more. For the first few weeks, we did indeed take £20, but then orders started to fall off. The first consignments of coloured china, not the plain white of wartime, began to re-appear in the shops.

Hoping to pull in more clients, we applied to the Board of Trade for a permit. This was refused, and it was pointed out that it was illegal to continue without one. Further desperate appeals were also refused, and since takings outside the china-painting were only a few shillings, the three ex-servicemen were understandably bitter. If we had said nothing and carried on without revealing ourselves to the authorities, we would at least have had enough to eat. It seemed that honesty was to be penalised.

We thought perhaps handwritten letters were beneath the notice of the officials we wrote to, but no way could we afford a typewriter. I was not told of the plan they devised until it was a *fait accompli*. Two of the partners spruced up their old R.A.F. uniforms, and drove out one night in our ancient banger to a camp near Edinburgh, choosing the right moment, they marched past the guard at the gate, snappily saluting everyone in sight, made their way to the nearest office and lifted the Remington. Their cover story was that they were taking it for repair, but amazingly no one prevented them walking openly out of the gate. I was unhappy about having stolen property in the shop, but as our dialogue with the Board of Trade progressed, I increasingly felt they were quite justified. No one was going to give us a chance, and it did not pay to tell the truth. Had we known about the vast sums going to the Nazis — !

For several more weeks we worked without pay, hoping the B.O.T. would relent. The other three were married with young families, and they started coming in with stories about their children crying with hunger. For the last five or six weeks I dug into my meagre savings to give them some relief, and hoping it might be possible to save the business. I had disbursed £50 or more when I realised I would be broke in a very short time, so I asked for my partnership to be dissolved. I was told I was a rat deserting a sinking ship, which I felt was rather unfair, as it would have sunk weeks before without my help. I could also have said that I had no savings anyway. There was no chance of my ever being repaid, but I was offered some of the shop stock instead. I accepted about £25 worth of paints — retail value — but this seriously depleted the goods for sale in the shop, and was, I suppose understandably, looked upon as a last stab in the back.

After this experience, I was quite determined never to go into partnership with anyone again, and vowed never to lend any of my hard-earned cash to anyone, no matter how heart-breaking the circumstances. The latter resolution has been broken several times since, and in some cases the persons helped reacted the same way. Few hard-luck stories have any effect on me now.

My total savings were now down to £70, plus a 'post-war credit', worth only a small fraction of its original value when it was refunded a few years ago. Post-war credits were receipts for money compulsorily deducted from the pay packet to help pay for the war. Naively, most of us expected to be repaid within four or five years, not, as it turned out only when we qualified for the old age pension. I struggled on with one or two small commissions, for freelance artists were at the mercy of the buyers. One book cover I designed for McDougall's Educational Co. was still in use when I retired from teaching. It was for a series called 'Ring up the Curtain', and I was paid two guineas for it, including a half-dozen preliminary designs.

Another commission came from the philanthropic Tom Curr. He asked me to do a series of drawings for a book on the Royal Mile. I had most of them finished when he informed me that the promised two guineas each would be paid only for the first four; the rest would be sixteen shillings. The *Radio Times* had for a time sent me commissions after I returned to Edinburgh, but usually dealing by post ruled out any work wanted the same week, and this source of income dried up.

128

My brother was now married. My two sisters were both working, and quite prepared to support me until my luck turned, and my mother wanted me to stay at home until I was happily married — her dearest wish. But I was now thirty. I could stay home no longer and still retain any self-respect. I resolved to take my bike and tent and spend some months looking for a croft, or even a cottage with a bit of garden, which would not cost more than my dwindling savings. The West of Scotland seemed the most likely area, but I searched from north to south without success. I continued south to visit the Lindleys in Anglesey. I financed my journey to some extent by helping in hostels, giving an occasional painting lesson or selling a small 'pot-boiler'.

For free food and sleeping accommodation, I worked for some time as an assistant warden at Patterdale Youth Hostel in the Lake District. One weekend I had three days off and decided to climb the nearest mountain, Helvellyn. The wardens, Fred and Gladys Frost, insisted I borrow a pair of climbing boots. I walked up the valley towards the foot of the mountain, loaded down with a rucksack containing tent, food and stove. Cuckoos called from the woods and the sun was warm, but ahead the sky was dark and lowering.

When I reached the foot, I was surprised to see there was no path, but it was obvious there was only one direction to go — up. The way became steeper and steeper, until it was like the side of a roof, and I had to use both hands to pull myself up. I never imagined grass could grow on such a steeply angled slope. Here I was glad of the nailed boots. My shoes would have had no grip at all. All this time I had not encountered a soul, but as the slope eased near the top I heard accordions playing, and saw a crowd of about a hundred holiday-makers milling around. I paused to look across at Striding Edge, the alternative route I had been urged to try, but rejected when they mentioned a rocky stretch which had to be negotiated. It was as well I had. Striding Edge was a knife-edged ridge of rock with drops of hundreds of feet on each side, and a steeply rough pitch to climb at the worst part, which I doubt whether I had the arm span to cover safely, even if I didn't get an attack of vertigo.

A black cloud had now covered most of the sky except for a small patch of blue to my rear, and a few large drops of rain started to fall. The crowd began to disperse rapidly, but I continued straight on. There was no path, but I aimed for the course of a little stream marked on my map, to follow it down to a valley and eventually a road. The rain fell in sheets. Going downhill, a blister on my toe became so painful I took off the ill-fitting boots and continued barefoot until I found a small level spot for my tent. Next day walking was torture until I found a tuft of lamb's wool caught on a twig. This I

129

wrapped round my bleeding toe and found I could walk again in comparative comfort.

Another day I went sketching on the east bank of Ullswater. About a third of the way along the lake, I saw a sheep not far above the footpath, running agitatedly here and there and making enough noise for a whole flock. I could see something was wrong and climbed up to investigate. From a wide cave mouth I heard a lamb calling. Obviously it had fallen in and couldn't find its way out. The cave 'floor' sloped sharply down, more like the entrance to a pot-hole. About thirty feet down was a slanting floor, on which the lamb lay. In spite of my fear of caves, I had to make some attempt to rescue the little beast. I climbed down and approached it with the expectation that it would shoot up the rocks like a mountain goat, but it just lay there. I examined it, and though there seemed to be no broken bones, its hindquarters were paralysed. Most likely a broken back. If this were the case there was nothing anyone could do, but I could hardly just leave it there. Somehow I got the lamb up on my shoulders. It was wet and heavy, being half-grown. It was not easy climbing back up with the unwieldy burden, a foolhardy thing to do. I could quite easily have ended up at the bottom with the lamb, and no one knew exactly where I had gone. Regaining the surface with some relief, I remembered seeing a cottage about a mile back. This turned out to be a shepherd's cottage, and I left the lamb with his wife. The ewe followed me all the way back, never coming too close, and carrying on a loud conversation with her lamb.

OVER the years we had got to know the Cunninghams of Grangehill Farm quite well, through calling at the farm for milk. When I mentioned I had been travelling, looking for a piece of ground I could live on, they suggested I could try to cultivate a piece of the Back Bents, if I could make anything of it, without charge. This was a 13-acre field too steep and rocky to plough, dangerous for stock after shale mining and sand pit operations, so they never used it. Most of it lay at a very steep angle, covered with bracken, weeds and coarse grasses. There were some bushes, and a few trees at the lowest point. Looking back, I think Mr Cunningham had not intended that I should actually *live* on the ground, but that was how I had interpreted the offer. In the light of subsequent events, if I had attempted to grow crops there while living elsewhere, I would most certainly never have harvested anything at all.

My plan was to buy a cheap hut and live in the country, trying to keep alive by growing my own food, or most of it. It seemed clear enough by now that I could never earn enough from art alone, and I was thoroughly disillusioned by society and wanted no more of it. There were several books around by people who similarly had 'got away from it all' and escaped back to the land, like Fraser Darling's *Island Farm*, though in the following years many of the escapees gave up and returned to the cities. My experience is that subsistence on the land is very difficult for one person. With two or more it could be rewarding, provided the participants remain fit.

The next problem was finding a hut at a reasonable price. Few if any new huts were being made for sale. A Polish friend living at Pettycur told me he had got a cheap ex-army hut at Leuchars. They had housed war prisoners. I had a look at the site. The smallest hut was 16 × 22 feet, and the price was £45. He and some husky ex-soldier Poles helped dismantle it and load it on a lorry. I gave them ten shillings for a drink, far too little, but it was all they would accept. I was grateful. Every penny had to count now. Some people had few complimentary words for the Poles who stayed after the war, but I remember their willing help when our own people and institutions seemed bent on destroying us. Orwell's *1984* seemed to be a distinct possbility.

The lorry driver was supposed to deliver the hut to my site, but when we reached Kirkcaldy it was too late and he refused to work overtime. Next day I guided him to my chosen spot. He complained about the condition of the track leading from the main road, with I suppose, some justification. But it was not too bad. The track had last been used some sixteen years previously, when the sandpit had been abandoned, but I had cut down some bushes and young trees which had grown in the centre, and scythed a clear way in through the tall grass. The short last section was uphill and impassable for the lorry, so all the hut sections were dumped on the level about sixty yards short of the site.

John Cunningham, his father, my brother and some friends all rallied round to help erect the hut some weeks later. The intervening time I spent partly levelling the site, which was a less-steep part of the slope where sand had been dug long ago. It would have been impossible to level the whole site singlehanded in the time available, so I stripped the sods from the ground and used them to build turf piers to support the main bearing beams. At the lower side they were three feet high, and the rear was at ground level. I guessed at how much weight they would have to bear, how far they would settle under pressure, and how much further as they dried out, so as to leave me eventually with a level floor. Fifteen years later they still stood, though I replaced the front ones with stone as I dug enough rocks out of the ground. John had brought his pony to help drag the heavier sections up the hill, and in an unexpectedly boggy patch it sank up to the hocks, but at last all the pieces were assembled. I had scythed down the bracken to give clear access. My helpers thought I should have put the hut down on the level track, which would have been much easier, but I had to live there, and I wanted a view. It was worth the extra trouble.

For heating and cooking I had the original cylindrical iron stove which came with the hut, and my primus stove. For lighting I had a storm lamp or candles. Water I got from a pipe which I stuck in a field drain about 300 yards away, about half-way back to the road. I already owned an adequate collection of gardening tools. It was quiet and peaceful, and I slept well, though at first I went to bed as it got dark. Reading by candlelight was not easy. I had an old three-valve radio, but it tended to fade out in the middle of a good programme as the batteries died.

After I had paid for the hut and transport and bought a few essentials, I had only £5 left. I could not claim the £1 unemployment benefit, because after thirteen weeks of unemployment it was discontinued. Poor Relief was granted the utterly destitute — if they could prove they were, but I was prepared to starve first. Now and again I managed to sell a few of my matchbox-sized miniature paintings of local scenes. These were hand-coloured prints in little plaster frames, selling at two and sixpence each. Nineteen different processes were needed, so it was hardly easy money. My biggest order was twelve, but I managed to scrape along without actually starving.

It was very hard work clearing a garden plot. Bracken grew four to five feet high everywhere, which indicated at least that the soil was well drained. I scythed down a clear strip, then dug it two-feet deep to remove the black, tangled cables of bracken roots, the growth of many years. My intention was to have a patch 10×30 yards ready for planting. Some romancer in a gardening magazine had claimed that bracken would die out if cut three or four times a year, so half-way through I decided just to scythe down the undug remainder, planting cabbages in the weedless duff under the ferns. I cut that bracken eight times in the first few weeks, and lost count after that. That winter I had to dig out the roots anyway. They were still quite robust and ready to shoot up the following spring.

In late August there was a tremendous gale which blew all day and night. Just after it started, I felt the hut being badly shaken, and the end wall with the door was visibly flapping in and out. The only wood I had was a two-inch thick driftwood plank, not enough for

132

four stays. It had to be cut into four lengths, and all I had was an elderly handsaw. This was hard work, and I sawed as fast as I could, momentarily expecting the hut to disintegrate in the howling blast. One heavy gust blew the wall in twelve inches, and I was sure this was the end. As I got each length cut, I nailed it across a corner at the height of the eaves, and when I had the four fixed, it stiffened the fabric considerably. I now worried that the roof would blow off, and went round wiring it to the top of the walls. But in spite of the terrible battering the hut stayed firmly on its foundations.

This experience convinced me that I must have shelter, and in October I transplanted some sycamore saplings from the foot of the hill, and took dozens of cuttings from a solitary sallow willow, putting them in what I hoped would be strategic positions all round the hut, but mainly on the south and west. By the time there was another gale of comparable violence, all the trees had grown tall enough to justify my trouble.

There were one or two small hawthorn bushes near the hut. In the *Countryman*, I found an article which said that in the 16th century it was common practice to graft apples on hawthorn stock. I begged a few cuttings from the farmer and grafted about six bushes. Six of the cuttings took, though not strongly; which was the reason for using hawthorn, as it acted as a dwarfing stock. They all died the following year except one which grew away beautifully, until it was blown off by a gale a year later. The article had not mentioned that the point of graft always remains weak, as I had noticed on the failures, which were more or less detached from the parent branch. Anyone trying this out should stake the trees very securely above and below the graft. Certainly a waste piece of ground covered by hawthorns could be converted to an orchard for no more than the cost of labour. But maintenance includes constant rubbing out of buds below the graft; hawthorn does not give up easily.

THE theory that you can live off what you grow by the sweat of your brow does not work in practice. Not near Burntisland. The soil was very sandy, comparatively easy to work, and with plenty of compost would grow almost anything. Everything I planted flourished. But rabbits burrowed under my wire netting fences, sheep or cattle from neighbouring fields stampeded through them, eating everything; stoats, rats and foxes decimated my ducks, geese or hens; crows stole eggs, ducklings and goslings. My potatoes, fruit and rhubarb were stolen by friendly locals as soon as they were ready; sometimes just pulled up and scattered. Once I let a goose sit on a nest only a few yards from the hut. I never knew her eggs had all been stolen until one night a fox killed her, burying the remains up the hill. No *animal* had taken the eggs, or there would have been signs of some sort. Had my garden been surrounded by a high electrified fence with guard dogs, no doubt I could have lived off the land.

A story must have gone around that I was an eccentric millionaire posing as a pauper. During the years I lived there, my hut was broken into no fewer than six times. There was never any money to be found, but the intruders always caused damage which cost money to repair. The police usually recovered my few paltry belongings, usually the worse for wear; no doubt the thief found them unsaleable. After the fifth burglary, I set a trap. I put six halfpennies in a piggy bank so the rattle would suggest a hoard of gold sovereigns, and added a dusting of gentian violet powder. I also left a purse conspicuously hidden in a drawer, stuffed with genuine pound notes drawn and painted by myself and generously sprinkled with more dye powder. The police found the sixth thief, a local from Kinghorn. He denied everything, but they found my old radio in his bedroom, and they found violet stains under his fingernails, 'It's almost impossible to get the dye off', said the detective, 'he must have scrubbed his hands raw all night to get them as clean as he did!' That I believe; for months thereafter I found violet specks on everything.

Apart from these tribulations, I was happier than ever before, living in close touch with the earth and the seasons. It seemed more 'right' than city living. And I was proving to myself that I could survive on my own, in spite of surely extraordinary circumstances, for there must be places where there are fewer thieves, and where natural predators can be controlled. The silence of the sandy, bracken-covered hillside was broken only by the occasional distant baaing of sheep, or the voice of a golfer on the fairway just over the wall. Sometimes I felt the language was quite unjustifiable, but full understanding came to me later when I took up the game myself. Would anyone but a golfer appreciate the proprietary name printed on some balls I got in America once — 'Oh Shit!' Anyway, the course was only busy at weekends; on weekdays all was peace.

My intention had been to continue painting and sketching, and occupying any spare time with various crafts, but I had no spare time or energy left at the end of the day. If it was too wet to work outside, I had a lot of tidying to do inside. I read at night. I gave up newspapers, which cost more than I could afford, and rarely had anything cheerful to record. I stopped buying them, and to this day I have never felt the loss.

The city dweller never sees the sky at night, and even during the day it is only a chopped-up geometrical indication of the weather in the immediate locality. Out here I could look from the distant lights of Edinburgh up into infinity; the Milky Way, thousands of stars north, south, east and west, and the moon with all space to sail across, not just the short interval between two chimney stacks. One freezing winter night I spent an hour standing watching in awe while the Aurora Borealis — the Heavenly Dancers — pulsed second by second from the horizon all around, to vanish into a black hole directly overhead. I had never seen anything like this formation, nor heard it described.

Several nights after Russia's first Sputnik was put into orbit, I went out to try to spot it. The news on the radio said this was possible. But there was no sign of it, and though they say there are thousands up there now, I still have not seen one. I was closely watching the area where it was to appear when my attention was drawn to a bright yellowish light which I assumed must be some sort of aircraft. It was travelling westerly from Edinburgh towards the Forth Bridge, just where a plane should be, over the airport, I estimated its height at about 1,000 feet. For about nine seconds it flew in a straight and steady path at the same altitude, then suddenly it expanded into a fireball about 400 or 500 feet across, then almost as rapidly faded into blackness. I waited horrified for the sound of the explosion. It was a still, clear night, and I counted the seconds to get an exact estimation of the distance. No sound came at all. I expected to hear next day about some large passenger plane disaster at the airport, but there was nothing on the radio, and none of my friends had heard of any accident. If anyone else observed the phenomenon, they didn't publicise the fact. In retrospect, I realise now that a plane's navigating lights at that distance, seven or eight miles, would hardly be bright enough to match what I saw. If it *had* been a blazing aircraft, then I should certainly have heard the explosion. There was no wind to carry the sound either towards or away from me. I have always hoped to see a genuine U.F.O. for myself, but if this really *was* one, then my evidence is as inconclusive as all the rest.

The summer of 1947 was a good one, and by its end I was fit, but always hungry. About this time I found I had no food left, only a quarter of a packet of tea. I could have taken a turnip or two from the next field, but felt it would be stealing. Had I thought to ask, the farmer would have given me a barrowload, and probably some food

135

too. But I hated the idea of begging for charity from anyone, including Poor Relief. Instead of using my last sixpence for oatmeal, which would have kept me going another week or two, I bought a twopence-halfpenny stamp and swallowing my pride wrote to my brother Charlie, asking if he could possibly let me have a few pounds to tide me over what I hoped would be a temporary phase. After a few days, he wrote to say he was sorry, but he had a young family to feed, and several other commitments.

In desperation, I bought another stamp and wrote to the Artist's Benevolent Association, explaining that I was very hungry, and would they please reply quickly. They did. Their 'benevolent reply' came by return post. They were sorry, but they could not see their way to helping me just then. As it turned out, I only starved for one week. (After four days or so, the craving for food eases off, and I imagine it would be fairly easy to starve to death.) Three of my miniatures sold at the end of the week, and I was saved. But I never again begged anyone for help.

The winter of 1947 was an exceptionally hard one, with six-foot drifts and hard frosts. One night I had my iron stove stoked up and glowing red, and decided it was time I had a bath. With my tin tub as close to the stove as I could get it, my back was comfortably warm, though my front was freezing. I finished, stood up, and bent down for the towel, forgetting how close to the stove I was. There was a sizzle, and I straightened up faster than I ever had before, branded for life. But having survived this unusually hard winter, I felt I could cope with any future bad weather. In the spring, breaking a new patch of ground beside the wall round the golf course, I became acquainted with Tim Low, head greenkeeper and steward of the Burntisland Golf Club, and his sons, who were his assistants. They were surprised to discover that I was a Scot. They had assumed I was Polish. Many expatriate Poles had found themselves plots of land and worked hard to establish themselves, and many of them with peasant backgrounds succeeded.

Hearing that I was finding it difficult to make ends meet, Tim offered me a job as assistant greenkeeper at £4 a week. By then I could see that I needed security guards to protect my holding, and I accepted gratefully. Each morning I would sweep the greens at my end of the course, then there were bunkers to weed and rake. I was given a hand mower for the teeing grounds. It was hard work, but on the whole pleasant, and the Lows were a friendly lot. Soon Mrs Low invited me to have tea with the family and each Saturday and sometimes oftener I would cycle along to the clubhouse for a meal and conversation or a game of rummy. Though before long I had to give up the job owing to arthritis, I remained friendly with the Lows, and I was allowed to have a proper bath there instead of using the old tin tub, with its drawbacks.

During the course of this job, I was converted to golf. Up till then, I had looked upon the game as an entirely fruitless occupation. As some would say, a good country walk spoiled. It seemed unncessarily difficult too; such a small ball to be hit so far with so small-headed a club into such an exasperatingly small hole. One summer evening after work, George and Sandy Low talked me into swinging an eight iron at a ball. The first try skittered along the ground. 'Told you so!' I said. But they got me to try again, correcting some of my faults. The next ball soared white and beautiful into the blue sky, exactly on line, and landed precisely where it had been aimed. From then on I was hooked. Even a rabbit occasionally makes a perfect stroke, and it is one of the most gratifying sensations I know. A great advantage of the game is that you can play alone against par, or your own previous best. It is one of the few games where an amateur can play against a pro on an equal footing, thanks to the handicap system. Possibly a companionable foursome is one of the most pleasant ways of combining exercise and enjoyment.

It was after I had given up this job and was again dependent on the sale of the occasional miniature that Mr Cunningham told me he had heard from a friend of mine. In his butcher's shop in Dysart, he kept one or two of my paintings on the counter. This artist had come into the shop for some water for his sketching, and asked who had done the miniature. When told, he wondered whether it could be the same person who had been at college with him before the war; if so, would I call on Tom Gourdie some day. He was a teacher at Kirkcaldy High School. The following week I called in just as he was dismissing a class at the end of the afternoon. I did not recognise him at first. I remembered Tom as a young student with a healthy crop of hair on top, and here I was confronted with an 'old' man with a bald head. But it was the same Tom. He took me home to meet his wife Lilias and their young family, and we brought each other up to date on our doings since 1938.

When he heard I had struck a sticky patch, he advised me to try teaching. 'Go and see the Director of Education,' he said, 'I'm sure he'll give you a job!' But teaching, I felt, was still out of the question. The thought of facing a class of forty urchins alone gave me cold shudders. I could imagine them jeering at me; and how could I possibly keep them occupied for an hour and a half? No thank you! '— and you'd get £6 a week as an uncertificated teacher!' said Tom. This was wealth untold. £6 would keep me for six weeks; surely I could just stand and endure for a week, then get out thankfully, even if slightly the worse for wear.

I made an appointment to see Grassie, the Assistant Director of Education, and turned up carrying a portfolio of my best work. After a short chat, he told me to start work at the High School the following Monday. 'But,' I protested, 'you haven't even looked at my work! How can you tell whether I *am* an artist or not?' He said he knew nothing at all about art, but things would sort themselves out when I actually got started at the school.

Next Monday morning I was in the staff room bright and early and full of trepidation. The head of the art department was George Bain (author later of a splendid book on Celtic decoration), and he was delighted to have me there. They were a teacher short; he would have welcomed anybody. He passed me on to Andrew Thorburn, a leading figure in the Fife gliding fraternity, who was to explain what I had to do. Said Andrew, 'There's your room; there's paper and paint in the cupboard along the corridor, I'm in this room if you want anything else; there's your class; I've got a class waiting for me; good luck!' Andrew had been at College the year after Tom and I.

My first class was sixteen 15-year-old girls from the less academically inclined of the school population. I tried to look as if I had been a teacher for years. Fortunately they had some uncompleted work left over from the previous week, and the monitor, Betty, was very helpful in organising papers, water, and paints and brushes, besides keeping me informed about bells, milk, dinner money, register slips, and so on. The behaviour of succeeding classes was equally good, and to my surprise and relief there was no problem with discipline. By the end of that first week, I had some inkling of what teaching was all about, and was kicking myself for not having the courage to join the profession before the war. With my present perspective, I know it was a good thing I had knocked around a bit outside the academic life, and learned something about the world outside. Too many teachers I have met went straight from school, to university, to training college and back to school, never leaving the atmosphere of the greenhouse. If every prospective teacher were required to spend at least a year in unrelated work, it could do nothing but good.

The job was temporary; I was only filling in until a woman teacher turned up, when I would be replaced. But I found the work so satisfying that I applied for more teaching appointments. It appeared there was always room for a peripatetic art teacher. This meant a great deal of bus travel which I disliked; up to fifteen miles in either direction, from Rosyth in the west to Denbeath in the east. I taught in both primary and secondary schools. Some of the primaries, though enjoyable, were hectic, as at Burntisland, where I had to do the impossible, three art lessons in one hour. It was only done by the

138

teachers having everything ready when I entered the room. Some of the classes actually cheered at my arrival.

In the secondary schools, I had the occasional difficult class, but there I had the advantage of having my own art room and equipment, instead of having to trek from room to room. To my great surprise I found I could control a large class simply by standing and looking at it — not even fiercely. Eventually though I did acquire a leather tawse from the traditional makers, Dickson of Lochgelly. It was only on the rarest occasions I ever had to use it; it was enough for the prospective trouble-maker to know it was there.

My mother was delighted that I now had a steady job, and in, as she believed, a highly respected profession. She never knew that at the beginning of the war I had taken steps to avoid going into teaching. She had spotted an ad in the papers asking for unqualified teachers, and got me to write to the authorities. In my letter I said, 'Please write and say you are unable to employ me. I never intended to teach, and could never face large classes. Only my mother has the confidence I can do the job!' They kindly replied that they were unable to use my services, much to my relief.

From then on I kept in touch with the Gourdies, and regularly visited for 'Scrabble', which we have played now for nearly forty years. Tom had started his campaign for better writing in schools, and made the point that as calligraphers we should be setting an example by habitually using italic writing ourselves. This made good sense to me. I had been using an italic-influenced hand up to now, but now I switched to pure italic. At that period most people had the impression that good handwriting was somehow reprehensible, and italic was 'precious', if not effete. It has taken more than thirty years, but at last the pendulum had started to swing the other way. I hope Tom and I have had some small part in influencing the movement.

Paper and art materials were still in short supply, and in some primary schools all they had was crayons and drawing books. One of my solutions was to get the children to bring in newspaper, wire and string and so on from which we could make various constructions from papier-maché to large sheets of paper for murals. All I had to do was supply paste and poster colours. One successful idea was Christmas angels; large papier-maché ones for the assembly halls, and smaller ones for tables.

Bob Morris, the art organiser for Fife, would drop in regularly for a chat and cup of coffee, and one afternoon, after I had been teaching for two years, he suggested I should return to art college in order to get the necessary papers to give me official status. Up till then I was employed on a temporary basis, which meant I was not paid for holidays. I had also encountered pretty blatant condescension and

139

even animosity from qualified teachers, one of whom went so far as to tell my classes that I was a 'spiv'. Some surely believed that if I had not taken the exams necessary to get the proper pieces of paper, then obviously I was incapable of doing so. 'Things are tightening up,' said Bob, 'if a qualified teacher asks for your job, I have to give it to him. You'll be the last to go, but as you are you've no security of tenure.'

Though I enjoyed teaching and knew I would miss it, I had to agree. I must qualify if I wanted to continue. A problem was finance over the year and half I expected to be away. Bob assured me I would get a grant, which in the event amounted to £90 for a year, a lot less than my teacher's salary. But I had plenty of practice in making money go a long way, and I was confident I could manage. It was settled; I would go through the prescribed hoops to become a qualified teacher. Had I decided on qualification just six months earlier, I could have done so by taking a mere six months training under the emergency recruitment scheme, and thereby saving myself much time and effort. Had I entered teaching by this sidedoor, though, there would have been some who could claim I was incapable of taking the normal academic route, and there would be no way I could refute this.

When the primary teachers heard they would not be seeing me again, some of them asked me if I could do a series of drawings which they could use when taking an art lesson. Few of them had any artistic bent, and inventing an interesting new subject every week was beyond them. Another problem was presentation; since they felt unable to turn out a passable drawing themselves, most of them thought there was no chance of getting good work from their pupils. I proved this was a fallacy by teaching without drawing on the blackboard, or drawing so very badly that anyone in the class could improve on it. Why not make a book, they suggested, with ideas for a whole session, and perhaps new ways of presenting each subject. This would supply the teacher with good ideas for a year, and thereafter they could repeat the lessons if I had not been able to do a series. I did go so far as to do a mock-up book which I submitted to several publishers, but none felt there would be sufficient sales to justify printing it.

DURING my first two years of teaching, I was given a good proportion of what were currently termed 'overage' classes. Periodically some brilliant educational psychologist decides that the

140

term is too specific, and instead of 'backward', suggests 'special', 'C-stream', 'Blue Group' — or, invent your own. No matter what they were called, I never encountered one of these classes which was in the slightest doubt about its place in the academic spectrum. I was not overjoyed at the artistic achievements of these children, but Bob Morris assured me they were exceptional. It may be that, not knowing any better, I *expected* them to do better. Most of them had been told so often that they were no good, they believed it. It took weeks of persuasion to induce them to try, when most of them began to enjoy art and crafts instead of just going through the motions.

One thing that always gave them a glow of achievement and started them off with confidence on a new track of self-expression, was when I showed them how to paint a free design. 'This design is yours only!' I told them, 'No one else ever thought about it. Nobody ever made one like it. Nobody will ever do it again — unless they copy yours!' Occasionally some artist would complain — 'Sir! He's copying my picture!' which was my cue. 'Good! That means you've done such a beautiful design, he knows he can't do any better! Let him copy it if he wants to. That's what you call a secondhand picture!' Upon which, hurt, the copyist would prove he could make a design of his own. This ploy worked just as well in normal classes. I never prohibited or punished anyone for copying, which is impossible for a child anyway, without considerable skills.

In most classes, but especially in primary school, praise can hardly be overdone. The veriest crumb of encouragement pays dividends. Most teachers could not understand why I never dismissed what they called the 'worst' drawings. To them a good drawing was representational, the more photographic the better. I had fun baffling those teachers by getting the children to make a purely abstract design, when they would find the most unlikely pupils coming up with the most inventive work. In art, as in all teaching, the principal aim should be making the child think for itself. Drawing skill is secondary.

Once, in a primary class of over forty, I noticed one little lad of seven sitting glumly with his arms folded, while the rest drew busily. The teacher was one of those who preferred to remain in the room during the art lesson. I asked her why he had no paper or crayons. 'Well, he used to get them like the others, but he made such a mess, I don't allow him to draw. He's M.D. you know!' Certainly he was. I never felt comfortable with handicapped people; mental or physical, they seemed to accentuate my own problems. But I had to do something for this pathetic wee soul. Really he should have been at a special school, but there were none within reasonable distance.

141

The teacher told me he always threw crayons at the others. I gave him a paper and box of crayons and told him to hurry up as he was behind the others. He was delighted. 'And if you throw your crayons at anyone, they'll get to keep them!' He never threw crayons again. At first his drawings were masses of scribbles, a glorious mixing of all the wonderful colours in the box, ending up a uniform grey all over. But towards the end of the term he was beginning to organise 'things' on the paper. I still recall a weird construction in white lines, on a coloured scribble background, intended to represent a scarecrow. It certainly showed some advance in his perceptions.

To be fair, the teacher agreed later that it had done him good to be allowed art, even though what he did was meaningless to her eyes, and he had improved in other subjects too. With more than forty-six in a class, it is impossible to give one individual treatment. With a class of even thirty, in one hour the teacher could only spend two minutes with each child. It is useless to complain about the standard of education until the number of children in each class is drastically reduced. This will never happen; as the number of children entering schools drops, fewer teachers are trained, so the ratio remains much the same. And how many ratepayers would countenance the employment of five more teachers, when *one* can cope with thirty children at one time? One problem was that the little lad thought the world of me, and he would follow me after school shouting 'Mr Tomsen!!' and would walk to the bus stop with me, grinning from ear to ear.

An unpredictable side benefit I gained from entering the teaching profession was that I could again use words of more than one syllable in everyday conversation, with some chance of being understood. This is not to say I found all my colleagues to be intelligent and literate. Many had closed minds and bigoted views. But in every school there were some who could converse on an adult level, and this I found remarkably refreshing. For years I had been disguised as a 'common worker' and had for so long limited my vocabulary in the way of protective coloration that I felt quite self-conscious when I used a word that was any way out of the ordinary. It was liberation for me again to come in contact with literacy and the art of conversation. Reading had provided a substitute, but had become progressively detached from what I was being conditioned to accept as real life.

WHEN I sent the application forms to Moray House Training College for Teachers, and the Edinburgh College of Art, it proved impossible to gain acceptance by either. Moray House would not accept me unless I had passed the university entrance exams, and had been accepted by the art college. On further enquiry, they said I could try to get the Prelims within the year, but still I would need to prove that I had already been accepted by the College of Art. The latter refused to accept me unless I had already been accepted by Moray House. A perfect example of bureaucracy in action. It seemed all doors were firmly closed. I was in despair, but a teacher friend, Jack Smart, had the answer. The Gordian knot was cut by writing simultaneously to both institutions, assuring each that I had been accepted by the other. I felt this must be slightly criminal, but as Jack pointed out, if it made them happy to believe the other stuck his neck out first, that was all I needed. Had I elected to become a teacher pre-war, there would have been no arguments anyway. The thing was to get in first and argue later if I had to. Anyway, the stratagem worked.

Now I was granted an interview with Robert Lyon, Principal of Edinburgh College of Art. I took a portfolio of work with me, not really the sort of stuff that would guarantee admittance by *his* standards. He had a few words with me, then showed me into the secretary's office, telling me to make myself at home, while he went to collect the heads of departments. I was quite on edge, and foolishly took his invitation literally. After waiting alone for about ten minutes, I lit a cigarette to pass the time. This was his cue to return, and immediately he pounced — 'How dare you smoke in My Presence! Put it out at once!' (He *did* use capitals.) I grovelled and stubbed out my desperate fag. I had determined that I would 'lout fu' low' and pull the forelock everytime it was necessary, no matter how much it went against the grain, just so long as I eventually got that piece of paper. It was every bit as difficult as I had anticipated.

They asked me what course I wanted to take. In retrospect, I should have asked which course *they* would recommend, and I would have had at least an even chance of the one I wanted. Since I had done design pre-war, I didn't want merely to recapitulate, and suggested drawing and painting or sculpture. Bill Gillies had known me and my capabilities before, but either he didn't remember me or was too diffident or browbeaten to put in a word for me; he was head of drawing and painting. Schilsky — sculpture — did not want me.

143

Dinkel, for design, I knew nothing about. Finally the 'big four' went into a huddle. I was told I would be entered for a design course, I was to understand that this arrangement was only for a probationary year. They considered it unlikely I could possibly reach their present standards, but if by some wildly improbable chance I *did* then I would be permitted to continue.

The four headmasters I had worked for in Fife had given me really first-class references, and I had a splendid one from Hubert Wellington, in which he said that in his opinion one year's refresher course would be more than sufficient. (I had reckoned on one year here, and six months at Moray House.) Lyon dismissed these as of no account. When I had attended college during Wellington's time, it had been an exceptionally poor period in terms of student quality (and obviously I had been scraped off the bottom of the barrel, he implied — any riff-raff could have got travelling scholarships then). Fortunately for me, I had not yet seen the college prospectus. Out of twenty-eight on the staff in the year 1950–3, a third were from that very period, and most of these precisely from my year.

The Principal in 1970, Sir Robin Philipson, started college the year after me. Some remarkably prominent names also came from my own year; William Gear, Charles Pulsford, Tom Gourdie, Henderson Blyth, James Cumming, Sir Norman and Lady Reid, John Hunter; and John Maxwell, George Mackie and Scott Sutherland and others were in the year or two previous to that. All these were of some status in the artistic community, William Gear and Sir Norman Reid both became curators, the latter of the Tate Gallery, London, and the former I believe in Birmingham. Some are now regrettably dead. Tom Gourdie was awarded the M.B.E. in the fifties for services to handwriting and has written many books on the subject.

Later on, I found that the sculpture department had preserved still my second-year modelled head. I might have mentioned this to Schilsky. And in one of the design studios, I found still hanging a framed illuminated map of Kew Gardens which I did after a vacation scholarship in 1935. The *only* example of calligraphy, from that or any subsequent period. Had I been aware of these unique relics, should I have pointed it out to Lyon?

My objections were brushed aside, and since it was of paramount importance simply to be accepted as a student, I did not pursue them. Dinkel led me upstairs to his office, where I was introduced to Nora Paterson. I knew her from pre-war, when she had taught first and second year calligraphy, but I doubt whether she remembered. They told me the requirements for a design student, then dug out a huge portfolio of 'plant form' drawings and paintings. This I remembered well from the early thirties, and it was obvious that the annual

144

increment since had been negligible. These were examples of work done by students over many years. One at least was from the previous century. Dinkel pointed out how beautifully they had been done, how masterly! Did I really think I could even approach this standard? I slipped up again. 'I think I can do rather better!' I had passed all exams in that area comfortably, and I had surely learned a *little* more since I left. Surely with my extra experience I could at least equal any student presently at college. But this was sacrilege. They were shocked; if I could even do as well, I would be very, *very* good.

From then on, I tried to remember to act like a little boy just out of school, knowing nothing compared to my tutors. Only once more did I make a serious boob. I was experimenting in the life drawing class with a combined pen and pencil drawing — not a very good one. Robert Lyon entered and made his regal tour of the class. Stopping at my easel, he remarked that one should never mix pencil and pen on one drawing. Though I knew many first-class artists had used this combination and others more bizarre, I agreed, 'you may be right, Sir.' Whereupon he exploded. 'What! If I say a thing is so, *it is so*!!' Let there be Light.

SINCE it was essential that I pass the university prelims the following March, to satisfy the college as well as Moray House, I had somehow to fit in a great deal of extra study. That July, I had approached Skerry's College in Edinburgh to ask if they would coach me for these exams. This could have been done by mail, which suited me, as I had no spare time to attend their day classes. Because of my age, I could be granted a Pass on only two Highers and two Lowers, instead of the three Lowers normally required. For some obscure reason, I was not allowed to make art one of my Highers, which would have been easier for me. And yet, if I had taken Higher art *at school*, it would have been perfectly valid. I was confident I could pass in Higher English, a compulsory subject in any case. As I had always been interested in Botany and Zoology, I felt I might just scrape a Higher pass. I chose Geography and History as my two Lowers, not because I had a lot of faith in my ability to pass, but I didn't know enough of the other subjects available — maths, physics and languages.

Anyway, Skerry's wrote saying that taking into account that I had left school some eighteen years previously without any recognised certificates, it would be quite impossible for me to pass the prelims with only six months' preparation, and it would be a waste of time and money to attempt it. I decided to have a go on my own. The English was to be on general questions, not set books, so I could leave it to look after itself. The Science had to be Botany and Zoology — my school science had been biased on the Chemistry side and quite boring. Alister Tulloch, one of my teacher friends at Kirkcaldy High, provided me with some old work books and an ancient textbook. This needed solid study. There was no time, nor had I the equipment, or inclination, to do the practical experiments on mice, frogs or dogfish, but I read the textbook for the hour it took the train to reach Edinburgh each morning. Reading on the return journey was impossible, I was too tired. Mrs Low, God bless her, had a cup of tea waiting for me when I cycled back up the hill after ten each night. It was a welcome break before I cycled on to the hut.

As for Geography and History, I found it impossible to fit in any time at all. I started to read up Geography only a week before the exam. There was no time at all for History; I went home at five the night before the exam, started reading, and went on till five next morning. I had two hours sleep, and at nine was sitting in the exam hall. The reason for this shortage of time was the sudden decision by the college that I must now pass the first and second year exams in *addition* to the third year ones as originally agreed. By great good fortune, some of my early exam results from the thirties still survived, though on the brink of being destroyed with previous years. I had no results for evening lectures or any of the third and four year exams, since I was not then a Diploma course student. This meant that the occasional free evening I had counted on now had to be used for extra subjects.

One of these last-minute extra impositions called for a portfolio of work which normally took a whole session to fill. I had to provide a selection of detailed copies of Historic Ornament. When I had left college previously, I had fat portfolios of a variety of subjects, but I had given them all away except a collection of illuminated capital letters. These were unfortunately now useless, since the shell gold (charged for as real gold) which I had used had turned green and black and greasy, and there was no way they could be repaired. With only a month or so to go, I could fit no extra work in without cutting down on sleep, already dangerously short.

I mentioned this final blow to Tom Gourdie, who generously offered to lend me some of the work he had done for the same subject. I could claim it was some of my lost work which had providentially just turned up. So I took in eight splendid watercolour studies of stained glass windows by Tom, which they had to accept as being quite good enough. They were actually well above standard. As they had by now seen the quality of my own work, there were no awkward questions about their authenticity. Later I returned them with thanks to Tom; he had passed the exam twice! This may have been sneaky and underhand, but in the circumstances I feel was justified.

Some years after I started teaching, I was giving some help and advice to my friend Arnold Runge, who was suffering similar tribulations at Dundee College of Art. He told me the following story. Arnold was over fifty when he started the course, and knowing what had happened to me, he was prepared for complications. He had been warned that if he failed any one of the many tests and examinations, he would not be allowed to continue. Normally students may re-sit any subject they were unable to pass first time around. But Arnold consistently ended high up in the results lists. Finally, someone hit on a foolproof way to get rid of him. At his age, and having to wear spectacles, it seemed a good bet that his eyesight would be deficient. Judging by his very individual use of colour, it was almost certain he would be found to be colour-blind too. This would mean instant dismissal.

So for the first time in the history of the college, all the students in Arnold's year had to take a test for colour blindness. They were all around twenty years of age, and had no worries about passing. There was only one student who scored the maximum points — Arnold! The student who was predicted to be the star of the group already knew *he* was colour-blind, and never turned up for the test. But neither he nor any of the others was failed, and the test was abandoned forever.

I was delighted when Arnold finally passed with first-class grades, and passed through Training College without incident to become a fully qualified art teacher. Sadly, he died only a few years later, but at least he had the satisfaction of winning against overwhelming odds.

I should here mention generous help from other students at this time — Stuart Barrie, Andrew and Con Chisholm and Fred Stiven. Andrew was appointed to the art college staff at the same time as Stuart. Fred taught at Aberdeen College of Art. One of my extra lecture courses was on the history of crafts, and each student was required to hand in a portfolio of notes for assessment at its conclusion. Had there been any spare time at night, I could perhaps have got them written out, but it was impossible. Stuart offered to let me copy out his notes, done the previous year. I accepted gratefully, but still had to find *some* time. This problem was solved by cutting short my tea break between four and five. I could fit in five minutes each evening before the five o'clock classes began. As they had left me only a few weeks in which to do all this, I wrote at top speed during my stolen five minutes, using ready-cut paper which I bound into a book at the end. I made a calligraphic pattern for the cover, so the outside looked good. Inside was the worst italic I ever wrote. It was legible, but only just, since it was also the fastest. Two-colour illustrations and headings helped to disguise the quality of the writing. It was admired by the lecturer, George Reid, one of the staff who was a student in the pre-war era. Nobody had ever made his lecture into a book before. Stuart has been on the staff of the college now for many years, and is also a member of the Society of Scribes (as, of course, is Tom Gourdie, who joined in the thirties).

Mardi Gatherum, who later married Stuart, commuted from Kinghorn, and we often got the same train home, when she would wake me up for Burntisland. Several times I slept on when no one woke me, and had to bus back from Kirkcaldy.

H AD the art college and university exams not overlapped in time, things would have been much easier for me, but I soon discovered that I had to pass nineteen exams in less than a month. The college graciously permitted me to do one of the extra subjects before the allotted date, because I had a full day at the university, followed by another college exam in the evening, and it was plainly impossible to be in two rooms at once. Higher English took the whole day, and I had thirty minutes to get back to the college, where I had only time to swallow a quick cup of coffee before starting the evening exam.

When at last all the results came through, I found I had passed every one except Higher Geography. Before the additional subjects were imposed on me by the college, I had opted for Higher, rather than Lower Geography, to give myself at least a chance of a second Higher in the event I failed in Science. I had, of course, counted on rather more than one week's study of the subject! Here was yet another problem. Even if I were accepted without the full prelims, I could not simply re-sit the one subject I had failed in; I would have to take another Higher as well.

Again Jack Smart came to the rescue. He advised me to write to the Universities Examination Board, explaining my circumstances, and enquiring whether they could grant me a Lower on the re-assessment of the Higher paper. I mentioned that a Lower was really all I needed, and I'd only had a week's study. I was quite confident I

148

could achieve at least a pass next year, when I should not have to cope with more than twenty exams in little over a month. I got my Lower pass. It was a great relief to know the first six months was over. The strain had been much more than I had been prepared for, owing to the unexpected additional demands made by the college after the session was well under way.

At the start of the session, I knew I could turn out work to the college standard at least, and in any style they might consider fashionable, and I also knew I could work fast enough and hard enough to produce a diploma show the following June. Once I had the diploma I could enter Moray House and be a qualified teacher before the end of the year. I set to, and among other things produced some composite sheets of plant studies which were shown to Dinkel and Elder Dickson, the Vice-Principal. They admitted the work was above average. This I had counted on; after all, I had already passed through college, and like my former peers, could surely now claim to be a professional artist. My paintings had been exhibited at the Royal Scottish Academy, an institution unlikely to exhibit rubbish. A first-time student could not be expected to equal the quality bestowed by experience.

Ah, yes! Splendid! But *unfortunately*, though they had a record of my first two years' attendances (what happened to the books I signed every day?), there was no other record, as I had not been an official diploma student. Before I would be permitted to take the diploma, I must have four complete sessions recorded, no matter how high my standard of achievement. I began to suspect that when at last they *did* allow me to take the exam, I would be disqualified anyway, on the grounds that . . . . (to be filled in by anyone who could invent a reason). So, although I did produce ample work for a diploma show in June, I still had to clock in for an extra year.

REALLY there is much to be said for a student's life. At the end of my college stint I felt I could happily have spent the rest of my life as a student, had it been financially possible, studying every conceivable subject. Under normal conditions, exams would be spaced out and therefore no strain. Should conditions ever arise to make it unnecessary for the human race to work for a living, so that its energies can be devoted to study, it can only be for the better. Anyone of mature age who may be worried that taking a new course of study might be beyond their powers should take heart. With less pressure on them to succeed, with more knowledge of real life and a working philosophy, it is likely they will make a better showing now than when they were at school and with far more enjoyment and satisfaction. It is a fallacy that one's learning capabilities deteriorate with age.

For some reason I was allowed leave of absence during the last weeks of the first summer term, so that I could fill a temporary teaching job at Cowdenbeath. This helped to replenish my dwindling resources. I had spent more than estimated on art materials, and since my pre-war stint, the term class prizes had been discontinued, so there was no way to top up. The job came through the good offices of Bob Morris. He had not anticipated that the college would demand more than a year's nominal attendance, and this allowed me to earn a few extra pounds.

The eight months strain had taken its toll. I had held up without any serious illness to keep me at home, but one afternoon I had just set a class to work when without the slightest warning, I went blind. Everything went a featureless grey, with a vibrating zigzag white line making an approximate circle. I could just make out a dim fraction of my surroundings from the outer periphery of my vision, very out of focus. This was the last straw. I sat there in cold despair. Everything was against me; why continue to fight the inevitable?

The class noticed nothing wrong. After an age of horror — it must have been at least half an hour — I noticed with a leap of hope that some vision was slowly returning. By the end of the afternoon it was almost normal again, apart from a residual effect of the zigzag white line. Much, much later I discovered that this was a typical migraine, without the pain. I had never heard of it before, or my despair would not have been so overwhelming. The occasional migraine afflicted me in later years, but at least I knew the loss of vision was only temporary.

With another year to spend at college, I could now afford really to work without having to pack in all sorts of extraneous subjects. Now I had a unique chance to do what I preferred, and hopefully acquire a few more skills I had not been able to fit in before. Obviously I could not make or save money, but the grant helped me to keep going.

During my second year I was informed I was a 'good influence' among the students, possibly because of my example; I tried to use every minute to the best possible advantage. I did not have to waste time, as every freshman student must, in developing techniques, finding out how tools and materials behave, and struggling with ideas which can't possibly work. With my extra years of experience I could do most things in a fraction of the time needed by a student. It

150

was entirely unrealistic and unfair to hold me up as an example, or to expect an ordinary student similarly to arrive complete and full-blown, like Venus from the scallop shell. If this sort of incentive should ever prove desirable, one can imagine every institute of learning planting an incognito instructor in every generation of students!

Though I had previously worked quite a lot in the sculpture department, I never had been able to try carving inscriptions. With Schilsky's permission, I now took a lesson or two from Allen, who only taught the subject in the evenings. I would be working during the day, when I started on my first effort. This was 'Gloria in Excelsis Deo', cut in a slab of Hopton Wood Stone, an English marble now sadly unobtainable. Letter carving proved to be much easier than I had expected, and quite enjoyable. I finished the inscription in three and a half days, to the disbelief of the fourth-year students, who had to design and cut an inscription as part of their prescribed course. On average it took them a whole term. Schilsky was visibly impressed, and now, too late, offered me a place in the School of Sculpture. This was tempting, but meant yet one more year at college. Had I not intended to return to teaching at the first opportunity, I might have taken the chance. I cut one more panel in Millstone Grit. It was in this class that I first met Tom Doyle, now principal art teacher at Buckhaven High School and a professional sculptor.

Stained glass, jewellery and glass engraving were three more crafts I had not had time to fit in pre-war, and I took classes in these whenever I could. I was not entirely welcome in Helen Turner's glass engraving studio; after a while I was told I was using time, equipment and materials which should be reserved for 'official' students. By then, however, I had learned enough to be able to carry on myself, given the opportunities.

With two years' attendances safely marked in, and with an ample store of finished work to choose from, at last I took the diploma exams. It was oddly sinister that on the first three days we were locked in the studios to perform our esoteric mysteries of creation. It seemed to imply a certain lack of trust in our honesty, or of faith in the assessor's ability to detect plagiarism. After that we were allowed time to finish what we had started. Then the diploma shows were put up, consisting of the exam work plus the best of the previous four years' work. All I needed was a simple pass mark, and I would have gone to very little trouble in displaying my work, but the place for a student's work was allotted from Above, and I was given the best position in the design studios. This was again manifestly unfair to the other students, but obviously the intention was to hit the assessors

151

with a favourable first impression. I did not object; if it made a pass more likely, fine. Then I could get out.

After the assessing, I was summoned to meet the assessors, one of whom was Edward Bawden, whose work I admired. As the blue-eyed boy of design, I was introduced to each. Shaking hands with Bawden was like holding a long-dead haddock. I was congratulated on my splendid work. All this I was expected to accept as a 'great honour'. I went along with the idea as far as I could, with my tongue firmly in my cheek. Those of my friends who were on the staff knew, of course, what was going on and went along with the charade. Then I was informed that I was one of the four offered a post-diploma award.

This complicated matters again. The perennial subject of whether Honours status for post-diploma students should be revived was again being aired in educational circles; it had been discontinued in 1939. I discussed possibilities with Bob Morris. He advised me to accept. So very much emphasis appeared to be placed on paper qualifications and honorifics that it now seemed unwise to reject the chance of an extra qualification. Already I had spent a year more than I had envisaged. One more would not make a great dent in my teaching career, but just might make a very considerable difference in salary and prospects. Hamish Rodger, one of my pre-war classmates, was one of the last post-diploma graduates to have Honours status. He eventually became headmaster of Braehead School. No ordinary student graduate could now become a headmaster, whether with or without the post-diploma endorsement. In theory, abolishing Honours status meant just the opposite; *all* art students were now eligible for such promotions. It didn't work that way in practice. While I might have this Honours equivalent now, I would not be entitled to a larger salary, but if legislation were changed I would get more in the future.

Immediately after the exams, I submitted a selection of my calligraphy and related arts to the Society of Scribes and Illuminators in London, and was honoured by election as a professional member and Fellow. I really should have applied years earlier in 1937, when Irene Wellington offered to sponsor me, but it was just impossible to afford the £5 membership fee. As the number of professionals has varied little from seventy since the society was founded, it will be apparent that not too many scribes qualify.

During the past year, I had been working on a handbook to teach italic handwriting, which I hoped would be useful when I resumed teaching. I submitted the idea to Penguin Books, who liked it, and the result was the Puffin Book, *Better Handwriting*, which became the bestseller in the series after only two years. It went into three or four editions in the first months. These two events boosted my status with Lyon and his associates, as you might expect, though in their attitude to me there was more than a hint of Pygmalion and his Ugly Duckling — to mix Greek and Danish.

No books on how to write italic were then available, though Alfred Fairbank had just published his *Dryad Writing Cards and Manual*, but many have been published since. I felt I might be able to use my teaching experience to devise a method of explaining every stroke to a complete beginner, and this I achieved by using hollow letters with arrows inside showing the order and direction of strokes. To my knowledge, this device had never before been used in any book, but just last year I came across a book published in Scotland by a Writing Master, James Thomson, who had done just that, though on a smaller scale. The date was 1746. Could we be related? Anyway, before Penguin allowed it to go out of print, it had sold a third of a million copies and was used in schools and colleges all over the world.

I asked Tom Gourdie for a sample of his writing for the book, and he suggested as he had intended for some years to write one on the subject, why not do it jointly? This might have been feasible had he mentioned it earlier, but the book was finished and accepted by Penguin as it was, and they were only waiting for his sample to start printing. The time was ripe for handbooks of this description; *Better Handwriting* was the first of a stream, subsequently joined by a dozen other writers.

At the end of the summer term, the Lord Provost of Edinburgh ceremonially presented the successful with their diplomas. We had to hire fancy dress for the occasion — cap, gown and hood. On a raised dais in the Sculpture Hall sat the staff in full glory, and the hall was filled with an invited audience of friends and relations. This ritualised event with its strong air of unreality aptly summed up my two years of hard labour. But it also provided the most heart-warming moment I had ever experienced. When my name was called and I marched up to receive my scrap of paper and metaphorical pat on the head, there was what can only be called an ovation from the assembled students. They had observed the pressures put on me, but until then I had not realised the depth of their sympathy. I was touched, and just a little of my lost faith in humanity was restored in these few minutes. The Lord Provost shook my hand and presented the diploma, but as the roar went on asked in some bewilderment, *'What's all this for?'* I said it was a very long story, and he should ask the people behind him.

My mother, glowing with pride, had brought my sisters to see me crowned. Elder Dickson chose a terribly inopportune moment to come over and congratulate me, and she attacked him like a hen

153

defending her last remaining chick. The Principal would have been better, but any representative of college authority would do. I tried to tell her that Dickson was not personally responsible for staff decisions, but that had little effect.

DURING my post-diploma year, a few commissions came my way, including two illuminated addresses to Queen Elizabeth, since it was Coronation Year. These illuminated addresses were written on calf vellum, and were decorated with coats of arms in full colour with raised and flat gilding. My highly finished and detailed flower and plant studies resulted in a commission for a series of illustrations for seed packets — bigger and better than life paintings of asters, beets and cabbages, through to zinnias. I think there were over sixty designs. When I was short of working time, I farmed out a few to student friends — always in need of ready cash — and they made splendid pictures, proving that with motivation, any competent fourth-year student could turn out first-class work.

The Arts Council of Great Britain, having seen my lettering, commissioned me to design a bronze door plate. I had to provide the working drawing for the firm which was to do the engraving. I was proud of it. It was nicely composed in a cool but lively Roman capital. They sent me a photograph of the finished plate. A good Roman alphabet has no straight lines in it — they only *appear* to be straight. But the engraver decided my lettering was all wrong, and using rulers, set-squares and compasses 'corrected' everything, and in the process killed the thing stone dead. The Arts Council, however, could see no difference between my drawing and the finished result, and paid up without demur.

During this period I found it possible to get down to some really solid research, the kind that is feasible only if you know exactly what to aim at, and which needs time — not just evenings, weekends or even an occasional entire week — but time outside the necessity to earn a living. The sort of time I had believed was forever out of my reach. I really appreciated this. Calligraphy was not the kind of work that resulted in a spectacular finale, the kind of show expected from a post-grad student. Space filling stuff. The tangible rewards for me were a handful of notes, a polishing of skills, and a certain clarification of aims. Had I aimed at top honours, I should have produced large, flashy, *clever* work, to impress the assessors.

154

Calligraphy with lots of gilding, colourful illumination and illustrations, 'arty' bookbindings and so on. But what I did was of more real value to me then and subsequently. My final show would look comparatively meagre, but since a simple post-diploma endorsement was all I needed, I could afford to leave the limelight to my three fellow students, who really were very good and would certainly put to good use any extras like money grants or travelling scholarships.

John Edmonston was doing textiles, Fred Macdonald — design, mostly murals, and Andrew Kirk — graphics. Andrew had, like me, opted not to take a diploma course, and theoretically should have had no chance of a post-dip award (he later became a captain in the army). It would be interesting to know how many more fitted this category, over the years. We had our own studios outside the college, and consequently saw a lot of what the others were doing. Fred was next door to me, and produced some really outstanding work in the way of murals. As he became dissatisfied with a design, he would paint another over the top of it. This was partly economic — he used the same backing instead of taking it down and putting up a new one. But it meant he lost several first-class designs which should have been in his final show. Some in my opinion were better than the final one, by far. He worked very hard, and it was a pity he could not keep and show all his work. He fully deserved his post on the college staff afterwards.

TOWARDS the end of the session, Nora Paterson asked me whether I would accept an appointment to the staff on a part-time basis, the usual preliminary to a full-time post. Since this would entail living in Edinburgh and less salary than I could get as a teacher, at least to begin with, I refused. First, I would never again willingly live in a town; second, though the smaller salary might well have been offset by more interesting work, I should again be forced into the rat-race of commercial art to which I had thankfully waved goodbye; third, I had found Lyon pretty insufferable while I was a nominal student, and I had not the slightest intention of trying him out as a boss. Added to these, I had some responsibility to the Fife Education Committee, which had helped with grants, and was expected to return there to teach, though there was no compulsion to do so. Admittedly the grants were niggardly compared with those now available, but open handedly generous compared with the bare fees pre-war. I just might have scraped by on my meagre savings for one year, but doubtfully for more.

After the assessment I was unexpectedly offered a travelling scholarship, again for £100. After my very low-toned final show, I had not thought I would get anything. Certainly it would have been very pleasant, and I could have fitted in a great deal of useful research abroad. Knowing now exactly what to concentrate on, my time would have been most profitably spent. But I was now very tired indeed. I had eased off a little in my post-diploma year, even to the point of taking the occasional afternoon or Saturday morning off to play golf with George, Gus and Andrew, which helped me unwind to some extent. But the scholarship had to be taken up before Moray House opened in September, and I knew if I worked as hard as I'd want to, I would be in no fit state when I returned. I desperately needed mental and physical rest now. In any case, I had been awarded my pre-war scholarship on straight merit, and had I accepted this one it would really be under false pretences; and some young student would be deprived of his chance, as only a limited number were awarded. So besides feeling dead virtuous, I had the great satisfaction of refusing a carrot they were certain I could not resist. Nora Paterson called it cutting off my nose to spite my face. It was a pity I had to let her down, as a successful student brought kudos to the school and tutors concerned.

Art at Moray House was fortunately still limited to six months. It purported to prepare a student to become a teacher, and to be legally acceptable as one, you *had* to have their certificate, no matter how prestigious your other qualifications might be. Now at least I was in without quibble, having attained far more than the normal requirements, plus authorship and Fellowship of the Society of Scribes and Illuminators.

After racking my brains to find something to indicate that teacher training was not all an utterly boring waste of time, the only mitigating circumstances I can recall were the English lectures of Doctor Oliver (of Oliver and Boyd). Interesting as they might have been to me personally, their connection with the teaching of art seemed rather tenuous. Obviously a good teacher should have a more than adequate command of English, but since Higher English was a prerequisite for admittance to the teaching course, it seemed rather a case of gilding the lily.

One of the other weekly lectures was on 'Health and Hygiene', for which we sat an exam at the term's end. After working under high pressure for so long, I found the exams almost childishly simple, especially as there were no conflicting studies to fit in. When I got the highest marks, the others christened me 'Doctor Thomson', (which

156

was also the name of the lecturer). I managed a first in English too, which helped boost my morale, but the poorest mark I was given that term was also the lowest in the class, and was awarded by Foreman, the P.T. instructor. Though it bored me to tears, I had faithfully turned up every week. Six of the others had never entered the gym, but they all had marks 30 to 40 per cent higher than mine. This made me mad, and throwing discretion to the winds, I tackled him about this. He pointed out that they were all magnificent physical specimens compared to me, which was true; therefore he'd given them better marks. I pointed out that none of them had done a cycle tour of thousands of miles, nor were they likely to. Had the College of Art applied this method of assessment, there would have been no need of all those extra years. I thought it was complete nonsense, and told him I would not waste one more afternoon in his gym, even if I failed to get my coveted 'piece of paper'. He said that was all right, but would I write out any notices he needed; and in the end I *was* given the minimum pass mark, unlike those glorious specimens of manhood who had spent their P.T. afternoons in the local pub, but all got top marks.

One of the forms we had to fill in on arrival at Moray House asked us to state our religion. It was strongly hinted that we should opt for a recognised religion, with Church of Scotland as the prime choice. For a very long time I had been agnostic, but I played safe and wrote in 'C of S'. Well, I could always recant later. Apparently the education authorities looked with disfavour upon unbelievers, who might later refuse to take classes in religious instruction, and thereby be legally entitled to a free period in the mornings. So, as with P.T., I had to take the prescribed classes, just in case.

Though many of us had trained to a very high standard in various crafts, we also had to take a crafts course. The objects we produced were stultifyingly primitive. Though crafts would have to be simple for schoolchildren, it did seem a waste of time to have trained stained glass or bookbinding experts making crushed paper mosaics, soap carvings and lentil-and-rice pictures, to the standard expected of eight-year-olds. Following the directions of our instructor, I made the worst bookbinding I have ever done. I had been doing bindings of professional quality for years, and shortly thereafter became a member of the Scottish Craft Centre on the evidence of my work in calligraphy, pottery and bookbinding.

At last this six months endurance test came to an end, and all of us got passes except one. At the end of the first term he decided he would take no more, and left with great relief. I believe most of us would have joined him, except that we had to have that 'piece of paper', and we felt things couldn't get a lot worse in three more months. When you have banged your head on the wall for five minutes already, five more won't give you two headaches.

We had been ordered to write a thesis, illustrated with paintings or models. Some students produced vast quantities of work. Their thesis was a volume, their illustrations an art gallery. One pair had collaborated on a huge scale model of Leith Docks, made with soap and cigarette cartons, and painted and mounted on a large board. I wrote my thesis on a single page, and used children's drawings to illustrate it. These I stuck in a scrapbook. Though Geisler frowned at this meagre effort, all I needed was a pass — and judging by past form, it seemed unlikely anyone would be actually failed at this stage. We were classified according to our promise as future teachers on five levels; fair, fairly good, good, very good and excellent. Two of us got the highest grade. I was put properly in my place with a 'fairly good'. This worried me not at all. I had a principal teacher's post waiting for me. At long last, I had the two indispensable 'pieces of paper' which 'proved' I was now a qualified teacher of art. (Why, thereafter, did no one ever ask to *see* them?)

Bob Morris was delighted I was now through, and came up with a brilliant idea. He commandeered a very large calligraphy panel which had been a centrepiece in my Diploma Show, and had it hung in Kirkcaldy Town House near the Education Department. It was an illustrated History of Writing, entitled 'Calligraphy', and had already been exhibited in various places including London, Bristol and Zurich. He assured me that having it on permanent display here would certainly bring me Town Council commissions, and possibly others through distinguished visitors who saw it. Several times over the years I tried to get it back, as no commissions ever came my way, but Bob refused; people were always interested in it, he said. But nobody ever mentioned to *me* that they had seen and liked it. Fifteen years later, Bob died, and I thought I would now go and reclaim my masterpiece.

Going into the front office of the Town House, I said I had come to collect my 'Calligraphy' panel. 'What's your name?' they enquired. I told them. 'Sorry! We don't have anything of yours here!' I said I could show them where it had been hanging for fifteen years, and led them along the corridors. 'I'm afraid you can't have *that!* It was done by Mr Tom Gourdie!' Taken rather aback, I asked them if that was the case, why was it clearly signed in the middle with *my* name? For all these years, this opus had been attributed to Tom.

AFTER Easter, I started teaching at Burntisland School, with full qualifications plus a few extras no one else had. It was a vast relief to know I no longer had to waste two hours daily travelling to and fro. The school was only ten minutes cycling distance away. The main drawback to being based in one school was being given a register class. I always hated filling in forms, totting up columns of figures and making graphs. But I was thoroughly run down after those years of concentrated effort, and very soon caught a cold — one of the teacher's occupational hazards. It became worse and developed into tonsillitis just a month before the summer vacation. This malady made me miserable for six weeks, but at the end I was pleased to hear my doctor say I would never get it again. The tonsils had completely broken down and vanished. During the weeks I had in bed, the Lows very kindly sent along one of their grandsons, Bob or Neil, with my groceries. My mattress was so soaked with perspiration after a series of fevers that I had to throw it out.

Each week I had to give my class Religious Instruction. I did try to avoid this, but Scott Christie, the head teacher, said I'd have to do it even if I was a 'Nonconformist Holy Roller Hottentot', or words to that effect. I began by following the lines laid down by Moray House, but could not counterfeit sincerity, and my class became almost as bored as I was. Then I started to talk about other religions, which went down a little better, though I doubt whether the local church congregations derived any benefit. Perhaps too, I should not have drawn their attention to the two quite different accounts of the Creation in Genesis, and that to believe every word in the Bible as Gospel truth (to coin a phrase), is to land yourself in deep trouble. There was a lot more interest when I got them to copy down the Lord's Prayer in different languages. They specially liked doing it in Latin — a *Pater Noster* in Roman Capitals.

Scott Christie worked diligently at presenting a tough, self-sufficient image; 'I'm all right, Jack!' or 'Step out of line and I'll throw you to the wolves'. But he had a carefully hidden soft centre. When he heard I was returning to college, he knew I had limited resources, and offered to loan me £20 for books and materials, to be repaid any time after I qualified. I had enough on hand, but thanked him gratefully for the thought. Another time he visited the widow of a friend to offer his condolences. When he left, she found a £5 note

159

tucked under the clock. I heard several other stories of the same nature, all done very quietly. He had high courage too. Latterly he suffered from heart trouble, and told me he had no intention of living on as a semi-invalid. He died of a heart attack during a game of golf. He collapsed on the second tee, but deliberately elected to carry on until a fatal attack at the ninth.

Most children are interested to know a word's equivalent in foreign languages. I would give them lists, and we painted inn signs with titles like Lapin Vert, Blaues Pferd, Aquila d'Oro or Rotes Haus. When I was at primary school, foreign languages were all Greek to me and sounded like Double Dutch. It was all the fault of those foreigners, who could understand English perfectly well if you spoke loudly and clearly. None of us ever needed to learn another language unless we needed them in business. The upper classes were only taught French and Latin so that they could sound superior.

One of the perks of being a register teacher is the privilege of being the first to see the original 'Note to the Teacher'. When a child was absent, the parent was supposed to send a letter of explanation. One lass brought me this: 'Please excuse Jeannie for being off school. She has had her legs under the Doctor for the last two weeks.'

A classic which turns up regularly in much the same form each time is: 'Please excuse Willy. He has had diarrhoea through a hole in his shoe for three days.' 'Dire hoe' was one version, but the most felicitous was 'Dire Rear', collected by my science colleague, Gilbert Johnston. He also told me of: 'Please excuse Johnny. He has not gone for four days. When he has went, he will come.'

Teachers may find their ex-pupils remember them too well. An old teacher of English who had retired and returned to teaching several times told me that she never really felt her age until one day she was stopped in the street by a former pupil who cried, 'Oh, hullo Mrs Annan! Ye ken this? Ye teached ma mither, an' ye teached me, an' noo here ye're teachin' ma bairn!' Mrs Annan was tempted to reflect that much of her teaching had been in vain.

On the whole I enjoyed my work at Burntisland, where I was acting principal art teacher, and officially so within the year. Alec Reid had been teaching art in the absence of a qualified teacher, but his subjects were woodwork and metalwork. He was a first-class craftsman, and now and then we saw examples of his work, like a miniature aero engine, beautifully finished. His art teaching was watercolours, based on his idol, Russel Flint.

He was near retiral, and many were the stories about him. He was notorious for throwing things at troublemakers. A girl who worked in the grocer's where I bought my weekly supplies had been one of his pupils. One day she had been chatting to a neighbour and

160

didn't hear him call her to order. He picked up the nearest object to hand, a wood chisel, and hurled it at her. 'I got an awful fright! But he had a very good aim — it stuck in the desk right between my fingers!' When I reminded Alec of this he confessed he'd nearly died of shock as soon as the chisel left his hand. His nickname for many years had been 'Sconnie', because he always wore a flat cap.

Only very rarely did I resort to using the tawse, though I had the reputation of being 'strick'. Once a student teacher was having trouble keeping order with her classes next door to the art room. The children, as with my teaching practice class, were well aware that students were not allowed to punish them, but usually they behaved sensibly after we explained that the student's chance of a future job depended on *their* good behaviour. I had told her to send any offenders in to me, and I would deal with them.

Next day while I had a free period, there was a knock on my door, and a lad came in. 'Mrs B. says I'm to be punished, sir.' This boy I had known for years. He was well behaved, a nice lad, and I had never heard of his being punished. I guessed he had been lumbered with someone else's transgression, or perhaps it was just a momentary lapse on his part. He was also six feet tall. 'If you think I'm going to climb up on a chair to belt you, you're mistaken!' I said, 'Kneel down!' And he did. But I had no intention of punishing him anyway. I reminded him that a third-year class should be *helping* a student, not making things difficult for the poor girl. She had no more trouble.

At first there was no proper art room, and I had to use an ordinary classroom above the cookery room, as I have mentioned above; with ordinary desks and no art equipment. Improvements came piecemeal, first art desks with drawing boards, then we had the end of the corridor bricked off to form a storeroom. I managed to get a kiln and kick-wheel for pottery, but the janitor was not at all pleased. The clay dust messed up his corridors. Several years later, I suggested we might convert one end of the dining hut, as only one end had been in use since the end of the war. The kitchen separated the two ends, so essentially I had a building to myself.

With much more light and space, two sinks, ample cupboards and storage and a concrete floor for easy cleaning, it was a vast improvement. The old room was allotted to my assistant art teachers, who normally stayed for two years or so before being moved on. It was also very convenient when I had to do dinner duty. There was a roster, and each teacher served for a week at a time. No one, I believe, actually enjoyed this duty. Most workers can enjoy maybe an hour's relaxation for a mid-day meal. Not teachers. Personally I found it made a very tiring day when I was on duty. We were allowed twenty minutes for our own meal, then we were in the dining hall until the last child was finished. So apart from the hurried lunch of twenty minutes, there was no let-up from nine till four.

Some teachers allowed quite of lot of noise in the dining hall, and even ignored a bit of horseplay. They just put up with it until their tour of duty was over. But I felt there should be a civilised quiet — not dead silence, but enough so that I did not need to scream to make myself heard. Also I wanted a modicum of self-restraint. I objected to scuffles at the table, or hammering the cutlery on the table tops to pass the time. First time in, the servers showed me a bowl full of wildly bent spoons and forks, à la Uri Geller. I took this around during the first meal, and promised to interview the first tableful who handed in even one more. The spoon-bending stopped.

Usually as the bell sounded, the hall filled with boisterous kids, six to a table, and pandemonium reigned, until a teacher called for silence and said 'For what —' upon which all recited grace and continued the row. I changed this. On my first day, the door opened and they charged in, fighting for the best tables. The place was full, and bedlam reigned. But slowly they realised that nobody was eating. I sat at the table nearest the serving hatch, saying nothing. They began to see that no lunches were going to be served until there was peace. The tables nearest to me fell silent, and the idea spread along to the far end of the hall.

'Well done!' I said, 'Now, while I am on duty, you will act in a civilised manner. If you want to make a noise, do, but we'll just stop serving. You may have to wait an hour to get your lunch; I don't mind. I've had mine!' This was a highly effective gambit. They wanted time to relax after lunch just as much as the teachers. Any hard case causing a disturbance had to wait until everyone had finished, and after the first day or two, few cared to take a chance. Conversation was kept down to a peaceful hum, as in a normal restaurant. Occasionally, Scott Christie came in to lunch with us, and the first time he came in when I was on duty, he asked 'What have you done to them! It's uncanny!' I said I'd just appealed to their better nature.

I had to stay off once with a nasty bout of 'flu. It took two weeks, and one of the side effects was a very sore and tender face, so that I was unable to shave. I had to let my beard grow. The morning I returned, I was waiting in the assembly hall for the children to come in, when Scott appeared at the far end. He stalked all the way up to me, stuck his face close to mine, and muttered, 'You look like Jesus Christ!'

My first class that morning was second-year boys, who had never seen me wearing a beard. They were impressed. One said, 'Sir!

You look Noble!' I thanked him for his kind comment and assured him he would get top marks in the next art exam.

Jack Smart was head of evening classes, later taken over by Eddie Ramage. He asked me to take a class in art. I was not too keen. After a school day, I was usually tired, and two extra hours at night did not appeal to me. The extra payment only paid for a packet of cigarettes, anyway. But I was persuaded. I would get home at four, have a cup of tea, and go to bed until seven, on the two nights each week on which I took classes. I taught pottery, basketry, painting, anything they asked for. It was fairly straight-forward when everyone opted for one subject, but teaching three or four was wearing.

Pottery was the most popular. Fortunately I now had an electric wheel as well as a kick wheel, so more people had a chance to try them. Many of my students found it impossible to pedal with one foot while still keeping their hands steady. They all started out with the intention of making a large and beautiful vase like the potter on the BBC *Interval* film, but inevitably their pots would develop a fatal wobble. Some found it easier on the electric wheel, where it was not necessary to keep a foot moving.

Demonstrating, I would make a pot, then introduce the well-known wobble, to the dismay of the watchers. 'Ah, but all is not lost!' I would say, discarding the ruined top, and steadying the remainder, from which I made another smaller pot. This process was repeated until I had only a tiny nub of clay left from which I made a minuscule pot or ashtray. Usually the learners ended up with yet another ashtray, but some became quite proficient.

Jock Pont from Aberdour was my most faithful student, and came to the classes every winter. One night, arriving early as he often did, he made his best pot ever, and slipped it on to a board to dry, displaying it proudly beside the wheel. One of the ladies, also early, saw this beautifully glazed grey pot — it was still wet — and exclaiming, 'What a lovely pot!' lifted it by the rim to look more closely. Of course it was all pulled out of shape. Jock said he could have killed her.

In succeeding years, I made plaster moulds, so that the more inept could at least have something fired and fit to take home. The class was so popular I was kept busy firing work in the kiln for both day and evening classes. Once or twice I forgot to switch off at four, and came in next morning to find a warm room and all the kiln contents melted to lava. For school use, kilns really should be supplied with time switches. These evening classes developed into a kind of social club, but I found them increasingly tiring, and in the end had to give them up.

163

I taught italic at some of these evening classes, long after I had stopped in the day school. During my first year, I found some children were keen to learn, and introduced it to my timetable. Some were so keen they even came to classes after four. But it was not long before one of the girls came and told me she had been punished for trying to use it in another class. The teacher claimed she could not read it. Since the classes had only been running for a few weeks, not many had managed the changeover from their old writing. Most found the old style too well rooted, but with a little more practice would have been writing at least passably. Scott Christie said they could write italic with me, and ordinary writing elsewhere, but it was quite unrealistic to try this, as the hand movements were quite dissimilar. It would have been like trying to juggle with cannonballs and balloons. So as I could not countenance the children being punished for changing their writing, I stopped the classes. Scott said I was wasting my time on any sort of writing, because everybody would own a typewriter within twenty years. That prediction did not come true. Jack Smart also advised me to forget italic writing, and to give up any interest in calligraphy, as nobody had or would have the slightest interest in such an outdated art. But for years now there has been a great and growing interest in the subject, especially in America. People find it a way of countering increasing mechanisation, standardisation and automation.

A S I remarked, I had a series of assistants who used my old room. Most of them were girls recently out of training college, and were moved on after a year or two. I got on very well with all of them, and we would part on the best of terms. One of my first assistants was Maggie Sutherland. She always wore her black hair long, in a pony tail. One rainy morning she got her hair wet, and was sitting in front of the fire in the ladies' staff room, with her hair hanging over her eyes to dry. One of the lady teachers came in and saw her, and taking her for a pupil said, 'My dear, you're not allowed to come in here! Shouldn't you be at your class?' And Maggie parted her hair, peered through and said, 'It's *me*, Mrs Robertson!'

Another of her stories is from a later date, when she had moved to Aberdour school. She had a class of infants, and the class next door was doing an examination, so she wanted them to be extra quiet. There was a shortage of crayons, so they were kept in a box on her table, and the children took the colour they needed, changing when

164

necessary. So Maggie said, 'Today I want you all to be *very, very* quiet! Don't make a sound when you come out! Just like little mice!' When they came out, she nearly choked. Every one came on tiptoe, with tiny little steps, holding their hands to their chests like a mouse's forepaws.

One winter I went down with a really vicious cold, and Maggie and Maggie Young, one of the primary teachers, and two others came up in the evening with a bottle of brandy to revive me. This worked very well, and as the party progressed, the girls decided they had to go and powder their noses. My bog was a bucket in a lean-to up among the bracken. The night was pitch black and my torch battery was low. I direct them to turn half left out of the front door, then follow their noses. We inside the hut heard a lot of bumping and giggling. They had turned sharp left and squatted in a patch of stinging nettles.

Around 1965, the secondary department of the school was closed down, and staff and pupils combined with two Kirkcaldy schools to make a new super-school, Balwearie. This was a large new glass and concrete construction of un-original design, the most up-to-date establishment in the county, standing in its own grounds. There were around 2,000 children. Most of us were less than delighted to move. Our own school was small, cramped, inconvenient and old, but it was a happy school, and everyone knew everyone else. In Balwearie, staff personnel were segregated in different staff rooms, and it was impossible even to know all the staff, let alone the children. But we had no say in the matter; we had to go where we were directed. Scott remained as head of the Primary School, though I am convinced he would have been an infinitely better rector than Belder, who was given the job. Still retaining principal teacher status, I was appointed assistant to Bob Duncan, who had been with Belder in their old school. He was much younger than I, but we worked at staying on a friendly footing. I did not enjoy having to requisition materials through a second party, but we managed.

In spite of Belder's super-organising, there were six art teachers and only five art rooms, which meant we perpetually shuttled from room to room. This did not work. We had all been used to having our own room, with our own stocks of materials, so we knew just how much stuff we had to work with, and where it was. Theoretically, I had the pottery room, but it was only a base. Everyone else used it too, with predictable consequences. I would have a class for pottery, only to find that a bin full of fresh clay which I'd spent time putting through the pug mill the previous day had all been used up. Belder's timetabling resulted on occasion with three art classes going on in one room. I found it impossible to teach with two other teachers talking to

165

their classes about different things. I am sincerely thankful I have never been called on to teach in one of the 'modern' open-plan schools.

To make things worse, the pottery room itself started to go mouldy. The architects had designed a first-class pottery room without bothering to consult a potter first. They *had* had the foresight to make a composition floor, waterproof. *And* it was designed with a slope so that surplus water would drain away to one corner. Brilliant stuff! Except they'd forgotten to put any drains in. The benches were also beautifully designed — and flush with the floor, so the slightest dampness seeped into their expensive wood, which rotted within weeks. And so on.

Because of all the moving around, there was no chance to use the printing machine and type I had brought from Burntisland. This included several fonts of my own which I added to the school stock before the amalgamation had been heard of, and it was impossible to separate them now. In one of the other rooms was my bookbinding equipment, never used because of the impossibility of carting unfinished work to and fro. Belder had been inspired to split up the day into twenty-minute segments, which was supposed to facilitate the dovetailing of timetables. This meant that the period bells sounded every twenty minutes too, and I for one became heartily sick of hearing them.

Long before a year was over I was considering leaving the profession for good. Up till now I had enjoyed my work, but in this glasshouse it had turned to drudgery. Belder was a 'new wave' educationist. He was not far short of retiral age, and as rector of this new school he was putting his advanced ideas into practice. Like the artist who sold a load of bricks to the Tate Gallery, he must have talked well to con the authorities into preferring him to Scott Christie or the other head teacher concerned.

At this school, I had far more boys' classes than girls. Up till then I had been teaching equal numbers of both, and this I found far less tiring, perhaps because I could teach a greater variety of crafts.

Belder had told me he didn't believe in corporal punishment. Or any other, since nothing was said to a class of delinquents. Not long after this incident, Belder had been called to an educational conference, where he was to lecture on 'School Discipline — Staff and Pupils'. It was after I left, but I heard the staff had finally rebelled and during his absence went on strike against the insufferable conditions he had created.

SIX months after I came to Balwearie, the Cunninghams' farm lease ran out. Grosset, the new owner, said I could stay on the same terms. I offered to pay him a suitable rent, but he refused. Some weeks later I noticed clouds of white smoke billowing past my window, and thinking someone had set the dry bracken on fire, as happened periodically, I went out to check if the hut was safe. Two men were burning a patch of grass just beyond my fence, and the flames had already killed a young hawthorn hedge planted two years previously. I protested, but they told me Grosset had given them permission to build a hut anywhere in the field to start a firewood business. Out of thirteen acres they had chosen a spot twenty yards from my hut, though there was a more level site much nearer the road.

Within a week they had set up a shanty containing a circular saw, and were carting in wood to cut up. The scream of the saw went on for hours at a time, but they preferred to start up after dark; nine, ten or eleven at night, and it was not unusual for them to go on until two in the morning. I grew desperately tired, because even when the racket stopped, I could never anticipate when it would start again. Inevitably I started oversleeping in the mornings and arriving late at the school. Belder's practice was to sit at the office window with a pair of fieldglasses, checking on teachers driving in late from the staff entrance. I had not believed this story when I first heard it, but subsequently I did see the binoculars on his desk.

I had been late several times, when one morning he came into my room just as a class of third year boys were preparing to leave. He reprimanded me for being late, and flatly rejected my explanation. That night I composed a letter of resignation, again giving the reason for my being late, and objecting strongly to being ticked off in front of my class. Any disciplining of staff should in future be done in private, if at all. He came and apologised, asking me to stay on. He did not think the class had noticed what he was saying anyway. I am quite sure they did. Though I accepted his apology and did stay on, I now believe I was mistaken — I should have walked out at the beginning.

The firewood merchants became thoroughly obnoxious, smashed a padlock and broke down my gate so they could drive up to the turning space beside my hut. This allowed my geese to wander at will. I only had two now. A thief the previous year had kicked one so badly it died, and another had been savaged by a dog brought into my garden by a local who refused to pay damages. One frosty morning they stole a hundredweight of coal to grit my part of the road so they could turn their van. Regularly they parked on my road in front of their shack and refused to move, so that I had to risk driving off the side to get past. I complained to the local police about this harassment, and discovered to my disgust that in Scotland, anyone may park in and block a private road. If the resident then asked him (nicely?) to move, and they refused, *then* he could apply for a court order, and if in due course this were granted, possibly something could be done.

Then I received a lawyer's letter from Grosset ordering me to leave by the end of the week, in three days time. Consulting a local lawyer, I found this impossible demand need not be taken seriously. I was entitled to a reasonable period in which to find another house. Actually with the excruciating saw and the obstruction of the firewood merchants, it would have been impossible to stay any longer anyway.

During my househunting period, I looked at several properties, trying to find one which fulfilled my requirements of quiet, garden space and a view, preferably with trees. One house with water, electricity and a splendid view would have been acceptable even though it had no garden. It was an ex-naval cottage at Dalgety Bay, and had been unoccupied for some considerable time. I contacted the authorities but was informed that the whole area had been classified as 'of outstanding natural beauty', and no one could be allowed to build or occupy any house there. Only a few years later the new town of Dalgety Bay covered those green acres. And shortly afterwards an oil terminal joined the town, all protests being over-ruled. So much for official protection of outstanding natural beauty.

Another site, very near the road at a place called Nine Lums, near Burntisland, where I could have built in a grove of trees, was a disused brick office with water and electricity. I could have made great improvements there by cleaning up the building, but I was refused permission for exactly the same reason. Last time I passed it was still there, more tatty and derelict than ever. Officially, I suppose it was continuing to be part of the outstanding natural beauty.

What I hoped to find was an old house of character, like one George Simpson lived in when he was a child. It was really exotic — it had a pear tree growing up through the middle of it, and in season, one could lean out of the window to pick a pear. As the trunk and branches were all in the same plane, he surmised that the tree had been an espalier on an outside wall, and later additions to that side of the house had enclosed the fully grown tree. He said that the children accepted it as quite commonplace, and probably everyone had one.

168

'Where's my coat?' someone would say. 'Oh, it's hanging on the tree!'

I was fortunate to find within a few weeks a cottage not far from Kennoway, with trees and an acre of ground, and a splendid view. No water or drains, but it had electricity. I hired a removal firm to move my goods and chattels. When the van arrived, the driver refused to come up my hill to the turning place near the hut. He had driven into the drainage channel at the side of my road, which itself was perfectly sound, as I had been improving the surface for years. I helped him dig out, but he would not try again, and backed all the way out to the main road.

It seemed the only thing to do was move the stuff myself, so for two days I shuttled back and forth with my minivan, until all that was left was a table and chair and a chest which wouldn't fit in. The firewood boys said they'd like to have the hut when I left. 'Make me an offer', I said. They were offering nothing; I was supposed to leave it out of the goodness of my heart. After all, they were only forcing me out of what had been my home for sixteen years. Rather than leave it to them, I would have burnt it.

Later I found a firm who dismantled the hut and brought it along to the cottage. But they had burned some of the things I had left, and 'lost' my water tank and gas fittings which I had not time to dismantle. They also brought my wooden garage, which had in the interim been broken into. I had to re-visit the site to retrieve the nuts and bolts for holding the sections together; they had been simply dropped and left, but I managed to recover most of them. During this time, all my carefully nurtured trees had been cut down for firewood and left piled in heaps. But the shack with its infernal saw had also gone. I suspect Grosset had only set them there to make me so uncomfortable that I would have to go. If so it could have been done in a more civilised manner.

Belder refused to give me a week off to do my removal, allowing one day only. When I returned exhausted after two days hard labour, he again told me off severely. It was the last straw, and this time I *did* hand in my resignation. I'd had more than enough of him and his school. The art organiser urged me not to abandon teaching. If I left now, I would get no pension. He suggested I should try peripatetic work again, retaining principal teacher status, but I knew how tiring that was and felt I could not face it. Then suddenly St Peter's school in Kennoway needed an art teacher. It was only about a mile from the cottage. It seemed ideal, and I accepted.

Here I found the principal art teacher was Harry Cartner, one of my pre-war friends along with Tom Gourdie, Hamish Rodger and the rest. At the first morning assembly, he gave me an embarrassingly

169

flattering testimonial in front of the whole school. We got on together just as well as in the past. I retained my status, but there was no hint of friction between us. We were the only non-Catholics on the staff of a Catholic school, but the staff were as friendly as the Burntisland lot. This of course was a small secondary school, but modern, having been built only a few years previously.

One morning I had a class of first year girls, and one of them asked why I never went to Mass. I explained that I was an agnostic. No one knew what that was, so I told them as simply as possible, and thought I had adequately presented the idea. But on their next visit, I overheard one say to another, 'Mr Thomson disnae believe in God — he's an Astronaut!'

Their opposite numbers in the boys' first year were a cheerful lot too. I came in one morning to find one of them showing his pals a girlie magazine. The full colour ladies portrayed were to say the very least well-developed. The lads involved fully expected instant and severe belting. I let them stew for a minute or so while I thumbed through this work of the Devil. Then I pointed out that I had made hundreds of drawings of nude women, and I could therefore tell them with some authority that these females were grossly malproportioned. So what was all the fuss about? They found naked women interesting? Fine. A natural instinct! They glowed. But did they really think they were old enough for this sort of thing? They thought they were. Then I pointed out that most of the models were old enough to be their mothers. 'If this one, for instance, came up to you right now and said "Give us a kiss!" you'd run for your life!' They had to agree. I gave the lad his magazine back and told him not to get caught again.

Some days later, one of them said 'Sir! Why is it you understand us, and the other teachers don't?' I pointed out that the other teachers understood them only too well; and in fact the staffroom had chuckled heartily at the story. They still wondered why they hadn't been punished, and no doubt if the visiting Padre had caught them they would at least have had to say a dozen Hail Marys.

For two more years I taught at St Peter's, but Balwearie had taken the joy out of the job, and I had suffered chronic fatigue ever since. Then, as had happened at Burntisland, it was decided to merge St Peter's with other Catholic schools. I was determined never again to work in a large school, and once more considered retiral. But this time I was persuaded to take a group of East Neuk schools, travelling every day. James Mowat, who had been at Moray House with us, was Bob Morris's successor, and had followed this route himself. All were primary schools, two of them very small, one and two teachers; the kind I found most enjoyable. But after a year of this, I was as tired as ever, and the constant travelling was no help. I told James I was

170

resigning whether I got the pension or not. But my friends thought I could be on the brink of a breakdown. Perhaps I was. After a couple of medicals, I *was* retired — on a much reduced pension, since I had not served long enough, but still, a pension. This was in 1967.

It was an immense relief to be free at last, but I felt so very worn I thought I would be lucky to survive for two more years. For these first two years I did indeed spend a great deal of time sleeping, on occasion for as much as twelve hours at a time. During these traumatic years, I greatly appreciated the moral support of my friends George and Pat Simpson. We had first become acquainted at College, where George had been one of the 'mature' students, a term applied to those who had their training interrupted by the war, and were consequently much older than the normal intake. For someone who had spent years in a Polish prisoner of war camp, the college and Moray House pettifoggery must have been exasperating. But he and others in the same category at least had the breadth of perspective which enabled them to cope with it.

I was welcome at their flat in Edinburgh, near Dean Village, and later when they moved to Lower Largo, I was appointed honorary Uncle to their two children, Simon and Judy, and greatly appreciated being accepted as one of the family on my weekly visits. For some reason, any time I went to see my own nieces and nephews, their parents always told them not to bother Uncle George. Phemia and I both loved children, and would have enjoyed being 'bothered', especially by children actually related to us. But no doubt we would have spoiled them rotten, given the slightest encouragement. Possibly it was a subconscious fear that achondroplasia might be contagious, but we have been delighted and relieved to see that no trace of it has showed in any of the children or their families.

The stone-built cottage I now lived in was an improvement on the hut. It was built in 1812 by a Kennoway stone mason, on three acres of ground, reclaimed from the Common along with other parcels of land at about the same period. Most of these, if not all, are now incorporated with Balgriebank Farm, including two of my acres. My cottage and the acre attached were never a part of the farm.

Before me, the cottage was occupied by Bogumil Imiela, a Polish ex-serviceman and his wife, who ran a mink farm. The acre of ground had been covered with dozens of wire mesh mink cages. A lot of these still remained when I took over. Bogumil used to collect fish waste from various places around Fife, and I am told the stink could be detected from miles away, depending on the wind direction. They stayed in the cottage for twenty years, until they had to move because of the wife's ill-health. The enterprise in any case had not turned out to be the money-spinner they had expected.

There were two advantages with the cottage. It had an electricity supply, and a well of its own. In periods of high rainfall, the water ran by gravity to a tap in the outhouse. At the hut, I had to carry all water 500 yards or so. When I first considered buying the place, I had a sample of the water tested. I was assured it was purer than most reservoirs in Fife, and well within European Common Market specifications. But when some years ago I applied for home improvement grants as a disabled person, the water inspectors who had previously passed my well as safe on several occasions now found various lethal substances in it, so each time the grant was refused. To qualify now, I would have to put in a pump and line from the nearest mains, nearly a mile away. At my own expense.

Presumably this would also apply to the farmer, Jim Young, whose water supply comes from the same strata, but from a spring further uphill than my well. When I first arrived, the farm was owned by a William Thomson — no relation — and when he died the farm was acquired by Jim, who had to abandon his farm at Banbeath, Leven, when the land was acquired for an industrial estate.

I had hoped my geese, bantams and ducks would be safer on my own acre, which was surrounded by the farm. I only had one pair of geese left, and one pair of ducks. One morning I went out to find the ducks had gone. I naturally suspected a fox, but going closely over the grass, I found only two feathers and several spots of blood. It was obvious some local sportsman had shot them, mistaking them for mallard. But a 'sportsman' who would shoot the proverbial sitting duck, since the domesticated ones don't fly. I had brought my two flocks of bantams, one black and one white. It is interesting to note that at dusk the black ones were first to come in to roost. Presumably the whites had greater visibility to each other in failing light. Some years ago, I introduced a brown cockerel to the flock, and now they are all brown.

Though I fenced the acre with wire netting, I still lost the occasional hen to foxes, which also threaten or kill Jim's lambs every year. The two geese died naturally after a few years, and I never replaced them, though I miss the annual crop of goose quills for calligraphy. Fortunately I acquired a shoot of dwarf bamboo from my friend Tom Doyle, head of the art department of Buckhaven High School, who was at art college with me in the fifties. They were only four feet high in the clump in his garden. My clump flourished, and is now fourteen feet high and spreading. I have enough to make bamboo pens forever!

Some of the trees round my perimeter had been blown down a year or so before I arrived, and I replanted the gaps with willow cuttings brought from the hut, which rooted immediately and grew well. I had also brought a few other saplings, ash, oak and poplar, and half a dozen larch about the thickness of a walking stick. These are now over thirty feet high.

Having space to plant and security of tenure, I bought five or six apple trees, though I doubted whether I would live long enough to see them fruit. But I have, and I have also found this is not ideal apple-growing country. I get plenty of blossom, but it takes a good summer to ripen fruit. I also did quite a lot of grafting, on proper stock this time, and now have four times as many trees as when I started.

In the days when I was fitter than now, I had quite a large area planted to vegetables, and enjoyed the digging during the winter. Birds attacked my fruit and greens, but my cats did their best to keep their numbers down. I eventually had to start murdering kittens to keep the number of cats down. At one point I had six! Due to deaths, possibly by poison or foxes, I now have only two.

With the material of the old hut, I built a cold greenhouse, and for the first two years grew great crops of tomatoes — about ninety pounds in the season. Then some sort of disease crept in, and I got very few. As an experiment, each year I kept seeds from the best plant, even if there were only one or two fruits on it. At the end of ten years, I had bred a tomoato plant resistant to whatever the disease was, and again got reasonable crops.

As I like almonds, I planted two almond trees during the first years, and they grew well. But they only flowered twice, and then very sparsely. No fruit at all. In the greenhouse, I grew a peach tree to fruiting age, from a peach stone. One year it set two fruits. In subsequent years it refused to flower. I gave it one more year, and when it again failed to produce, turned it into a walking stick. I had more success with my vine and fig. These plants incidentally are very easy to propagate. The vine grew from end to end of the greenhouse, but again it needs a sunny summer to ripen fruit, and these seem to get more and more rare. The fig was much more successful, and produces delicious fruit every year, which is the more welcome as they come two or three at a time, not all at once like apples. I already had a fig plant, grown from a cutting begged from George Simpson when he lived at Court House, Lower Largo. Their fig was reputed to be over 100 years old, but never fruited. Nor did my cutting, though it was inside a greenhouse instead of in the open like its parent. Again I tried my grafting skills, and shoots from my bought 'Brown Turkey Fig' all took, and this tree is now bigger than the original, and fruits well.

For several years, while I could still operate a mower, I maintained a little three-hole golf course which gave me a lot of enjoyment. I was able to practise approach shots and putting, though there was not enough space for a full drive. Now the surrounding undergrowth is encroaching all around.

In one corner of my acre I dug a small pond: it had occurred to me that I could emulate the ancient monastic practice of keeping fish in special ponds to supplement the diet of the monks. The main species they bred was carp, and I stocked my pond with about a dozen bought at a local pet store. I added a few sticklebacks and some tadpoles, with water plants gifted by Ian Hamilton Finlay, for whom I was carrying out commissions in wood, stone and calligraphy at that period. The fish grew and flourished, but the pond froze over when winter came, and when the ice melted, all the fish floated belly up. I tried re-stocking in subsequent years with species supposed to be more hardy, like loach and catfish, but they met the same fate. As a last resort I tried goldfish, which I knew survived in open-air pools in other parts of the country. But the result was the same. Though the pool was four feet deep, and measured nine by thirty feet, it seems it was not big enough. Some winters it appeared to be frozen completely solid.

At 600 feet above sea level, I have a splendid view to the south over the estuary of the River Forth to Edinburgh, Prestonpans and the hills beyond. On a clear day I can see beyond the Bass Rock and Berwick Law, nearly sixty miles, and around the same distance from the North Sea in the east to the Forth Bridge in the west. There are enough trees around now to break the force of the gales, but during my first year here one of the largest firs at the eastern corner of my land was blown over by a strong westerly wind. As it helped to protect my garden from the east wind, I thought I might try to save it, at least to keep it growing. The roots had lifted a large slab of earth which stood at right angles to the ground, while the trunk lay over the hedge horizontal to the ground. I felt that if I could cut off the trunk high enough to save some lower branches, I could lever it back into position, and the tree would continue to grow. It did, too. But something very unexpected happened. I put up my ladder resting on the lower end of the trunk, and sawed through without incident. But as the two pieces of tree parted, the weight of the soil held by the roots snapped the shortened trunk back to vertical, and I was flipped into the air like a tiddlywink to fall from a height of twelve feet or so, landing flat on my back, fortunately not across the rest of the tree. I lay winded for a minute, then got up. I was amazed to find nothing broken, and was none the worse except for a few bruises.

WHEN I retired in 1967, I felt at such a low ebb I expected only to have a year or two of life left. All my energies had been exhausted during the last few years of teaching, though from the beginning I rarely had any spare time or energy left to use on projects of my own, either painting, calligraphy or follow-ups to my first book. Early on I had suggested a companion book to *Better Handwriting* to Penguin Ltd. but they already had one in hand, and I went no further.

There is a saying among artists, 'Those who can, do. Those who can't, teach'. Amended, I should say 'Those who teach, can't,' because if they are doing the job well, they will be too tired. I never felt the six weeks' summer vacation long enough. I had only just started to unwind when it was time to go back.

But after two years' rest, it was like beginning a new life. My peaceful surroundings, the sights and sounds of nature, working the soil, all helped to restore my soul. I felt the stirring of re-born creative energy, and started painting and writing again to some effect. I had intended to play a lot more golf, now my favourite recreation, but with progesssively worse arthritis, had to limit myself to nine holes only.

During my college years in the thirties, I had written several manuscript books as part of my calligraphic training, and several more in the fifties, most of which I sold for negligible sums. Two I remember which were exhibited at the Society of Scottish Artists shows sold for five and eight pounds — much less than the price of many of today's paperbacks.

My friends George and Pat Simpson now suggested that a Scottish recipes collection would make a splendid manuscript book. I agreed, and set about collecting old recipes. The real traditional ones I thought would fit the calligraphic medium best. I think it was Pat who said 'Why not try and get it published, then instead of only one copy, hundreds of people could buy and appreciate it?' My original intention had been to make and bind the book for my own pleasure and satisfaction. I knew it would be next to impossible to sell it at a price which would justify the amount of time and labour spent on it. I hawked the book round several publishers, all of whom praised it but didn't want to print it, until at last one suggested I should send it to Canongate of Edinburgh. They said they loved it, and it was published in 1976.

Around 1972, I revised *Better Handwriting*, but Penguin decided against a reprint because of the recession. I offered it to a small American publisher who promised to publish it within six months, kept it three years, and in the interval printed his own book on handwriting. When at last I managed to get the book returned, Canongate published this too.

During this decade I was also carrying out commissions of varied sorts — illuminated addresses, presentation scrolls, stone and wood carving, title pages and so on. I also carried on writing more books, trying to pin down in black and white something of what I had learned in a lifetime and pass it on before it was too late. It is as if these bonus years since I retired were a special gift of time, that I must put to the best possible use. One book was not intended for publication — *Scribe*. This was a collection of many scripts from various sources that I had built up during my student years. It was written on handmade paper and I bound it in hand-tooled full leather. There was some criticism because the examples were not in chronological order, and did not include historical examples necessary for continuity. This was to miss the whole point of the book, which was to satisfy *me* and to record only *good* writing in the serendipitous fashion I had found them. It is a good book to handle, and just to dip into for pleasure; the published book has preserved much of the charm of the original.

Other manuscript reproduction books were *Christmas Recipes* and *Traditional Irish Recipes*, the latter with illustrations in the style of the artists who decorated the Book of Kells in the ninth century.

Rubber Stamps originated in a curious way. I was invited to visit Florida in the late seventies by Professor Margaret Rigg, who taught art and calligraphy in Eckerd College, St Petersburg. She wanted me to demonstrate some of my skills, which I did over a period of a month or more. She had been making stamps from hand-cut erasers, and I was inspired to try some myself. During my pre-war spell at college, I was known as the 'Linocut King', and I had experimented with rubber cutting then. But I gave up because the rubber distorted under the cutting knife, and I could not get the fine detail I wanted. This was the case with my new attempts too, but it came to me that a fine needle might be the tool to solve the problem. It worked beautifully, and I cut many eraser designs. The final result was the book. Like *Better Handwriting*, it was written because no one else had done it first, and there was no handbook to show anyone how to do it.

Two recent books are *The Calligraphy Work Book* (Thorsons) and *The Art of Calligraphy* (Treasure Books), a version of the same. Of recent years, I have had to curtail my book writing and calligraphic

176

activities due to worsening arthritis. Age takes its toll, and I have been sharply reminded of this during the past few years, which have seen the loss of a sister and a brother, and several good friends. Charlie died in 1985, and Phemia in 1987; Pat Simpson also in 1987.

When Charlie left school, he became an apprentice in a firm in Edinburgh which made gas meters. On finishing his apprenticeship he was seconded to Trinity House, which administers all the lighthouses round our coasts, as a lighthouse fitter. He rose through the service over the years to become administrative officer, and looked thoroughly official in his nautical uniform. In his early days, he had an accident while servicing the machinery of one light. The gears moved unexpectedly and sliced off the tip of one finger. His mate fished the finger-tip out of the dust and brass filings under the machinery, washed it clean, and held it in place with a bandage. Charlie was rushed to hospital where the finger was stitched. It healed up perfectly. Another time he went down with appendicitis on a remote skerry light off the coast of Scotland. This time he was mentioned on television news when he was flown to the mainland on a helicopter. He married Cathie McKinnon in 1946 and had a family of four children.

When Charlie was eight or nine, he joined the Life Boys, and later the Boys' Brigade, where he learned to play the drums and bagpipes, though he did not continue very long. About this time too he had an evening job, along with a friend, working in Leggat's chip shop. This consisted of washing and peeling potatoes and general tidying up, for which he got sixpence a week, and lots of chips.

During the last few years of his life, he suffered one or two strokes. When I last saw him not long before his death, of a heart attack, he looked fragile and had a slight speech impediment. But like Phemia, he remained cheerful to the end.

Phemia, as I remarked earlier, was like me achondroplasic, but always had more difficulty in walking. When she left school, she was found a job in a lampshade making factory by the Cripple Aid Society. This was a very poorly paid post, and after a few years she managed to get work with Butterworth's, a wholesale and retail opticians, who were known to employ disabled persons. They did not overpay these people. After many years, during which she learned all the processes in the making of spectacles, an opening appeared for a chargehand in her department. As she had years of seniority, she fully expected to be promoted, which would have meant a raise in pay. The employers put another girl in charge, who had only worked there for six months, but who was not disabled. They told Phemia they didn't want to put her under extra strain. This was a poor excuse, and Phemia found herself each day with a pile of rejected spectacle frames from this girl's workplace to be corrected.

She and Betty had joined the Brownies as children, and went on to become Girl Guides. Phemia continued her connection with the organisation until in her later years she was confined to a wheelchair, as a 'Tawny Owl' — second in command to the 'Brown Owl' in charge of a Brownie pack.

She took several aspirins a day, and two at night for as long as I can remember, to kill arthritic pains. For her it worked, and she had no obvious side-effects. But she became unwell in 1987 and rapidly got worse. Within only a month or two she died, of colonic cancer. This I attribute to the daily dose of aspirin.

On leaving school, Betty served an apprenticeship in book-binding, but the firm's practice was to sack the girls on its completion. She then worked for some years in Nelson's Printing Works, and just before the war worked on a boring job in Milne's Meter Works, which had switched to war work. She was glad to leave this and then joined the Women's Auxiliary Air Force — she was in the catering corps. Betty married James Alexander in 1951, and they had two children. These two, Betty and James, attended Balwearie School while I was a teacher there, and I took their classes for Art. Betty herself is happily still with us, though her husband died in 1985. We both started smoking cigarettes during the war. I stopped nearly twenty years ago, but I cannot convince her to.

My father died of a heart attack at the age of 54, and my mother, who never stopped grieving for him, at the age of 76, so none of us has reached her age yet. The Thomsons are not a long-lived tribe, though the Lukes, on my mother's side, have several surviving into the eighties. I am in the process of compiling a family tree, a fascinating occupation which I understand many more people today are beginning to adopt.

IN the winter of 1977, before my first visit to Florida, one of Professor Rigg's students, Ruth Pettis, came to me for special tuition in calligraphy, her major subject. She was especially interested in British calligraphy, and felt it would be good to work under someone who was in the main line of the art, since I was a student of Irene Wellington's, who learned directly from Edward Johnston. She struggled up the hill to my cottage every day for a week or more, through a foot of snow and deeper drifts, in one of the worst spells of weather for years. Ruth was very enthusiastic, a quick learner and hard worker. She is now a practised scribe in the Johnstonian tradition, and worthy to carry on to the next generation, having assimilated the *spirit* of true calligraphy and added her own personal touches. On my second visit to America, she had more tuition from me, this time in more pleasant climatic conditions.

This second visit was in 1979. Becky Blue from Sacramento had bought one of my vellum panels in the Scottish Craft Centre during the mid-seventies, and had been writing to me for some time. When she heard I had gone to Florida, she said I now had no excuse to put off visiting California — which I had been for some time. I was invited to stay with her and her parents for as long as I wished. I would pay for my keep by teaching Becky calligraphy and art. On my way home I was again to stay with Professor Rigg. The whole visit was prolonged for six months, and Ken and Helen Blue treated me like one of the family.

At week-ends Ken would drive us to various interesting spots. One was Sutter's Fort, a relic of the pioneering days and the gold rush. This has been restored, with set pieces illustrating life there during the 1870s and thereabouts, when Indians lived around the area. I especially remember a visit to an ancient Indian site, still sacred, as it is used to this day for religious ceremonies. Nearby were many huge oak trees, one really vast — it occupied a whole acre of space by itself. The trunk must have been ten feet in diameter. Next to it was a large sloping area of bare rock, pocked with hundreds of depressions maybe a foot across. Here the women used stones to pound the acorns from the oaks, one of their staple foods.

I think my first impression of America and the one that persists, is its sheer size, compared with Britain, and this really hit me when we drove to Oregon for Christmas with Becky's married sister Karen. This was a journey of over 400 miles, covered in one day. Even the climate changed. While I never saw snow in Sacramento, for the last 100 miles of our journey the land was snow covered, though the road had been efficiently cleared for normal traffic.

The second impression was the excessive use of advertising in the towns. Billboards, three-dimensional signs in the poorest taste, posters, and shop and business signs in colour and neon. These cluttered every view. Thankfully this visual pollution was effectively curtailed over here in Britain during the fifties.

While the weather in California was not greatly different from our own winter, it was a new experience to step off the plane in Florida and immediately notice that the place smelt like a greenhouse. Winter there was like a hot summer here, and some nights I found it

179

too hot to sleep. During the day butterflies and red cardinals could be seen, and lizards basking on the walls and tree trunks.

Professor Rigg had given me a small caravan to stay in not far from the house. It was like having a house of my own, and even had a refrigerator. There was a gas stove, but water had to be carried from the house, which worried me not at all. Nearby was a fine 'Olde American Privy', 'approved by local authorities'. Once I saw a coral snake vanish into it under a crack in the cement floor. There were several other types of snake around, a copper coloured one and a black one. The house was in four acres of ground, mostly grass, with Australian pines and palm trees, paper-bark trees and live oak draped with Spanish moss, and surrounded on three sides at that time by palmetto scrub. Now the area is being 'developed', and ruined, no doubt.

My best golf story must not go unrecorded. Margaret, who doesn't play, fixed up a foursome for me with a keen young golfer, Debbie High, Jo Ann Whitaker and a friend. Margaret had an exaggerated idea of my prowess. Jo Ann was a former lady champion, and her friend was almost as professional, and they were playing on their home course. Debbie and I knew we could not possibly win, but it was a unique chance to play on a first-class course with members. Casual visitors could not get on this course. It was beautifully kept, with palm trees and orange groves, and lagoons with alligators. We saw a big one in a pool near the second tee.

On the first tee, with a critical gallery of spectators, I was given the honour, as a visiting Scot. I put up a fervent prayer to Saint Andrew, and hit a beauty straight down the middle, to end up with an easy par four. The three ladies could all outdrive me, and did for the rest of the round, but my borrowed clubs did not let me down, especially the putter. During the second nine holes, I had seven single putts. I even won one hole, a par three. All the ladies were through the green, and I was in a bunker beside and short. I holed my bunker shot for a two.

At the last hole, a long lagoon beside the fairway trapped any hooked shots. My drive was as usual short of the rest. The next stroke had to be played left and over the lagoon. I mis-hit, skied the ball and helplessly watched it drop six feet short of the far shore. Just as it struck, an alligator raised its head, the ball hit it and bounced high and safely over to the fairway beyond. I chipped on to the green and holed an eight yard downhill putt for my par four.

Jo Ann made me a gift of that magic putter, and when I protested showed me a long wall back at her house in Crystal Springs. From side to side it was stacked with dozens of clubs of every description. 'If I feel like giving one away', she said, 'I can afford to! And anyone who can use a putter like that deserves to keep it.' I still have it as a memento of a fabulous day.

Everyone I met in America seemed to be friendly, though we know this can't apply to the whole population, as everywhere else. It may be because I only met friends of friends. Practically all the people I spoke to had an ancestor or relation in Scotland. Rigg I thought *should* be a Scottish lowland name, but apparently not. The Blues trace their ancestry back to the Dutch Blaue. Maybe the first Blaue lived in New Amsterdam!

I should have liked to travel again to America, and indeed visit many other places, but it is not to be. Television has served as a substitute for physical travel. Like every other medium, it has its proportion of trash, but I believe it does much more good than harm, especially those items which show how other people live. The more we identify with others, the less likely we will be to wipe them out. Television is probably the best hope that this planet will be saved, with its many illustrations of what has already happened, the incredible beauty and complexity of life, and what might still be done to preserve it.

OVER the past three score years and ten I have tried to build up some sort of philosophy of life. This is still in the process of building and changing, but seems to have some satisfactory sort of shape even now. As I may have remarked earlier, I found Scottish Presbyterianism to be a religion that did not fit what I observed around me, and after the age of fourteen started to investigate and read all I could find of other religions, the Torah, the Koran, Buddhism, Hinduism, and on to Shamanism, animism and many 'primitive' religious beliefs.

I concluded very soon that those peoples who worshipped or believed in the spirits which inhabited rocks, springs, animals, mountains, or whatever, and respected the land they lived on, believing it should be held in trust for future generations had a deeper understanding of the Cosmos than Christians, Muslims or Jews. (Truth is not a monopoly of any one religion.) These three believe man has domination over the material world, animal, vegetable and mineral, which can be exploited with immunity, 'Go forth, be fruitful and multiply' was fine some 6,000 years ago. Not now. Man is now so numerous that the other flora and fauna of the planet are being crowded out, though their pedigrees are as long as humans and they are surely entitled to existence too. But a rising tide of pollution threatens to poison the whole earth, to the extent that even the climate is changing. A part of atmospheric pollution is actually caused by our insatiable appetite for meat. Vast herds of animals raised for food produce methane, more than would naturally occur.

Should the earth eventually be so completely poisoned that all higher life became extinct, still there could be optimism. Some bacteria would survive and thrive even on the poisons, and evolution could re-start with some billions of years head start on the first time, when no micro-organisms at all existed. The planet is after all young, a molten sphere of rock with a thin film of crust on which life can exist, and this crust constantly re-cycles itself. If consciousness again develops, then things may go better second- or third-time around.

The sun, source of all life, still has billions of years of existence ahead, and man has not been able to tamper with it yet. It is my belief also that nothing is wasted. Matter is constantly metamorphosing into something different and new. Even if all life is wiped out on some planet, everything that life has experienced, constructed or thought is somewhere stored in consciousness, and will play its part, no matter how small, in the final resolution.

The Cosmos, I think, must evolve towards complete consciousness of itself. Life on our own planet demonstrates this beautifully. Where living things have had billions of years of uninterrupted evolution, as in tropical rain forests, where there are many thousands of plant and animal species, proliferating and diverging into ever more complicated relationships, and many of them interdependent or even symbiotic. This latter state, carried to the nth degree, is what I picture the final result of cosmic evolution, when all is known to all of creation. In temperate climes, the number of species is relatively limited, owing to the repeated interruption of evolution by ice ages, the land being wiped clean each time of any vestige of life.

My theory ties in fairly well with that of Teilhard de Chardin's, mentioned in earlier pages. He gives prominence to the birth of Jesus Christ and its importance, which narrows the scope of his vision. But the conception of a 'now' which embraces the moment of creation and its end I can fully endorse. Thanks to the mathematicians, the Big Bang seems an accepted fact, though most people would find it impossible, as I do, to conceive of all the billions of galaxies in the universe being concentrated in a space a zillionth of the size of the full stop at the end of this sentence. This is as near to creation from nothing as I can imagine. And what sparked off the explosion, and what was there before? So you end up, no matter how scientific or pragmatic or agnostic, with something which for want of a more explicit term we call God.

This God, force, or entity, I cannot envisage in terms of any religious belief. I am inclined to believe this force is biased to the side of good, without any proof and therefore irrational; but I am sure there is a dark side to it too, the Devil if you like. The Chinese concept of the universe as Yin and Yang, good and evil, light and dark making one perfect whole, is quite persuasive. A point to consider is, without its opposite, neither can be visualised. Each is necessary to the other, and we have the choice which side to favour.

Entities on this planet (and elsewhere) with intelligence or consciousness are seeking to merge with the ultimate consciousness of the entire Cosmos. When that happens, creation will have been fulfilled. But after that, you might ask? I have no doubt there will be some other mighty project for the super entity thus created. Too many anthropocentric thinkers believe that Homo sapiens (sapiens!) is the ultimate in intelligence — patently untrue when one looks at the state of the world today. My understanding is that life is in everything, and intelligence and consciousness innate in all living things and most likely in the mineral world also, since all are formed from the same basic materials. The simplest element, hydrogen, is built up through successive processes in the formation of stars, their growth and death, to the complex elements necessary to build life forms on this planet, and which we could not live without. This applies to everything from whales to bacteria, to silica and common metals.

Life on this planet I find endlessly fascinating, and the more we discover of the solar system in our own back yard, and the universe beyond, the more intriguing it all becomes. It does seem as someone once said, that God must be a mathematician, and our mathematicians seem to be on the track of Truth, at last. Every atom in the cosmos, they tell us, has a gravitational effect on every other. Infinitesimal, no doubt, but there nevertheless. So it should not be too difficult to accept that what one individual *does* must affect others, for better or for worse. My choice is to try to use my influence to do good, to *be*, trite as it may sound, good. As the wiser religions postulate, God/force is in everything, and we must respect this force, as when a hunter apologises to and thanks the animal he kills in order to live, or when someone picks a fruit and similarly gives thanks. It is of course impossible to live without killing or harming other entities, but one must do it with as much compassion and grace as possible. Personally I find it very difficult to live up to this ideal. I try, and hopefully I have taken a step or two along the Way, and helped a soul or two in the process.